BlackBerry©
Made Simple!™

For Full Keyboard BlackBerries
Including: 5800, 6200, 6500, 6700, 7200, 7500,
7700, 8700 Series and Related Full Keyboard Devices
("Full Keyboard" = One letter per key)

If you have a "7100 Series" BlackBerry (two letters per key)
please check out our "7100 Series" Edition of this book.

Ned Johnson
and
Martin Trautschold

Second Edition
November 2005

www.blackberrymadesimple.com
**See the electronic version of this Book (Adobe PDF format),
Video Clips, Web Training, Free Email Tips, Great BlackBerry Links,
Contact the Authors, and more.**

BlackBerry® Made Simple!™
for Full Keyboard BlackBerries

This book is intended to help owners of the 5800, 6200, 6500, 6700, 7200, 7500, 7700, 8700 Series and Related Full Keyboard BlackBerries ("Full Keyboard" = One letter per key)

If you have a 7100 Series BlackBerry (Two letters per key), including: 7100g, 7100i, 7100r, 7100t, 7105t, 7100v, 7100x, and related 7100 Series Devices, please look for our "7100 Series BlackBerry" version where you found this book. If you cannot locate this published guide, please check out our electronic versions at www.blackberrymadesimple.com

Published by
CMT Publications, Inc.
25 Forest View Way
Ormond Beach, FL 32174

Copyright © 2005 by CMT Publications, Inc., Ormond Beach, Florida, USA

Library of Congress Control Number:
ISBN: 1-4196-1740-0
Published Date: Nov-1-2005

Published in the United States of America

10 9 8 7 6 5 4 3 2 1

Trademark Acknowledgements

Images
BlackBerry images courtesy of Research In Motion, Ltd. (www.blackberry.com)

Contact Us
Contact the authors at
 info@blackberrymadesimple.com
For Free Email Tips, and the Electronic Version ("Ebook") in Adobe PDF format, please visit
 www.blackberrymadesimple.com

Tired of reading?   Rather watch the video?

Check out our New Video Clips
We are developing a full set of "Video Clips" viewable on your personal computer that bring to life the information found in this book. Each clip will be between 3-6 minutes long and will show you on the screen exactly how to do the setup, tips and tricks! We also will add new Video Clips all the time. To learn more, please visit:
 http://www.blackberrymadesimple.com/videos/videos.htm

Want an Expert to Train You or your Team?

Check out our New Live Web Training
We provide standard or customized web training classes. Visit our web site to learn more.
    http://www.blackberrymadesimple.com

About the Authors

Ned Johnson is a technology project manager, trainer and author whose experience ranges from the management of large scale web site projects, to the launch and subsequent sale of a BlackBerry wireless software company whose products are being used today in companies big and small, around the world. Ned gained his BlackBerry expertise by leading hundreds of BlackBerry training sessions, managing a customer service team devoted to BlackBerry users and writing hundreds of pages of knowledge base articles and other instructional materials for BlackBerry users. Ned holds a Master's Degree in Library & Information Science from Wayne State University and a Bachelor's Degree in English from Wittenberg University.

Ned Johnson

Martin Trautschold is an entrepreneur, author and consultant who lives in Ormond Beach, Florida. Together with Ned, he co-founded, developed and then sold a BlackBerry wireless software company. Martin managed the international software development team, marketed and sold to Fortune 500, small companies and individuals, provided technical customer support, training and wrote dozens of technical "how to" knowledge base articles. Martin has over 15 years of technology and management consulting experience with several of the largest consulting firms. He holds an MBA from Northwestern University and a Mechanical Engineering degree from Princeton University. He is devoting his time to creating a series of Video Clips based on the books, providing training via the web, writing and promoting new BlackBerry Made Simple books and consulting projects. He can be reached at martin@blackberrymadesimple.com.

Martin Trautschold

Authors' Acknowledgements

To all our inquisitive readers of previous editions of this book (which was sold only in electronic downloadable format), and their wonderful questions which have inspired new tips/tricks and sections of this book. Also, thank you to all the students of our Live Web Training classes for your great questions and unique perspectives. Finally, thanks to the Web Master and contributors of www.pinstack.com who have answered some tough technical questions and provided some great ideas!

From Ned

To my wife for patiently listening to "BlackBerry speak," for years, and to my co-author and brother-in-law Martin Trautschold for his devotion and hard work in our BlackBerry ventures.

From Martin

To my talented co-author, Ned Johnson, for his great assistance developing this book and our related web site. To my loving wife, three daughters, parents, and mother-in-law for all their support, insights and encouragement during this and all my BlackBerry endeavors. It has truly been a family effort!

Tip!

Press the ALT (half-moon key) together with rolling the trackwheel to do all sorts of interesting things!

QUICK REFERENCE: Full Keyboard BlackBerry

The BlackBerry is simple to use but learning a few key navigation tips from the start will help you in every application on the BlackBerry.

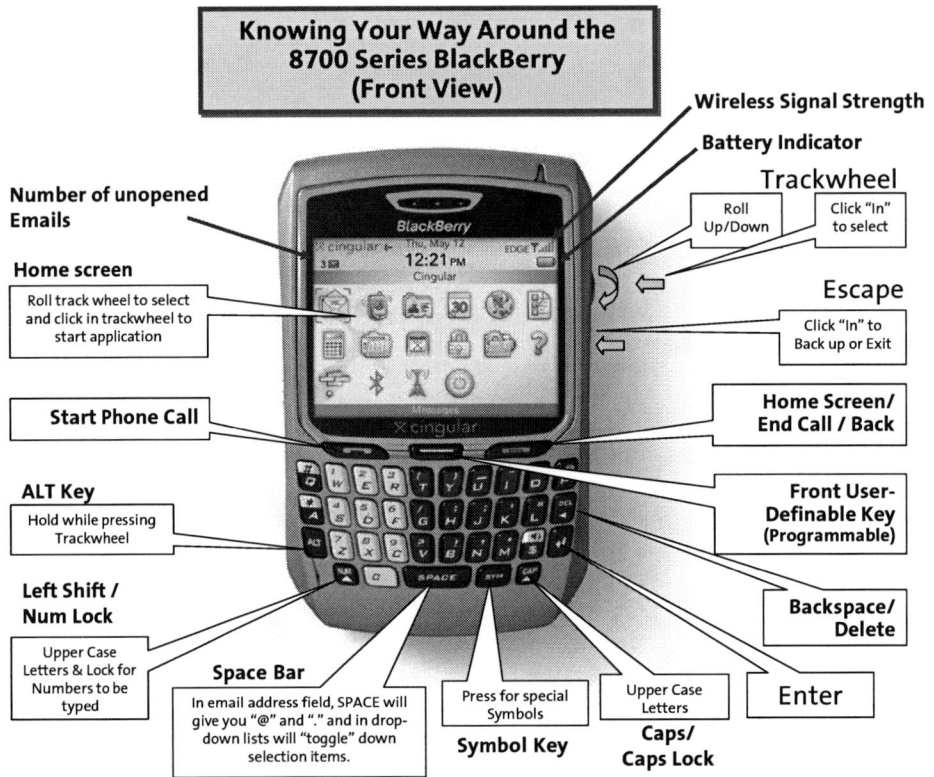

Knowing Your Way Around the 8700 Series BlackBerry (Front View)

Wireless Signal Strength

Battery Indicator

Number of unopened Emails

Home screen
Roll track wheel to select and click in trackwheel to start application

Trackwheel — Roll Up/Down — Click "In" to select

Escape — Click "In" to Back up or Exit

Start Phone Call

Home Screen/ End Call / Back

ALT Key
Hold while pressing Trackwheel

Front User-Definable Key (Programmable)

Left Shift / Num Lock
Upper Case Letters & Lock for Numbers to be typed

Backspace/ Delete

Space Bar
In email address field, SPACE will give you "@" and "." and in drop-down lists will "toggle" down selection items.

Press for special Symbols — **Symbol Key**

Upper Case Letters — **Caps/ Caps Lock**

Enter

Knowing Your Way Around the BlackBerry 8700 Series (Top and Side Views)

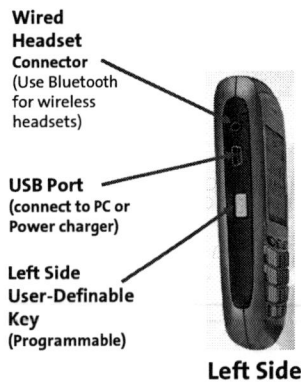

Power/ Backlight   Phone Key

Message Light (Flashes when you Receive new messages)

Top View

Wired Headset Connector (Use Bluetooth for wireless headsets)

USB Port (connect to PC or Power charger)

Left Side User-Definable Key (Programmable)

Left Side

Trackwheel — Roll Up/Down — Click "In" to select

Escape / Back Key — Click "In" to Back up or Exit

Right Side

Knowing Your Way Around the 8700 Series BlackBerry Icons

Number of Unopened Emails

Phone
Place & Receive Phone Calls

Address Book
Names, Addresses, Phone #, Emails, etc.

Calendar
Day, Week, Month, Agenda Views

Inbox
All Received & Sent Email, also Phone & SMS Logs

Web Browser
Wireless Internet – Google, etc.

Applications (sub-menu)

Memo Pad

Search

Browser

Pictures (view pictures From Email)

Password Keeper

Task List

Settings & Tools
Date/Time, AutoText, Text Size, etc.

Help

Calculator

Power
Turn Power Off

Keyboard Lock
(Prevent inadvertently typing keys.)

Brick Breaker Game

Configure Bluetooth headset or car connection

Bluetooth

Turn Radio Off / On

Wireless Radio

Adjust Ring/Vibrate/None for Phone, Email, Calendar, etc.

Profiles (Sounds)

Knowing Your Way Around the BlackBerry (v4.1) Icons

Inbox
All Received & Sent Email, also Phone & SMS Logs

Battery Strength

Number of Unopened Emails

Date/Time change in "Settings"

Wireless Signal Strength
You need all uppercase "NXTL" to send/receive email & browse the Web

Enterprise Activation

Phone
Place & Receive Phone Calls

Address Book
Names, Addresses, Phone #, Emails, etc.

Calendar
Day, Week, Month, Agenda Views

Task List

Memo Pad

Web Browser

Calculator

Alarm Clock

Password Keeper
(Store important Passwords)

Profiles (Sounds)
Adjust Ring/Vibrate/None for Phone, Email, Calendar, etc.

(Scroll down to see the rest of the icons...)

Keyboard Lock
(Prevent inadvertently typing keys.)

Pictures
View pictures saved from email attachments. Customize home or standby screen with your pictures.

Settings & Tools
Date/Time, AutoText, Text Size, etc.

Wireless Radio
Turn Radio Off / On – when on an airplane, sometimes helps regain wireless data signal

Turn Power Off

Search
Find any text in Inbox, Address Book, Tasks, Calendar or MemoPad

Knowing Your Way Around The 6200, 6500, 6700, 7200, 7500 and 7700 Series BlackBerries Icons

Inbox
All Received & Sent Email, also Phone & SMS Logs

Phone
Place & Receive Phone Calls

Address Book
Names, Addresses, Phone #, Emails, etc.

Calendar
Day, Week, Month, Agenda Views

Web Browser
Wireless Internet – Google, etc.

Saved Folders
Saved Emails from Inbox

Compose
Write Emails

Task List

Calculator

Memo Pad
Take Notes, Store Lists, etc.

Profiles (Sounds)
Adjust Ring/Vibrate/None for Phone, Email, Calendar, etc.

Turn Wireless Off

Pictures
Any Pictures saved from Email Attachments

Power
Turn Power Off

Find text in Inbox, Address Book, Calendar, etc.

Search

Date/Time, AutoText, Text Size, etc.

Settings

Turn Radio Off / On

Wireless Radio

Knowing Your Way Around
The 6200, 6500, 6700, 7200, 7500 and 7700 Series BlackBerries

Phone / 2-Way Radio
(2-Way Radio-6500, 7500 Series)

Trackwheel
| Roll Up/Down | Click "In" to select |

Battery
5 bars = full
1 bar/red = empty, radio
will turn off

Escape
Click "In" to
Back up or Exit

Home screen
Roll track wheel to select
and click in trackwheel to
start application

Forward / Back Cursor
Press ALT + keys for
forward/back 1 character

ALT "Half-moon" Key
Hold while pressing
Trackwheel

Backspace/Delete

Enter

Left Shift
Upper Case
Letters

Space Bar
In email address field, SPACE will
give you "@" and "." and in drop-
down lists will "toggle" down
selection items.

Right Shift
(caps lock)
Upper Case
Letters

Power/ Backlight
Hold to turn off, press quickly to turn
on/off back light

Check out the free VIDEO CLIP which shows you how to navigate around your Full Keyboard BlackBerry here: http://www.blackberrymadesimple.com/videos/videos.htm

**Knowing Your Way Around
The 6200, 6500, 6700, 7200,
7500 and 7700 Series
BlackBerries
(Top and Side Views)**

Phone or 2-Way Radio
(2-Way radio on 6500, 7500
Series models)

Message Light
(Flashes when you
Receive new
messages)

Antenna
(Only on 6500,
7500 Series
models)

Top View

Tip!

Press the ALT
(half-moon key)
together with
rolling the
trackwheel to do
all sorts of
interesting
things!

**Wired
Headset
Connector**
(Some
models have
Bluetooth
for wireless
headsets)

USB Port
(connect to PC or
Power charger)

Trackwheel
| Roll Up/Down | Click "In" to select |

Escape / Back Key
Click "In" to
Back up or Exit

Left Side

Right Side

Quick Tips & Tricks

- **Trackwheel:** The trackwheel is the main way you navigate the BlackBerry. Rolling the trackwheel moves the 'cursor' or allows you to highlight icons. Clicking or pushing in on the trackwheel makes a selection or opens an application (much like clicking your computer mouse).

- **Escape key: ("ESC")** Located on the side of the device underneath the trackwheel, pressing the escape key takes you out of the current view or brings you go back one screen at a time.

- **ALT Key: ("ALT")** In the lower left hand corner of the keyboard, (some models have a 'half-moon' icon on the ALT key), the ALT key is often used in tandem with the trackwheel and escape key to affect the way the cursor moves. For example, rolling the trackwheel while holding the ALT key while typing an email will cause the cursor to move back or forth one character at a time to allow editing.

- **Power/Backlighting:** Pressing this key briefly will toggle the backlighting on/off for the keyboard and the screen. If you hold this key for a few seconds, it will power-off the BlackBerry. ALT key lets you move the cursor horizontally when editing text as in an email.

- **Space Bar:** While reading an email, will "Page Down"; While setting the time on a calendar event, will "move down" one day, hour, etc.; Will insert a "@" and a "." When typing an email address "test@company.com"

- **How to Call Voicemail?** Open the phone Icon, Click the trackwheel and select "Call Voicemail"

- **Can I set Voicemail to a single key?** Yes, Open the phone icon, click the trackwheel and select "View Speed Dial List" – roll up/down to select any letter, say "V" for voicemail and click the trackwheel and select "New Speed Dial" – then enter your own BlackBerry Phone Number – that will call voicemail.

- **Can I check the calendar while on the Phone?** Yes! Press and hold the "ALT" (Halfmoon) Key while pressing the "Escape" key (under the trackwheel) to bring up a window with icons – select the Calendar, or if you don't see it, select the HOME icon and then go to the calendar. Then you can use "ALT-ESC" after you've checked or scheduled your calendar event.

- **Can I call a restaurant I find in Google on my Web Browser?** Yes! If you're using www.google.com from your web browser and you locate a restaurant, then when you see their phone number underlined "333-123-4444" just highlight it and click on it to call them from your BlackBerry!

Troubleshooting Your Wireless Signal
(If Email / Web / Calendar wireless syncing not working)

○ Check your wireless signal strength – do you have at least 2 bars? If yes, do you see "1X", "GPRS", "NXTL", "EDGE" (key to look for is all UPPER CASE letters / numbers)? If no, then try to turn off then on the radio using the Wireless Radio Tower Icon (see Icon images above).

○ Try a soft reset – press and hold 3 keys simultaneously – ALT (Halfmoon) + CAP + DEL (press 2 or 3 times until you see the hourglass and the screen goes blank for about 1-2 minutes)

○ If that doesn't work then try going to the Wrench Icon (Options) select "Host Routing Table" (If it's not listed, go to "Advanced Options" first, then select "Host Routing Table", Click the Trackwheel and select "Register Now"

○ Finally, do a "Hard Reset" – turn off the BlackBerry, remove the battery, wait 30 seconds and then re-insert and power-on the BlackBerry.

Finding Answers to Frequently-Asked-Questions

FIRST TIME SETUP:

Q: I just received my BlackBerry, where do I start?
  A: Installing BlackBerry Desktop Manager (p. 22)

Q: How do I put my Names, Addresses (email addresses), Phone #'s on the BlackBerry?
  A: Putting your information on the BlackBerry (p. 67)

Q: How do I set up my BlackBerry email the first time?
  A: Setting Up Your BlackBerry Email (p. 25)

Q: How do I tell what type of BlackBerry Internet Service Email web site I have?
  A: Determining your Type of BlackBerry Internet Service (p. 25)

Q: What is the web site address so I can setup my BlackBerry Internet Service Email?
  A: See: BlackBerry Internet Service Web Site List (p. 26)

Q: How do I move around on the BlackBerry – what is a "trackwheel"?
  A: See the Quick Reference Guides (p. 4)

Q: How do I send an e-mail from my BlackBerry?
  A: Sending Email from Your BlackBerry (p. 55) and Receiving Email (p. 54)

Q: What if I can't send email because it says "No Email Services, connect to PC..."?
  A: Get Error message when try to send Email Message from BlackBerry (p. 62)

Q: My 'sent from' address is some weird email address – how do I fix it?
  A: Fixing your 'Sent-From' E-Mail Address (p.65)

Q: How do I quickly erase the entire BlackBerry Address book, task list or calendar?
  A: Quickly Erase or Restore Address Book, Calendar, or Other Data (p. 72)

Q: How do I fix the date/time on my BlackBerry?
  A: Setting the date/time (p. 75)

Q: How do set the BlackBerry to ringing or vibrate?
  A: Profiles: To Vibrate or not to Vibrate! (p. 78)

Q: Can I set my BlackBerry to Alert me a special way when I receive email from a specific person (or people)?
  A: Setting your BlackBerry to Notify You for VIP Email (p. 134)

Q: How to tell if I can Send/Receive Email and Browse the Web?
  A: Understanding when you can Send/Receive Email & Web Surf (p. 56)

Q: What are some good ways to test my email setup?
  A: Testing your Email Setup (p. 66)

New Videos & New Web Training

Check out our New Video Clips Series and Live Web Training on our web site at: www.blackberrymadesimple.com

UTILITIES AND BASICS:

Q: What version of BlackBerry Software am I running on my handheld?
  A: See "Checking Your BlackBerry Systems Software Version" (p. 77)

Q: What are some great web sites for the small BlackBerry web browser?
  A: Great Stuff on your BlackBerry Web Browser (p. 110)

Q: 8:00am Tee off time canceled after you arrived at the course?
  A: No problem. Use Google local to find another course. (p. 111)

Q: How can I do more than one thing at a time ("Multi-Task")?
  A: Multi-Tasking with your BlackBerry "ALT-ESC" (p. 84)

Q: I've lost my wireless signal, how do I get it back?
  A: Wireless Connection Troubleshooting (p. 57)

Q: How do I check how much free memory I have left?
  A: Checking your memory (p. 95)

Q: How do I reset my BlackBerry to free up memory and improve connectivity?
  A: How to Soft Reset (p. 60) /   How to Hard Reset (p. 61)

Q: How do I Move and/or Get Rid of Unwanted Home Screen Icons?
  A: Home Screen: Hiding Icons (p. 85) /
      Home Screen: Moving Icons (p. 85)

Q: Can I make the BlackBerry type frequently entered text for me?
  A: Teaching the BlackBerry to type for you! (p. 101)

Q: How do I change the font size to see **LARGER** or smaller characters?
  A: Adjusting Font Size (p. 90)

Q: How do I quickly move to the first message or last message in the Inbox?
  A: Navigating your Inbox (p. 92)

Q: Is there a way to take notes while on a Phone Call?
  A: Yes, See Taking Notes on a Call (p. 96)

Q: How do I extend my Battery life and what are other battery tips?
  A: Getting the most out of your Battery (p. 99)

Q: How do I find "lost" information on my BlackBerry (in Address/email/Memos/Tasks)?
  A: Searching – Finding anything on your BlackBerry (p. 163)

Q: Is there a way to organize or "filter" my contacts into key groups?
  A: Yes! Learn about Categories. (p. 206)

Q: How Do I Set the Programmable Keys on the 8700c?
  A: Yes! Read Here. (p. 91)

Q: Can my BlackBerry 7520 accept voice commands?
  A: Yes! Read Here. (p. 91)

Tip!

Many times to get your wireless signal back, just cycle your radio antenna off / on!

Tip!

Charge your BlackBerry every night especially if you use it as a phone.

ADVANCED EMAIL TIPS:

FAXING Tip!

Visit the **Partners Section** on our web site to sign up for "eFax" services so you can send, receive, view, and forward Faxes right from your BlackBerry! www.blackberrymadesimple.com (See the last pages of this book for more information.)

Q: Can I receive and view a **FAX** on my BlackBerry?
   A: Yes, see receiving a FAX on your BlackBerry (p. 129)

Q: Can I send a **FAX** from my BlackBerry?
   A: Yes, see Sending a FAX from your BlackBerry (p. 131)

Q: How can I receive email up to 95% faster using the Web Client?
   A: Check this out. (p. 137)

Q: How can I stop the SPAM from getting to my BlackBerry?
   A: Go to: Stopping SPAM from getting to your BlackBerry (p. 126)

Q: How do I get rid of that signature 'Sent from my BlackBerry Handheld'?
   A: Go to: Fixing your Reply To and Default BlackBerry Signature (p. 65)

Q: How do I move around the BlackBerry email Inbox?
   A: Moving Around in BlackBerry Inbox – Fast! (p. 92)

Q: If I delete an Email on my BlackBerry, can it automatically delete in my inbox?
   A: Yes, if you have a specific type of email and Wireless Email Reconciliation Turned On (p. 93)

Q: Can I view e-mail attachments?
   A: Yes, See E-Mail Attachment Viewing (p. 144)

Q: Can I send an e-mail "mail merge" from my BlackBerry?
   A: Yes, with a few manual steps. (p. 146)

Tip!

Yes – you can view (most) e-mail attachments!

Q: Is there a way to be more responsive with marketing literature?
   A: Yes! Check out this tip. (p. 148)

Q: Can I setup and use an e-mail mailing list on the BlackBerry?
   A: Absolutely! (p. 148)

Q: How do I increase or decrease the font size in my e-mails?
   A: Adjusting Font Size in E-Mail (p. 90)

Q: I've lost my wireless signal how can I get it back?
   A: Wireless connection tips. (p. 57) / Resetting Your BlackBerry. (p. 60)

Q: Can a low battery stop my e-mail?
   A: Yes! You need to keep it charged. (p. 99)

Tip!

Did you know you can setup and use an email list on your BlackBerry?

Q: How can I put a scheduled call phone number into my calendar from email?
   A: Here's how. (p. 155)

Q: Can I teach my BlackBerry all my signatures and then easily choose one?
   A: Yes! Check out this tip. (p. 101)

Q: I need to find an email, how do I do this?
   A: Use the "Global Search" Icon (p. 163)
   or Email Inbox Search (p. 106)

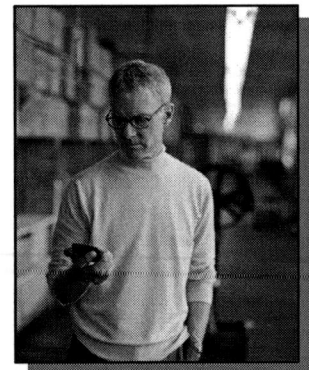

ADVANCED PHONE TIPS:

Q: How do I see my call logs (received, placed, missed calls) in my Inbox?
   A: Here's the answer! (p. 152)

Q: What is the fastest way to dial frequently used phone numbers (e.g. Home, Spouse, Friends, and Work) on the BlackBerry.
   A: Check this out: Speed Dial from Home Screen. (p. 177)

Q: How do I dial voicemail with one keystroke?
   A: See here. (p. 179)

> **Tip!**
>
> Dial voicemail with a single key "V"!

Q: How do I adjust my ringer or vibrate setting for my Phone?
   A: Look at Profiles. (p. 180)

Q: What is a great way to use the calendar to remind me of a conference call and even dial the number?
   A: Check this out! (p. 155)

Q: Can I view the address book or calendar while on the phone?
   A: Absolutely! Check out this tip. (p. 84)

Q: Is there a way to dial the phone from the calendar or a ringing alarm?
   A: Yes! (p. 160)

Q: Can I dial from text in an e-mail message or Memo Pad item?
   A: Yes! (p. 168)

Q: Can I dial from an e-mail address on a message I've received?
   A: Yes! (p. 168)

Q: Can use the BlackBerry as a Speakerphone?
   A: Yes! (p. 170)

Q: Is there a way to take notes while on a phone call?
   A: Yes. (p. 96)

Q: Can my BlackBerry be a portable conference call?
   A: Yes! (p. 173)

Q: How do I find that restaurant's number on my BlackBerry?
   A: See here. (p. 163)

Q: I seem to have lost wireless connectivity, how to I get it back?
   A: See our Wireless Connection Troubleshooting. (p. 57)

ADVANCED CALENDAR TIPS:

Q: What is the fastest way to schedule calendar events?
    A: Use the "Quick Entry" feature! (p. 182) or
        Quickly scheduling In Day/Week View (p. 186)

Q: What's the quickest way to move around in the calendar?
    A: Finding a specific day. (p. 184) /   Scrolling a Day-at-a-Time. (p. 189)

Q: Can I View scheduled TASKS on my calendar?
    A: Yes, if you are running v4.1 or higher BlackBerry Software (p. 197)

Q: Can I see with the calendar when I'm on the phone or in e-mail?
    A: Check this out! (p. 84)

Q: Is there a way to dial the phone right from the calendar ringing alarm?
    A: Yes! (p. 160)

Q: Can I see my driving directions right when I need them (when my alarm rings)?
    A: Yes! (p. 191)

Q: I use conference calls a lot, is there a way my BlackBerry can dial for me?
    A: Yes! See here. (p. 155)

Q: I like **Week View**, can I have the calendar start in **Week View** all the time?
    A: Yes! (p. 195)

Q: I have a lot of evening appointments, but my calendar ends at 5pm can I fix it?
    A: Yes! Read here. (p. 194)

Q: I cannot read the font in the calendar (it's too small), how do I fix this?
    A: Adjust your font size here. (p. 90)

Q: I know I have that name or phone number in the calendar but I can't find it.
    A: Use the search command – read here. (p. 163)

Q: When I leave my BlackBerry on my desk, I miss calendar alarms – help!
    A: Adjust your "Profile" here. (p. 78)

Q: Do you sell an **electronic searchable PDF version** of this BlackBerry book?
    A: Yes! (p. 18) and
    Visit: http://www.blackberrymadesimple.com/

Q: Do you sell **on-screen videos** with information from this book?
    A: Yes! See our new videos. (p. 20)
    Visit: http://www.blackberrymadesimple.com/videos/videos.htm

Q: Do you offer **web-based training** for BlackBerry End Users and Help Desk / Support Personnel?
    A: Yes! Visit our web site for the latest information and to sign up today!
    Visit: http://www.blackberrymadesimple.com/

> ## Tip!
>
> Just start typing on the calendar day view to schedule a meeting. Use the cap key to change START time and the trackwheel alone to change END time.

BLACKBERRY AS PERSONAL LIFE ORGANIZER:

Tip!

Use your calendar with alarms to remind you of all your personal commitments – don't use the task list, use the calendar instead!

Q: Is there a way to put a phone number in the calendar and have it available when the alarm rings?
    A: Yes! Read here. (p. 160)

Q: Can the BlackBerry type frequently entered information for me (like directions)?
    A: Yes! See here. (p. 101)

Q: What is the fastest way to schedule calendar events?
    A: Use the "Quick Entry" feature! (p. 182)

Q: How can I send a group email from my BlackBerry (e.g. Baby Birth)?
    A: Read here about Creating E-Mail Groups. (p. 148)
       And sending them. (p. 200)

Q: Can my BlackBerry help me remember my Grocery List while on a Call?
    A: Yes! Use the Memo Pad as your List for each Store you Visit. (p. 204)

Q: How can I get rid of all those Icons I don't use on my BlackBerry?
    A: See here. (p. 85)

Q: Is there a way to organize or "filter" my contacts into key groups?
    A: Yes! Learn about Categories. (p. 206)

Q: I never seem to get my important things done during the week?
    A: Yes! This can help you. (p. 210)

Table of Contents

Top 5 Reasons To Read this as an Electronic Book

Visit www.blackberrymadesimple.com

1. **Easily Search the Entire Book** – Search for any phrase or word instantly in the book using the Adobe Acrobat Reader™ text search command.

2. **Navigate Quickly from the Table of Contents** - Click on any Table of Contents entry to jump to that page!

3. **Instantly go to the "Answers" pages** - Click on the Answers text in the Frequently Asked Questions section and instantly jump to the answers page(s).

4. **Read Anywhere without Lugging the Book** - Have the entire book accessible with you anywhere on your laptop computer.

5. **Instantly access the web** - Much of the information is web-related, you can click on any of the web links throughout the book.

● ●

Testimonials:

"With this training, your handouts, and the Blackberry simulator I feel confident that I will be able to help most end-users with any questions they might have!"

S. Schmelzer
BlackBerry Help Desk
Company with over
400 BlackBerry Users

"I found it very helpful!"

R. Donelson
Technical Support
HNI Corporation

Martin Trautschold

Expert Web Training For End Users or Help Desk Personnel

Visit www.blackberrymadesimple.com

1. **Save travel costs and time!** You are trained right at your desk.

2. **Have the Expert show you!** Via web conferencing, you see on the Trainer's BlackBerry on your screen.

3. **Fully Interactive!** Ask the Instructor any question you have.

4. **Learn by doing!** Follow along with exercises on your own BlackBerry.

5. **Be Trained Anywhere!** You could be at home, your office, a hotel, anywhere you have a phone and high-speed Internet!

Who is the trainer?

Martin Trautschold is the instructor. He is one of the co-authors of this BlackBerry Made Simple!(TM) book and has spent 1,000's of hours with BlackBerries since 2001 selling, supporting, training people, providing customer service and writing documentation. Martin co-founded a BlackBerry Software company in the fall of 2001 which became one of the earliest BlackBerry Alliance Member companies. He also has attended and co-hosted a booth at Research In Motion's Annual BlackBerry Wireless Enterprise Symposium conference. Early in 2005, he sold the software company and focused his attention exclusively on BlackBerry Made Simple books, e-books, videos and training. Martin has helped 100's of people get up and running with their BlackBerries and is passionate about helping people understand and do more with their BlackBerries! **To ask Martin a question**, please send an email to: martin@blackberrymadesimple.com

...where Blackberry _Professionals_ Connect!
PinStack.com

Top Reasons to join PinStack.com, *a BlackBerry Made Simple Preferred Partner*

1. Quickly Find Answers to BlackBerry Technical Questions – no matter how simple or complex.

2. Learn about all the newest BlackBerry Devices including product reviews.

3. Quickly find information about Tips, Tricks and FAQs.

4. Listen to what people are saying about pinstack.com:

"I just discovered Pinstack.com and it's awesome! I browse many of the other major Blackberry forums but this one is definitely unique." - Chris, USA

"This is a nice community and very professional. I work in the Wireless industry and many people I meet have mentioned Pinstack.com." - Andrea, Canada

"Pinstack.com is one of my favorite member-run Blackberry related online resources. Lots of forums, where members (Pinstack.com calls 'em "stackers") can state their opinions and ask for advice on pretty much anything RIM Blackberry." – Russell, USA

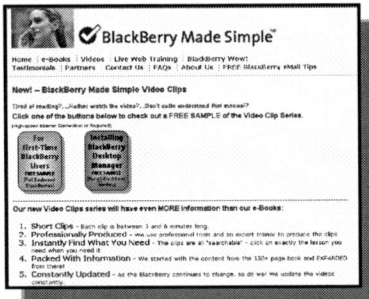

"NEW" BlackBerry Made Simple Video Clips

http://www.blackberrymadesimple.com/videos/videos.htm

✓ Professionally produced on-screen videos make the book come to life!

✓ Great for people who don't want to read the book.

✓ See on the Screen EXACTLY how to do what's in the book.

✓ Some people are more visual and auditory learners – videos are a great answer.

✓ AND MUCH MORE!

If you want to be notified via email as soon as the Video Clips are ready, please sign up for our Free Email Tips at www.blackberrymadesimple.com.

Visit the "PARTNERS" section on our web site to...

http://www.blackberrymadesimple.com/partners/index.htm

✓ Find answers to (those few) technical questions you didn't find in this book! (From the most basic to the most challenging – find answers using the BlackBerry Discussion Forums)

✓ Sign-up to use the same eFax service, and other services used by the authors! (Click the links)

✓ Find all sorts of accessories and software for your BlackBerry (Using on-line retailers)

✓ Even make money from selling the Electronic Version of this book (Put our Affiliate links on your Web Site and setup a PayPal account), And MORE!

✓ If you want to become a partner or have any questions or comments, please contact us at info@blackberrymadesimple.com.

Who should read this book?

You should read this book if:

- Just purchased or received a new BlackBerry
- Want to learn all the most useful BlackBerry tips/tricks
- Are interested in undocumented tips
- Need help setting up your email or getting your names/addresses on your BlackBerry
- Want to avoid waiting on hold for 45 minutes to talk with technical support
- Are interested in eliminating SPAM from your BlackBerry.
- Are interested in FAXING to or from your BlackBerry.
- Want to get the most out of your BlackBerry!

How long will it take?

It depends on how much you want to learn today!

With 15 minutes you can setup your email

With 30 minutes you can get your names/numbers on your BlackBerry

You could also use the "Section-A-Day" Method! Just take 5-10 minutes to read a section a day.

Have a question that is not answered in this book?

Send us your Questions:

Please send them to   info@blackberrymadesimple.com and we'll do our best to answer them. If we like them so much we may include them in a new book!

Find Answers in the Partners Section of our Web Site:

You may also find a wealth of information in many of the BlackBerry Discussion Forums and other sources of information in the Partners section on our website: www.blackberrymadesimple.com

Read This Section IF...
- Desktop Manager is not installed OR
- You <u>are not</u> using a BlackBerry Enterprise Server
- Your email is outsourced (usually with a POP3 server)

Installing the BlackBerry Desktop Manager

Blackberry Desktop Manager is usually required to:

☑ Synchronize contacts, calendar and tasks.

☑ Backup or Restore Data from your BlackBerry

☑ Install/Uninstall programs from your BlackBerry

Skip This Section IF...
- Desktop Manager is already installed AND your BlackBerry email is working OR
- Your organization has setup your Desktop Manger for you or told you not to install it.

See the VIDEO of how to install Desktop Manager!

Check out the free sample video clip on our web site here:
http://www.blackberrymadesimple.com/videos/videos.htm

This is the software that came on the CD when you purchased your BlackBerry.

TIP: Many times, the CD is out-of-date when it ships.

If you are not sure if you have the latest version of your Desktop Manager Software, then first go to your Carrier's web site, if you cannot locate the software there, then go to this screen:

http://www.blackberry.com/support/downloads/index.shtml

1. **Try your carrier's web page**
2. **Try this link from BlackBerry's web site:**
   http://www.blackberry.com/support/downloads/index.shtml

CAUTION

If your BlackBerry was issued by your company, please check with your IT department for the right version of Blackberry Desktop Manager.

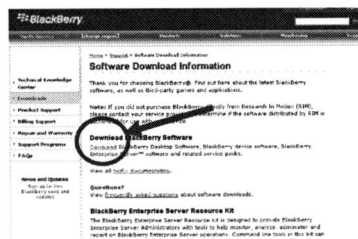

Click the "Download" link

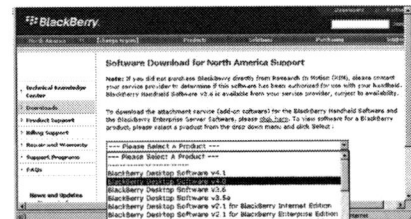

Select the appropriate version of BlackBerry Desktop Manager for your organization.

Then follow the instructions to download the software (you'll have to supply contact information and agree to the legal terms.)

If you are ready to move forward with the install, just insert the CD and follow the onscreen instructions. Move to the next section of this guide when you are prompted to choose your **"Email Integration Options."**

Choosing your type of E-mail System

When you are installing the BB Desktop manager from the BlackBerry CD, you will be prompted to choose what type of email system you want to integrate your BlackBerry with. Several screens into the installation process, you will see a screen like this:

<table>
<tr><td>

When to Get More Help...
- You don't know what kind of email system you use.
- You don't know the settings for your e-mail servers.
- Your organization has issued you your BlackBerry and plans to set it up.

</td></tr>
</table>

Knowing what type of email configuration to choose is important. If you do not know what choice to make, contact your IT department or wireless carrier for help.

BlackBerry provides the following Help Screens when making this choice:

The BlackBerry Enterprise Server or BlackBerry Desktop Redirector Option

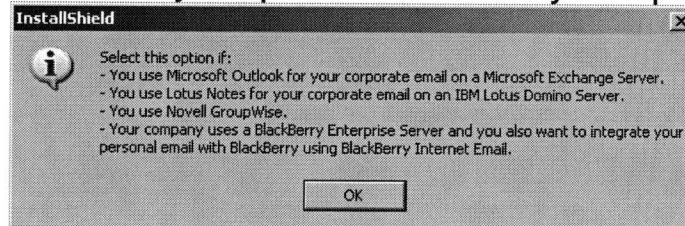

The BlackBerry Internet Mail Option

InstallShield [x]

Select this option if:
- You use a new email account provided by your BlackBerry service provider, for example userid@serviceprovider.com.
- You want to integrate your existing ISP email account with BlackBerry.
- You want to integrate your corporate email account with BlackBerry, but your company does not use a BlackBerry Enterprise Server.

OK

Again, if you don't know which to choose contact your IT support or call your wireless carrier for help!

Follow the remaining onscreen instructions to complete the installation of BlackBerry Desktop Manager.

Setting Up Your BlackBerry Email

The BlackBerry can receive email from (or be integrated to) up to 10 email accounts using the BlackBerry Internet Service (also known as "BIS") Email web tool. This BIS tool allows you to integrate and configure your email accounts including signature, "reply-to" address, filters and other things.

There are two types of "BIS" sites: "**Separate**" (which is a separate web site from your carrier's with a yellow/orange bar across the top of the screen) and "**Imbedded**" (which looks like part of your carrier's web site and has a black bar across the middle of the screen and your carrier's web site across the top of the screen). On October 1, 2005, T-Mobile was the first North American BlackBerry wireless carrier to launch this new "IMBEDDED" BlackBerry Internet Service site as part of their main "My T-Mobile" site. As of this date, other North American BlackBerry carriers still had the "Separate" (or Standard) BlackBerry Internet Service Web Sites. We believe that others carriers around the world will start to have IMBEDDED sites soon.

Do I have a "Separate" or "Imbedded" BlackBerry Internet Service site?

The **"Separate" BlackBerry Internet Service** site looks like this and is typically separate from your BlackBerry Carrier's main web site.

The **"Imbedded" BlackBerry Internet Service** site looks like this image and is a window "imbedded in" or part of your carrier's main web site:

This is an **"Imbedded" BlackBerry Internet Service Site** (a "window" inside the carrier's main web site.)

Your Carrier logo will be here

The **"Imbedded"** site will have a BLACK BAR across the middle of the screen

BLACKBERRY INTERNET SERVICE WEB SITE LIST:

See the table below showing which carriers have "Separate" or "Imbedded" web sites as of October 10, 2005.

If your BlackBerry Carrier is…	The Type of BlackBerry Internet Service site (10/10/05)	This is the link to The BlackBerry Internet Service E-Mail Configuration (*) (As of 10/10/05)
Cincinnati Bell (US)	Separate	https://webclient.blackberry.net/WebMail/Window.jsp?site=cinbell
Cingular & AT&T (US)	Separate	https://webclient.blackberry.net/WebMail/Window.jsp?site=mycingular
Nextel (US)	Separate	https://bwc.blackberry.net/WebMail/Window.jsp?site=nextel
Sprint (US)	Separate	https://webclient.blackberry.net/WebMail/Window.jsp?site=sprint
T-Mobile (US)	Imbedded	http://my.t-mobile.com/Login/
Verizon (US)	Separate	https://webclient.blackberry.net/WebMail/Window.jsp?site=vzw
Rogers (Canada)	Separate	https://webclient.blackberry.net/WebMail/Window.jsp?site=rogers
Telus (Canada)	Separate	https://webclient.blackberry.net/WebMail/Window.jsp?site=telus
Bell Mobility (Canada)	Separate	https://webclient.blackberry.net/WebMail/Window.jsp?site=bell
Cable and Wireless (Cayman Islands)	Separate	https://bwc.blackberry.net/WebMail/Window.jsp?site=cw

(*) NOTE: Web-links: We have verified all web links and type of Web site (Separate or Imbedded) at time of writing, however sometimes the links do change. If you notice one of the web-links is incorrect or broken, please email us at: info@blackberrymadesimple.com Thanks!

You may also find updates for these web site links at the bottom of this BlackBerry.com web page here: http://www.blackberry.net/support/client/index.shtml

Setting Up Your Email for the "SEPARATE" Type BlackBerry Internet Service Email Web Site:

Do you have a "Separate" or "Imbedded" BlackBerry Internet Service site? See how to tell the answer earlier in this section. (If your carrier has an Imbedded site, then please go to the **Setting Up Your Email for "IMBEDDED" Type BlackBerry Internet Service Email Web Sites** section later in this book – click here if you are reading the electronic version to jump there)

First, Register and Create your Account on your BlackBerry Internet Email Site

1. Open up a web browser on your computer and enter the appropriate link from the table above to go to the BlackBerry Internet Service site for your BlackBerry – you should be able to locate the correct site from your BlackBerry Carrier's web site. If not, then give the carrier customer service a call and ask for help.

2. You will see a screen like this:

3. Click on the **Create New Account** button to see this screen asking you for your PIN and IMEI from your BlackBerry.

Account Set-up　　　　　　　　　　　　　　　Pg 1 of 3

To set-up your account please enter your handheld PIN and IMEI. Click here ⑦ if you require assistance locating the PIN and IMEI of your handheld.

PIN: [＿＿＿＿＿＿＿] ⑦
IMEI: [＿＿＿＿＿＿＿]

Submit　Cancel

NOTE: If your carrier does not provide a "Create New Account" link, please call the Customer Service number listed and ask for help.

4.　To find these PIN and IMEI numbers:
Quick Method: On your BlackBerry, go to the **"Help Me"** screen by simultaneously pressing ALT (halfmoon) + CAP + "H" keys.
You will need to scroll down to see your **PIN:** and **IMEI:** numbers.

A Little Longer Method: If you have trouble getting to the **"Help Me"** screen, then go to To find these PIN and IMEI numbers: On your BlackBerry, go to the **Options** screen (wrench icon)

Options

Tip!

On most menus and list screens like this OPTIONS screen, typing the first letter of the item will "jump" to it. Hit an "S" to jump down to the first item starting with "S"

5.　Choose **Status**

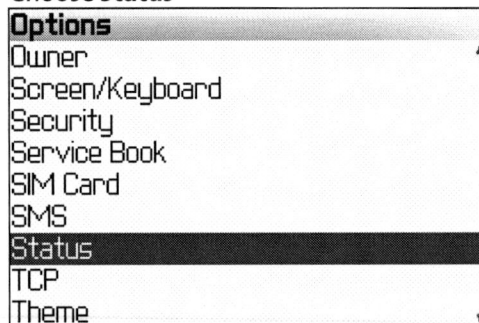

Options
Owner
Screen/Keyboard
Security
Service Book
SIM Card
SMS
Status
TCP
Theme

6. Scroll to the bottom of the **Status** screen to find your PIN and IMEI numbers

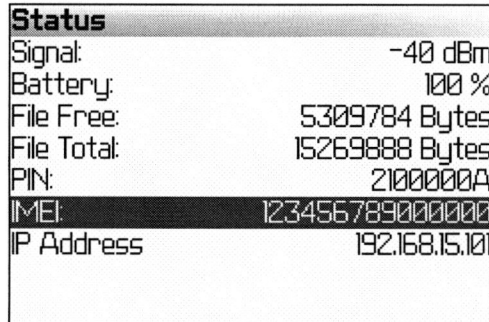

Status	
Signal:	-40 dBm
Battery:	100 %
File Free:	5309784 Bytes
File Total:	15269888 Bytes
PIN:	2100000A
IMEI:	123456789000000
IP Address	192.168.15.101

7. Enter those numbers in this screen and click "Submit"

   NOTE: DON'T enter the periods in the IMEI number even though you may see them on your BlackBerry.

> **Tip!**
>
> If you see error messages, after clicking Submit then verify you entered then PIN and IMEI correctly, if you have entered correctly, then please call you carrier for assistance.

BlackBerry.

Account Set-up   Pg 1 of 3

To set-up your account please enter your handheld PIN and ESN. Click here ⑦ if you require assistance locating the PIN and ESN of your handheld.

PIN: 2100000A   ⑦
ESN: 123456789000000

[Submit]   [Cancel]

Copyright@2001-2005 Research In Motion Limited. All rights reserved. Additional Legal Information.

Done   🔒 🌐 Internet

8. Then on the page pictured below click "I Agree"

BlackBerry.

Account Set-up

Please carefully read the Legal Terms and Conditions.

> BlackBerry Internet Service End User Agreement
>
> 1.   Acceptance of Terms
>
> This BlackBerry Internet Service End User Agreement (the "Agreement") is a legal agreement between you and Research In Motion Limited ("RIM") (together the "Parties" and individually a "Party"). BY CLICKING ON "YES" BELOW, YOU ARE AGREEING TO BE BOUND BY THE TERMS OF THIS AGREEMENT AND YOU ACKNOWLEDGE THAT YOU HAVE READ, UNDERSTOOD AND AGREE TO ABIDE BY AND COMPLY WITH ALL TERMS, CONDITIONS AND NOTICES CONTAINED IN OR REFERENCED BY THIS AGREEMENT, AND THAT YOU HAVE

Do you agree to be bound by the Legal Terms and Conditions?

[I Agree]   [I Disagree]

Tip!

You can change your "Reply To" Email address to your own "standard" desktop or Internet email address in the Web Client options screen!

Next, Create the Default Email Address for your BlackBerry

9. Enter your USER ID (**this becomes your BlackBerry's Default email address**) and other information:

BlackBerry.

Account Set-up   **Pg 3 of 3**

Please enter the following information to complete your Web Client account setup and click Done.

User ID:	⑦
Friendly Name:	
Password:	
Re-enter Password:	
Secret Question:	
Secret Answer:	

[Done]   [Cancel]

Your User ID will become the email address of your BlackBerry in this format:

If you entered	Then your BlackBerry Email Address "Handheld Email Address" would be: (varies depending on your Wireless Carrier)
User ID [johndoe] Friendly Name [John Doe]	John Doe < johndoe@tmo.blackberry.net> for T-mobile John Doe < johndoe@mycingular.blackberry.net> for Cingular John Doe < johndoe@rogers.blackberry.net> for Rogers Etc...

9. Next, you'll want to send an email to your BlackBerry.

Go ahead, give it a shot. From your computer send an email to the address you just set up (e.g. johndoe@tmo.blackberry.net - *We will refer to this address from now on as the 'Default Email Address,' as it is the actual email address of the BlackBerry handheld.*) and you should receive it on your BlackBerry in a few seconds.   If you need help receiving or sending email on your BlackBerry, take a look at these sections later in the book: (click on the section titles if you have the electronic version, or see the table of contents for exact page numbers)
>"Receiving Email on Your BlackBerry" Section
>"Sending Email from Your BlackBerry" Section

Make sure your BlackBerry is properly charged, the BlackBerry radio is turned on you have the correct BlackBerry email data plan with your wireless carrier.

If your message arrives – then you've been SUCCESSFUL!   Your first test email worked! Reply from your Blackberry so you can see if that works.

Then back on your Desktop, reply to the message and check to see the email address that shows up when you reply from your desktop. It should be the default email address, so you'll need to fix that and make it your desktop email address.

Now, Fix your "Sent From" / "Reply To" address for your BlackBerry

1. You should still be logged in, but if not, login to your BlackBerry Internet Service site (See the "BlackBerry Internet Service Web Site List" earlier in this book for the correct link – or click here to jump to the list if you are reading the electronic version of this book)

2. After you log into your BlackBerry Internet Service, click on the **Profile** link on the top.

3. Then click on the "Sent From" address on the "Profile" page as shown (arrow)

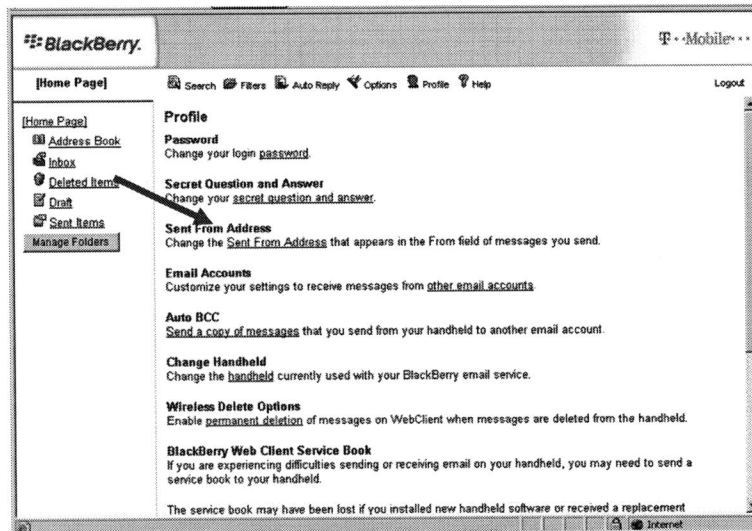

4. Then you'll be on this **Sent From Address** page. You'll want to click on the bottom radio button (see circle) and type in your main email address (home or office).   Then click "**Submit**." This will fix the problem when you "reply" to messages from your BlackBerry of the strange

"Default" email address (johndoe@tmo.blackberry.net) showing up in the "From" field.

Sending Email and Web Browsing Service Books

While you're on this Profile page, you should scroll to the bottom to see the "Send Service Book" buttons and click on both of them to ensure your BlackBerry is correctly registered on the wireless network to receive Email and Browse the web.

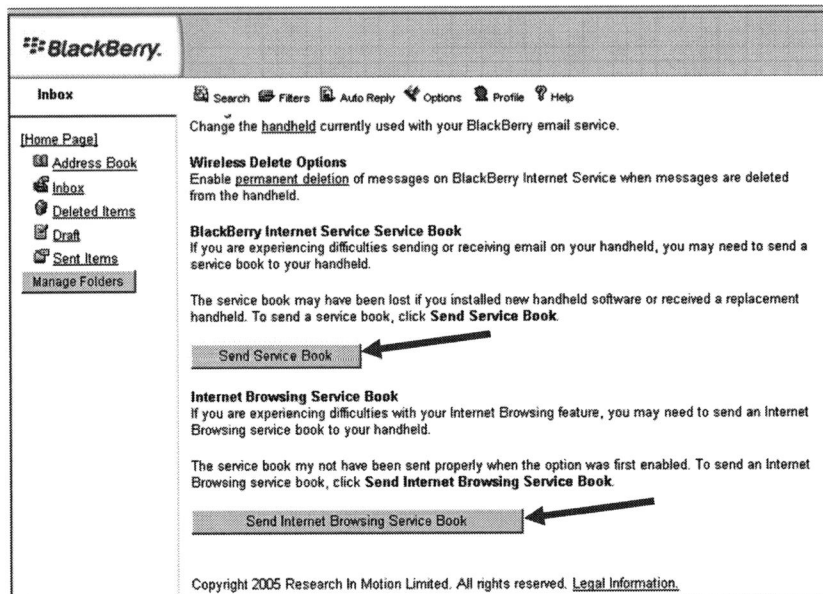

5. If you want to test this setting, go ahead and Compose a message on your BlackBerry to your desktop email address. When that message arrives on your desktop email account, you should now see the correct "From" email address and not your default BlackBerry address (like johndoe@tmo.blackberry.net)

Next, you'll want to integrate your home and/or office email accounts so you can receive them on your BlackBerry...

Configure your Home or Office Email Address(es) for your BlackBerry

1. You should still be logged into the BlackBerry Internet Service (Separate Type) account. Go back to the home screen of the BlackBerry Internet Service and click the "Email Accounts" link (see arrow):

2. Then you'll see this page, click on the "Add Account" button (arrow)

3. Next, enter your e-mail address, and the username and password you use to login to your email server and → **click Submit**.

You will then see your new email address added to the list of Email accounts and will now start receiving email sent to that address on your BlackBerry.

If the BlackBerry Internet Service cannot login to your POP3 Email Account, it may ask for your mail server name. See the box above which shows how to find out your email server name if you have Outlook™ or Outlook Express™

The final step is to adjust your Signature for your BlackBerry email

The default signature is "Sent from my BlackBerry handheld." You might want to change that to your name, organization, telephone and email address and even a tag line if you desire.

TIP: If you want more than one email signature, then you'll have to use the **AUTOTEXT** feature on your BlackBerry. If you're going to do that, then you'll need to either erase this signature on the BlackBerry Site or make it very "generic" – e.g. just your Name or email address. (Click here to jump to the AutoText section if you're reading the electronic book, or check the table of contents for the exact page number.)

1. You should still be logged into the BlackBerry Internet Service (Separate Type) account. If not, check above on how to login.
From the BlackBerry Internet Service home screen click the "Options" link (see arrow)

Tip!

WANT MULTIPLE EMAIL SIGNATURES?

You can do this with the "AutoText" feature of your BlackBerry Options/Settings Screen. (Check the table of contents for the page number, or click here if you're reading the electronic version to jump there.)

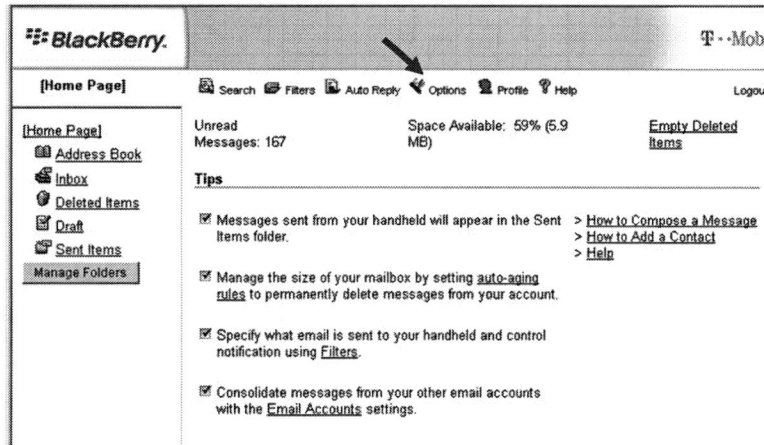

2. Enter your new email signature in the block on the screen and click the check box next to "**Include auto signature in outgoing messages**"

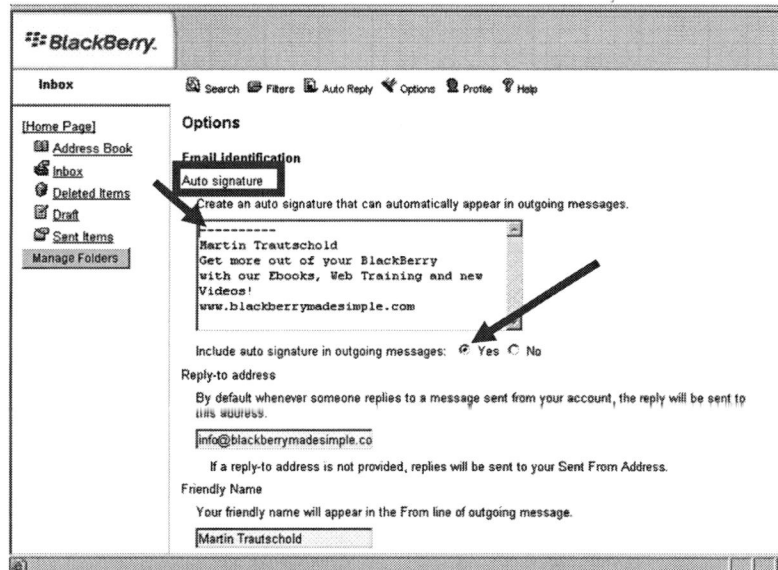

3. While you're on this page, you should also fix the **Reply To** address, **Friendly Name** and **Time Zone** as shown below.

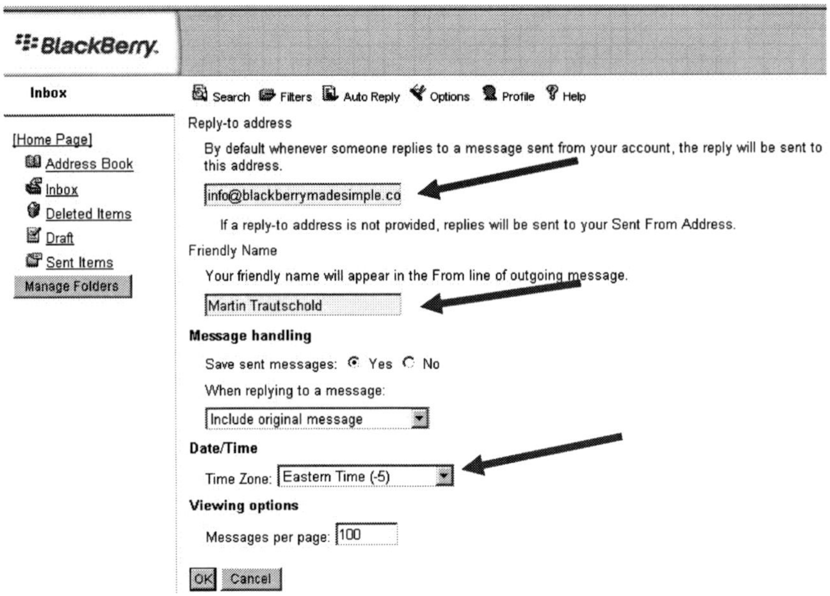

4. Finally, click "**OK**" to save your new settings.

If you desire to have an email sent to everyone who sends you an email – an "AUTO REPLY", then you can configure that as well by clicking the "Auto Reply" link at the top of the BlackBerry Internet Service as shown here. Just type in your Auto Reply and click "Save." We recommend using this sparingly as people may get annoyed by receiving the same email every time they send you one.

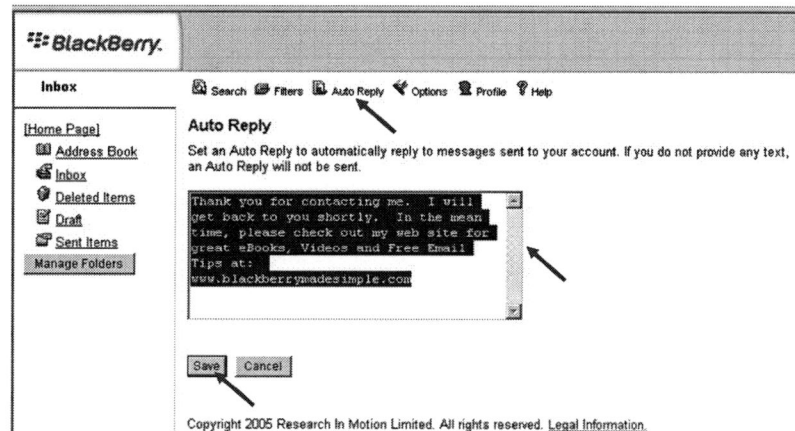

CONGRATULATIONS! You've now successfully:
o   Registered on your BlackBerry Internet Service Email Account
o   Setup your BlackBerry Default Email Address
o   Fixed your "Sent From" and "Reply To" address for your BlackBerry
o   Integrated your Work/Home Email address to your BlackBerry
o   Set up your new Signature for all outgoing BlackBerry messages.

Now, you should go to the "Receiving Email on Your BlackBerry Section" (click here if you are reading the electronic version)

Setting Up Your Email for the "IMBEDDED" Type BlackBerry Internet Service Email Web Sites:

Do you have a "Separate" or "Imbedded" BlackBerry Internet Service site? See how to tell the answer on page 21. (If your carrier has a Separate Type site, then please go to the **Setting Up Your Email for "SEPARATE" Type BlackBerry Internet Service Email Web Sites** section later in this book – click here if you are reading the electronic version to jump there)

First, Register and Create your Account on your BlackBerry Internet Email Site

1. Find and click the "Register" or "Sign Up" link on your carrier's web site
(See the "BlackBerry Internet Service Web Site List" earlier in this book for the correct link – or click here to jump to the list if you are reading the electronic version of this book)

Find the "Register" or "Sign Up" link on your carrier's web site like this one.

2. Enter your BlackBerry Phone number to receive your temporary password on your phone:

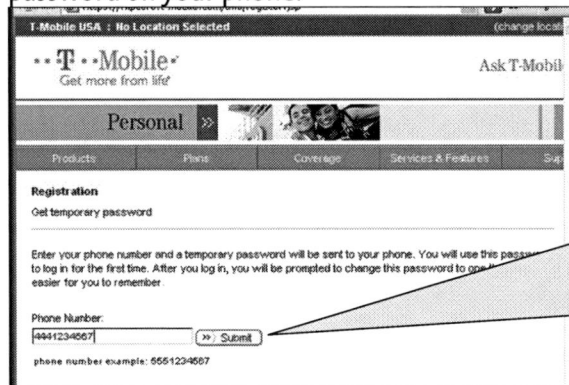

To register on this site, enter your BlackBerry phone # to receive your temporary password on your phone. (Your carrier may be slightly different)

3. Now, using that Temporary Password from your BlackBerry, log in to the web site:

If you're registering on the site, login with the temporary password you received on your BlackBerry. Otherwise, use your regular password.

4. Once logged in then scroll down to set up your BlackBerry Internet Email:

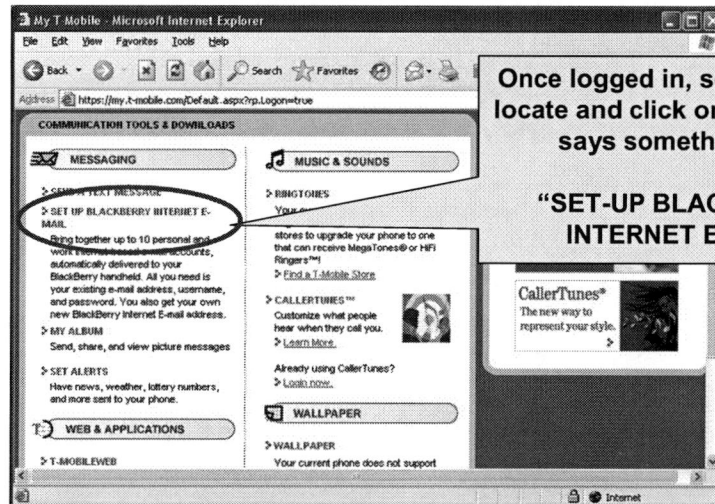

Once logged in, scroll down to locate and click on the link that says something like:

"SET-UP BLACKBERRY INTERNET E-MAIL"

Next, Create the Default Email Address for your BlackBerry

5. Now you are looking at the BlackBerry ("Imbedded") Internet Service site. You need to first create your BlackBerry default email address:

The first thing you'll want to do is create your new default BlackBerry Email Address. Click here.

6. Then choose a username for your Default BlackBerry Email address.

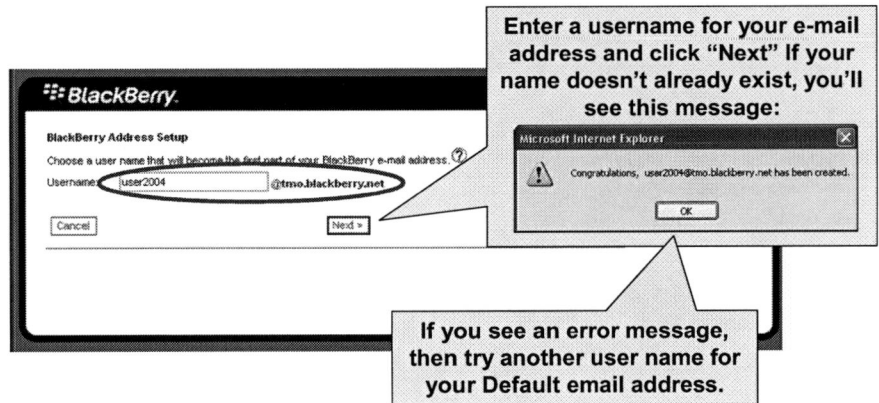

Enter a username for your e-mail address and click "Next" If your name doesn't already exist, you'll see this message:

Congratulations, user2004@tmo.blackberry.net has been created.

OK

If you see an error message, then try another user name for your Default email address.

Now, Fix your "Sent From" / "Reply To" address and your "Signature" for your BlackBerry

7. In this example the email address for the BlackBerry is:
    user2004@tmo.blackberry.net
Most people won't want people to see that address when you compose or reply to emails from your BlackBerry, so you'll need to fix your "Reply To" address as by clicking the "EDIT" icon as shown below.

Now you need to configure or "Edit" this default BlackBerry Email Address. So click "Edit"

Tip!

WANT MULTIPLE EMAIL SIGNATURES?

You can do this with the "AutoText" feature of your BlackBerry Options/Settings Screen. (Check the table of contents for the page number, or click here if you're reading the electronic version to jump there.)

8. Now you can make all the adjustments required to fine-tune your BlackBerry default email address.

TIP: If you want more than one email signature, then you'll have to use the **AUTOTEXT** feature on your BlackBerry. If you're going to do that, then you'll need to either erase this signature on the BlackBerry Site or make it very "generic" – e.g. just your Name or email address. (Click here to jump to the AutoText section if you're reading the electronic book, or check the table of contents for the exact page number.)

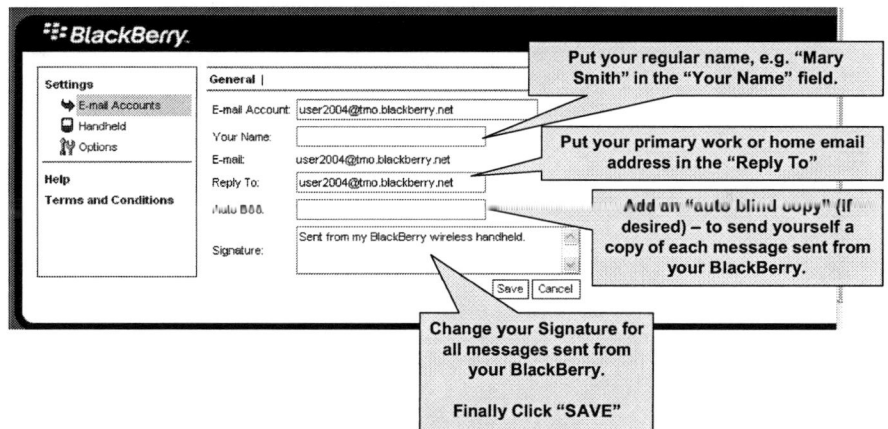

Put your regular name, e.g. "Mary Smith" in the "Your Name" field.

Put your primary work or home email address in the "Reply To"

Add an "auto blind copy" (if desired) – to send yourself a copy of each message sent from your BlackBerry.

Change your Signature for all messages sent from your BlackBerry.

Finally Click "SAVE"

Now, you've successfully setup your Default BlackBerry Email address, now you need to work on integrating one or more work or home email addresses:

Finally, Configure your Home or Office Email Address(es) for your BlackBerry

9. Click the "Add Account" link:

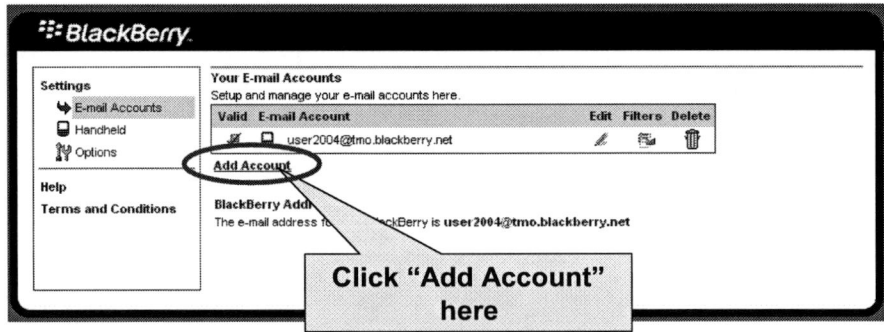

Click "Add Account" here

10. Enter your work or home email address and password, click "Next". The BlackBerry Internet Service will now try to login to that account. If it's successful, then you're done! If not, you'll have to continue to provide more information...

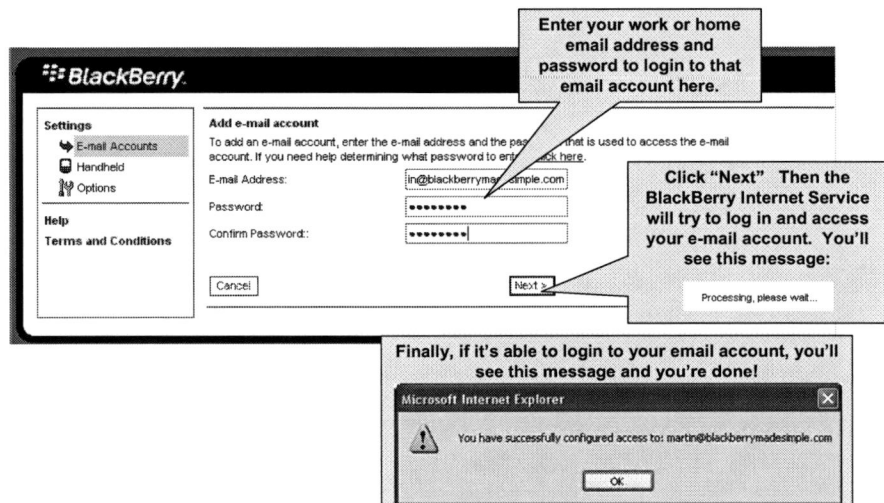

Enter your work or home email address and password to login to that email account here.

Click "Next"   Then the BlackBerry Internet Service will try to log in and access your e-mail account. You'll see this message:

Processing, please wait...

Finally, if it's able to login to your email account, you'll see this message and you're done!

Microsoft Internet Explorer

You have successfully configured access to: martin@blackberrymadesimple.com

OK

11. (Only if you see an error message do you need to continue here)   If you see the error message that it cannot configure your email account, then first click "BACK" to try re-entering your email address and password.

If you see this error message:

First, click "Back" and verify your email address and passwords were entered correctly.

You'll be brought to the "E-Mail Wizard":

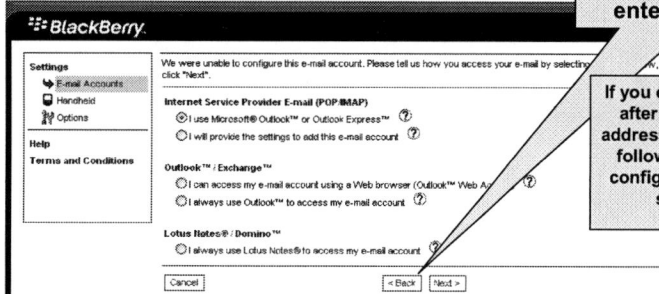

If you end up the same place after verifying your email address and passwords, then follow the Wizard to try to configure your accounts as shown in step 6.

Working with the new "Email Wizard" on the BlackBerry Web Site

If you tried your email address and password again, and still end up on this screen, then you'll have to complete this email Wizard to complete your email integration. Don't worry, it's been well designed to have programs help you determine your settings. (It's an upgrade from the "Separate" type BlackBerry Site)

This is the new "E-Mail Wizard":

Click any of these "?" (question marks) for help.

Use this if you have a POP or IMAP email service and use Outlook/Outlook Express on your PC.

Use this if you have a POP or IMAP email service and know your email server name, account and login password.

Use this if you use MS Exchange mail server and can login from "Outlook Web Access"™

Use this if you use MS Exchange mail server and only login using Outlook on your PC.

Use this if you want to integrate to a Lotus Notes e-Mail from your PC.

See 11(a)
See 11(b)
See 11(c)
See 11(d)
See 11(e)

11(a) – Internet Email with Outlook or Outlook Express:

Step 11(a): Wizard: When you select: Internet Email "Microsoft® Outlook™ or Outlook Express™" option…

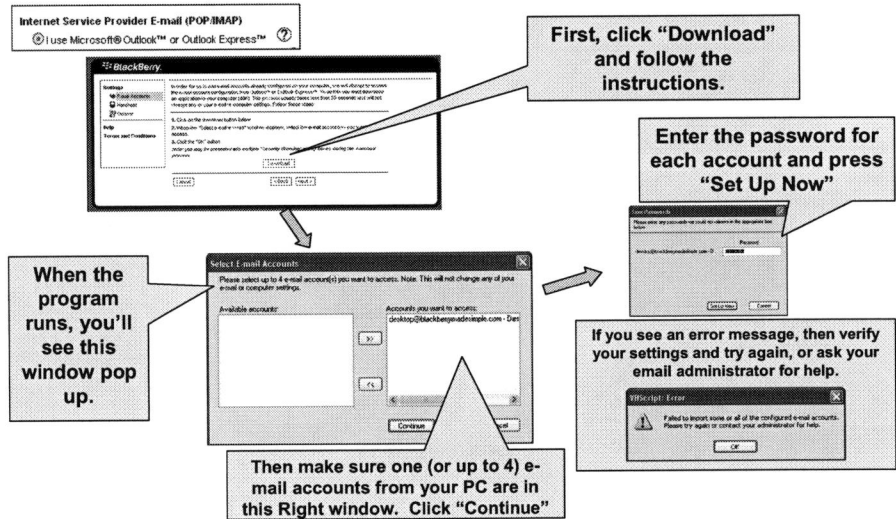

If you see a security warning or error message after clicking "Download", then click at the top of your web browser and "Install Active-X Control" as shown

Then, click "Install" when you see a window like this… to install the program.

If you are successful, then you will see a "Success message" like this:

and be returned to the main list of email addresses configured for your BlackBerry –
Now, Go To Step (12) to finish the account setup.

11(b) "Internet Email - I will provide my settings" Enter the settings as shown below:

Step 11(b): Wizard: When you select: Internet Email
I will provide the settings to add this e-mail account option…

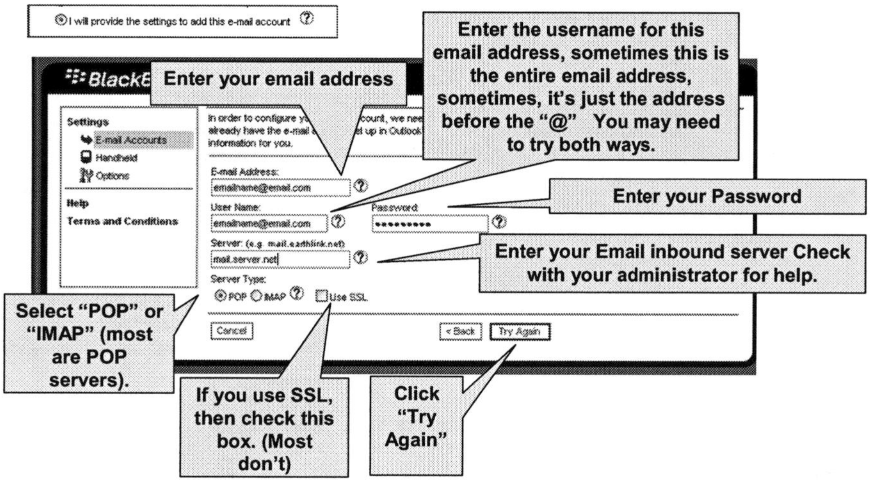

If, after you click "Try Again", you see this error message, then contact your Email Administrator for help.

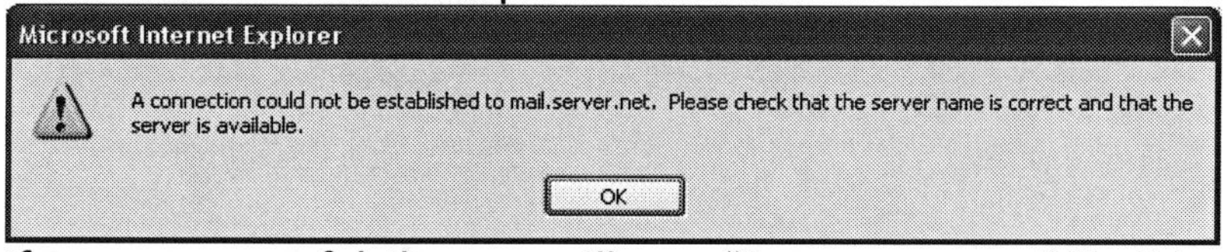

If you are successful, then you will see a "Success message" like this:

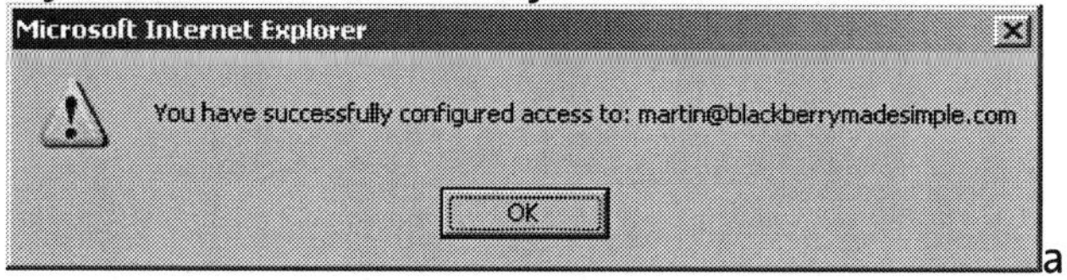

and be returned to the main list of email addresses configured for your BlackBerry –
Now, Go To Step (12) to finish the account setup.

11(c) Outlook/Exchange with Web Access:

Step 11(c): Wizard: When you select: Outlook/Exchange
I can access my e-mail account using a Web browser (Outlook™ Web Access) option…

If, after you click "Try Again", you see this error message, then contact your Email Administrator for help.

If you are successful, then you will see a "Success message" like this:

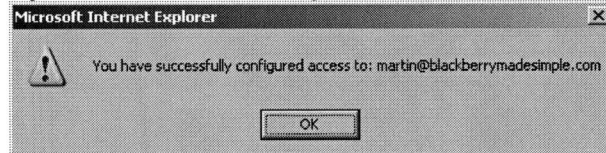

and be returned to the main list of email addresses configured for your BlackBerry –
Now, Go To Step (12) to finish the account setup.

11(d) Outlook/Exchange using Outlook only. Now you'll be using the new "Mail Connector" (replaces the "Desktop Redirector").

You have two options:
Option 1: Install your own Mail Connector on your PC
Option 2: Share a Mail Connector already installed on a co-worker's PC

Why might you want Option 2 - Share someone else's Mail Connector?
- This allows you to turn off or take your PC with your (e.g. Laptop) and still receive your email on your BlackBerry.
- Reduce the "load" on your computer
- Avoid the hassle of installing the software yourself.

Step 11(d): Wizard: When you select: Outlook/Exchange "I always use Outlook™ to access my e-mail account" option

If you are successful, then you will see a "Success message" like this:

and be returned to the main list of email addresses configured for your BlackBerry –
Now, Go To Step (12) to finish the account setup.

11 (d) Outlook/Exchange using Outlook only. Option 1 (continued)

Outlook™ / Exchange™
○ I can access my e-mail account using a Web browser (OWA)
● I always use Outlook™ to access my e-mail account ②

After the installation is complete, you will see this screen.
Leave as "Outlook" and click "Next"

Remember: To have a Mail Connector work on your PC, your PC must be:
(1) Turned ON
(2) Connected to your Network
(3) Connected to the Internet

Note: You can still "Share" your mail connector, even if you did not do it when you first installed it.

Settings
  E-mail Accounts
  Handheld
  Options
Help
Terms and Conditions

Username: Martin Trautschold
Password: ●●●●●●●●
Domain: MYDOMAINNAME
☑ I want to allow others to share my Mail Connector ②

You can "Share" your "Mail Connector" with others in your organization if you complete this information and check the box on this page.

Click "Next"

If you are successful, then you will see a "Success message" like this:

Microsoft Internet Explorer   ✕

⚠ You have successfully configured access to: martin@blackberrymadesimple.com

[OK]

and be returned to the main list of email addresses configured for your BlackBerry –
Now, Go To Step (12) to finish the account setup.

11 (d) Outlook/Exchange using Outlook only. Option 1 (final step)

Settings
  E-mail Accounts
  Handheld
  Options
Help
Terms and Conditions

We were unable to configure this e-mail account. Please tell us how you access your e-mail by selecting an option, click "Next".

Outlook Profile: (your Profile Name)

MS Exchange Settings: (required if your Profile name does not appear)
Exchange Server: (required if your Profile name does not appear)
Exchange Mailbox: (required if your Profile name does not appear)

Username: (for your computer or domain)
Password: (for your computer or domain)

Domain: (your Domain or Computer name)

[Cancel]   [< Back] [Next >]

The final step is to input your Outlook Mail settings to allow the Mail Connector to "See" your Outlook Mail Box.

You may need to contact your Email or System Administrator for more help with some of these answers.

A unique Mail Connector ID must be assigned, then you're done. You know everything is set up when you see the Email screen with your email account listed.

If, after you click "Next", you see an error message similar to this one, then contact your Email Administrator for help.

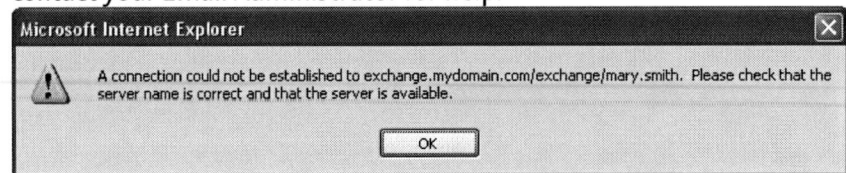

Microsoft Internet Explorer   ✕

⚠ A connection could not be established to exchange.mydomain.com/exchange/mary.smith. Please check that the server name is correct and that the server is available.

[OK]

11(e) Lotus Notes / Domino Server

Now you'll be using the new "Mail Connector" (replaces the "Desktop Redirector").

You have two options:
Option 1: Install your own Mail Connector on your PC
Option 2: Share a Mail Connector already installed on a co-worker's PC

Why might you want Option 2 - Share someone else's Mail Connector?
- This allows you to turn off or take your PC with your (e.g. Laptop) and still receive your email on your BlackBerry.
- Reduce the "load" on your computer
- Avoid the hassle of installing the software yourself.

Step 11(e): Wizard: When you select: Lotus Notes®/Domino™
"I always use Lotus Notes® to access my e-mail account"

If you are successful, then you will see a "Success message" like this:

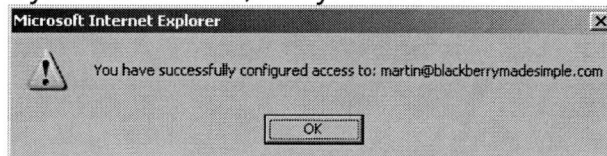

and be returned to the main list of email addresses configured for your BlackBerry –
Now, Go To Step (12) to finish the account setup.

11(e) Lotus Notes / Domino Server - Option 1 (final steps)

After the installation is complete, you will see a screen asking to confirm your Lotus Notes configuration and Password and whether or not you want to "Share" this Connector with others.

Remember: To USE or "Share" your Mail Connector, your PC with Outlook has to be:
(1) Turned ON
(2) Connected to your Network
(3) Connected to the Internet

Note: You can still "Share" your mail connector, even if you did not do it when you first installed it.

You can "Share" your "Mail Connector" with others in your organization if you complete this information and check the box on this page.

Click "Next" to Finish.

If, after you click "Next", you see an error message similar to this one, then contact your Email Administrator for help.

Microsoft Internet Explorer

A connection could not be established to exchange.mydomain.com/exchange/mary.smith. Please check that the server name is correct and that the server is available.

OK

If you are successful, then you will see a "Success message" like this:

Microsoft Internet Explorer

You have successfully configured access to: martin@blackberrymadesimple.com

OK

and be returned to the main list of email addresses configured for your BlackBerry –
Now, Go To Step (12) to finish the account setup.

12. Finish the New Email Account setup.

A Successful Email Account Setup will show this message:

And you will then see this main page. Click "Edit" to adjust the settings on this new account.

To complete the setup of this new email account, edit your Account settings, "Name"(sometimes referred to as 'Friendly Name'), "Reply To", "Signature" on this screen and "Save".

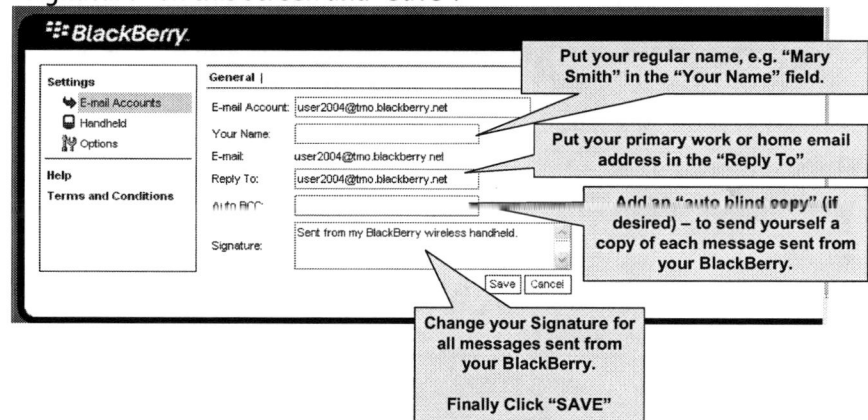

CONGRATULATIONS! You've successfully:

- o Registered on your BlackBerry Internet Service Account
- o Setup your BlackBerry Default Email Address
- o Fixed your "Sent From" and "Reply To" address for your BlackBerry
- o Created a Signature for all outgoing messages from your BlackBerry
- o Integrated your Work/Home Email address to your BlackBerry

Now, you should go to the "Receiving Email on Your BlackBerry Section"

Receiving Email on Your BlackBerry

Receiving Email is easy and instant on the BlackBerry with the "PUSH EMAIL" system. Emails are PUSHED to your BlackBerry. You do not need to dial up or query for emails – as soon as emails are sent to your address they are forwarded onto your BlackBerry.

1. On your BlackBerry, go to the 'Messages' Icon

2. Just look at your email messages come flying in!

Tip!

You can speed up delivery of email to your BlackBerry by forwarding it immediately from your e-Mail Server.

NOTE: You'll see PHONE icons (☎ = PHONE call log - made or received) as well as messages icons (✉ = EMAIL received)

Remember, the BlackBerry Web Client logs into your email server *__only every 15 minutes__*. So if someone sends you an email it will take up to 15 minutes to receive on your BlackBerry and sometimes more, depending on network congestion.

Want to receive email faster on your BlackBerry, read our tip in this e-book on speeding up BlackBerry E-mail delivery! (click here to jump there if you are reading the electronic version of this book)

Sending an Email from Your BlackBerry

Sending email from your BlackBerry is simple. Just follow the steps outlined below. Note that with BlackBerry System Software v4.1 and above, you now have the option to compose your message before addressing it – which is more similar to regular desktop or web-based email systems! *(How do I check my BlackBerry System Software version? – Check the FAQ pages or Table of Contents for help on doing this.)*

Sending an Email from your BlackBerry

1 Click Trackwheel to select "Messages" (Inbox). Your Icon might look slightly different, look for the word "Messages".

2 Click Trackwheel and select "Compose Email"

Tip: Roll to the Date Line separator and click the "Enter Key" to start composing!

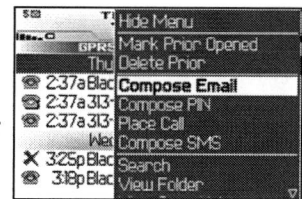

For BlackBerry Software v4.0 or below (check in this book how to determine your software version)

3 Select an email address for your "To:" <u>before</u> you compose.

4 Write your email message...

5 Click the trackwheel and select "Send"

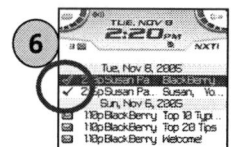

6 Look for the "check mark" -- your message was sent!

For BlackBerry Software v4.1 or above (check in this book how to determine your software version)

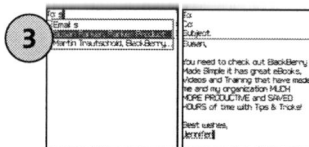

3 You have the choice of addressing your message or composing it first!

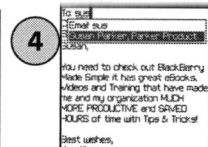

4 Then compose or address your message. To address, roll up and start typing next to the word "To:"

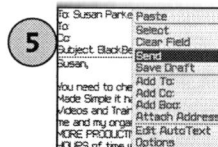

5 Click the trackwheel and select "Send"

6 Look for the "check mark" -- your message was sent!

How to tell if I can Send/Receive Email and Browse the Web?

Wireless Data Connectivity (When you DO have it:)

You will see in the upper right corner of your "home screen"
2 or 4 upper case letters (and/or numbers) -- These will show you can:
Send/Receive Email
Browse the Web
(and if you have the correct configuration, you can also
Wirelessly Sync Contacts, Calendar and other Data)

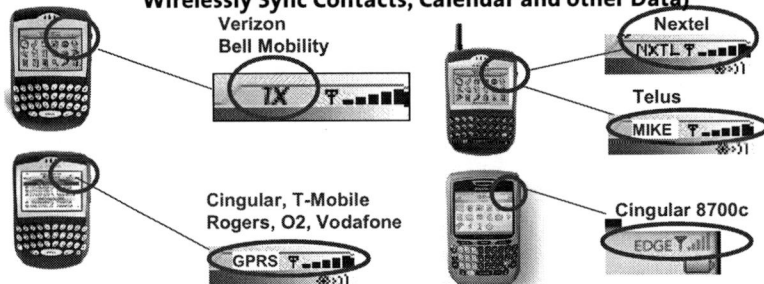

Verizon
Bell Mobility

Nextel

Telus

Cingular, T-Mobile
Rogers, O2, Vodafone

Cingular 8700c

Your Carrier, if it's not listed above will most likely have one of the above
characters. If not, then look for all uppercase letters / numbers
(except "GSM" – that means voice calls only, no data)

Wireless Data Connectivity (When you don't have it:)

If you see any of the letter / number combinations below,
Then you cannot: Send/Receive Email, Browse the Web, or Wirelessly Sync
Contacts, Calendar and other Data

All these letters next to your wireless signal strength mean **NO wireless data coverage:**
"edge" "GSM" "1x" "X" "OFF" "nxtl" "nXtl" "cdma" "GSM" "gprs"
"Searching for Network"
"No Coverage"

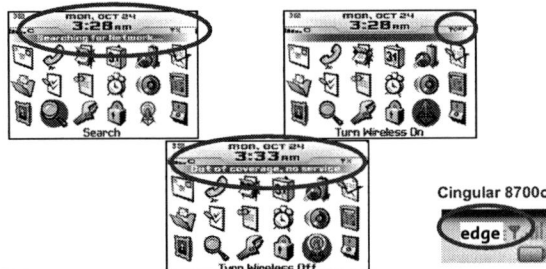

Cingular 8700c

Tip!

Did you know that if you are away from a wireless signal for a long time (e.g. several hours) your BlackBerry will stop trying to find the network and turn OFF your radio in order to save your battery. If you see this, then just turn on your radio as shown in this section to get back up and running.

Wireless Connection Troubleshooting – What If I cannot send/receive email or browse the web?

Wireless networks are far from perfect and signals are inexplicably lost sometimes. If you lose wireless coverage on your BlackBerry you will see an "X" in the upper right hand corner of the home screen. (If you see an "OFF", then your radio is OFF and you just need to turn it back on by clicking on the radio tower ICON – see the images at the beginning of the book for which icon you need to click)

Cingular 8700c

All these letters next to your wireless signal strength mean <u>NO</u> wireless data coverage: "edge" "GSM" "1x" "X" "OFF" "nxtl" "nXTl" "cdma" "GSM" "gprs" "Searching for Network" "No Coverage"

Getting your wireless signal back

To try and get your wireless signal back, or to attempt to find a stronger signal, follow these steps:

1. Get to the Radio Off/On selection by following these steps:

Cycle your Radio OFF/ON

Sometimes helps regaining wireless data connectivity

Tip!

Sometimes all it takes to get your wireless signal back is to cycle the radio off and on!

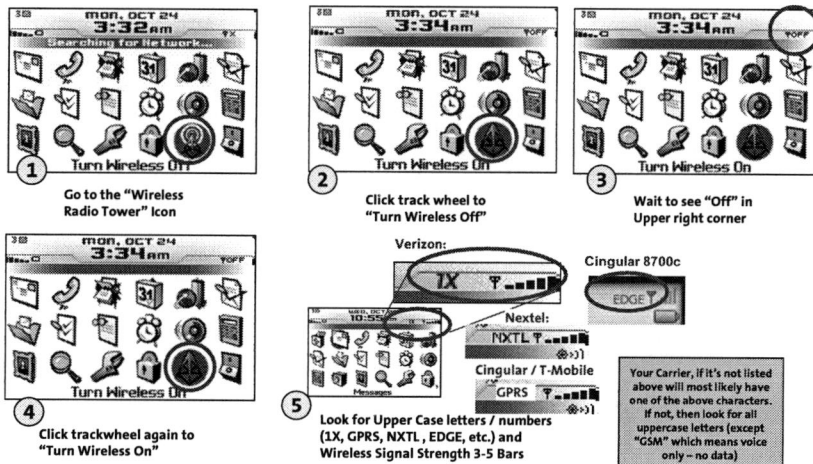

1. Go to the "Wireless Radio Tower" Icon
2. Click track wheel to "Turn Wireless Off"
3. Wait to see "Off" in Upper right corner
4. Click trackwheel again to "Turn Wireless On"
5. Look for Upper Case letters / numbers (1X, GPRS, NXTL, EDGE, etc.) and Wireless Signal Strength 3-5 Bars

Verizon: 1X
Cingular 8700c: EDGE
Nextel: NXTL
Cingular / T-Mobile: GPRS

Your Carrier, if it's not listed above will most likely have one of the above characters. If not, then look for all uppercase letters (except "GSM" which means voice only – no data)

Look for Upper Case letters / numbers (1X, GPRS, NXTL , EDGE, etc.) and a Wireless Signal Strength 3-5 Bars.

If you still see an "X" or not all uppercase letters, follow the instructions in this book called "Resetting Your BlackBerry".

Tip!

Sometimes the only way to reconnect is to do a "Hard Reset" of your BlackBerry by removing the battery, waiting 30 seconds, then re-inserting the battery.

If that didn't work and *you're reasonably sure you're in an area where you should be able to receive a good wireless signal* then, cycle the power on your BlackBerry by pressing the button on the top of your BlackBerry as shown:

Cycle the Power Off / On –
Sometimes Helps Get Wireless Data Connectivity Back

6200, 6500, 6700, 7200, 7500 and 7700 Series BlackBerries

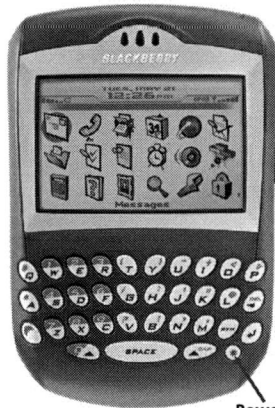

8700 Series BlackBerry

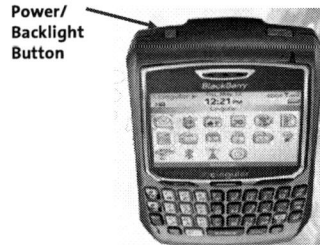

Power/ Backlight Button

Power/ Backlight Button

1. Turn OFF the BlackBerry: Press & Hold the Power/Backlight Button for 3 seconds to turn off.
2. Turn ON the device: Press & release the Power/Backlight button.

Next, *if you're reasonably sure you're in an area where you should be able to receive a good wireless signal... try to "Register Now" from your Options Host Routing table as shown:*

"Register Now" from the "Options > Host Routing Table"
Sometimes Helps Get Wireless Data Connectivity Back

(1) Go to the "Options" Icon

(2) Go to "Host Routing Table"
(If you don't see it listed, then go To "Advanced Options" It Will be listed under that.)

(3) Click the trackwheel And select "Register Now"

(4) You should see this message.

Then, you might see your web browser icon (yours may look different than this one) disappear and re-appear. After it comes back, you should have wireless data connectivity again so you can Send/Receive and Browse the Web.

FINALLY, if all else fails... *and you're reasonably sure you're in an area where you should be able to receive a good wireless signal... you'll need to do a soft reset.*

Resetting and other BlackBerry System Information

Just like on a Windows computer is it occasionally necessary to see what's going on behind the scenes on a BlackBerry, or the device might just need a good, swift reboot. This section outlines some key BlackBerry system tips.

"Soft Reset" Of Your BlackBerry

Occasionally your BlackBerry might not maintain a good wireless signal or it will run out of memory and really slow down, at these times, or any other time you think the device would benefit from a clean start don't hesitate to soft-reset your BlackBerry. It's just like rebooting windows, you don't lose any information.

> **Tip!**
>
> Sometimes the only way to reconnect is to do a "Soft Reset" of your BlackBerry (Like Ctrl-Alt-Del on your PC)

To soft-reset your BlackBerry, follow these steps:

1. press and hold the ALT (half-moon key)
2. press and hold the CAP key
3. press and hold the DEL key
4. With all three keys held down simultaneously and pressed in

BlackBerry "Soft Reset"

Press & Hold

(1) ALT "Half-moon" Key

(2) CAP Key

(3) DEL Key

You may need to press the 3 keys twice. A full "Soft Reset" requires 1-2 minutes, the screen goes blank and the hourglass pops up.

the above mentioned order, the BlackBerry screen will go blank, then an hour glass will appear and reset within about 1 to 2 minutes. press ALT+CAP+DEL keys simultaneously until you see the screen go blank.

5. WARNING: With most new BlackBerries, you'll need to press the ALT-CAP-DEL several times to really see a reboot happen. (Should be a blank screen and hourglass for at least 1 minute)

"Hard Reset" of Your BlackBerry

Occasionally your BlackBerry might not maintain a good wireless signal or it will run out of memory and really slow down, at these times, or any other time you think the device would benefit from a clean start don't hesitate to reset your BlackBerry. It's just like rebooting windows, you don't lose any information.

To do a HARD RESET, you remove the battery, wait 30 seconds, re-insert the battery, and power on the BlackBerry as shown:

"Hard Reset" of Your BlackBerry

Helps when you've tried everything else – cycle power, radio off/on, soft reset.

6200, 6500, 6700,
7200, 7500 and
7700, 8700 Series

7700 Series

1 Turn the
BlackBerry
Power Off

2 Push button and slide open the battery door on the back of the unit (some models slide down, others slide to the right)

3 Gently Tap your BlackBerry
Gently in your hand until
The Battery comes out

**Wait
30 seconds**

4 Wait 30 seconds...
Then Re-insert
your Battery

8700 Series
BlackBerry

5 Then Turn
Power Back On

6 After turning
Off/On, look for
3-5 BARS and
UPPER CASE 2-4
letters/ numbers
here.

Error Message When Try to Send an Email or Cannot Browse the Web on Your BlackBerry: "No e-mail services..."

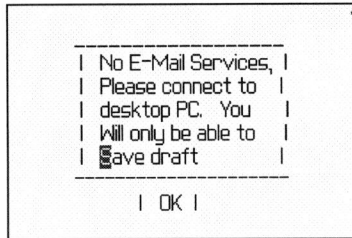

If you see the above error on your BlackBerry, and you see that you have 3 or more "Bars" of wireless coverage on your status indicator in the upper right of your BlackBerry home screen, you'll need to "Send a Service Book". Follow these steps:

1.   Open a Web Browser on your PC and go to your BlackBerry Internet Service site (See the "BlackBerry Internet Service Web Site List" earlier in this book for the correct link – see the Table of Contents for the exact page or click here to jump to the list if you are reading the electronic version of this book)

2.   Login using the **BlackBerry Internet Service User ID and Password.**

3.   Click **"Yes" or "OK",** if you see a security alert.

4.   Depending on the type of BlackBerry Internet Service ("BIS") web site (SEPARATE OR IMBEDDED TYPE), you'll need to follow slightly different steps. Follow those images that look closest to your BIS site:

For SEPARATE Type Site	For IMBEDDED Type Site
Click the Profile Button (see arrow in image below)	**Click the Handheld Link** in the left column (see arrow in image below)
When you see the following screen, **Click BOTH of the Send Service Book**	When you see the following screen, **Click the Send Service Book**

buttons (see arrow in image below)	button (see arrow in image below)

5.   Logout of the Blackberry Internet Service site.

6.   Make sure your BlackBerry Radio is on and you are connected to the wireless network (You can tell if you're connected by looking in the upper right corner for the radio tower signal with BARS next to it and UPPER CASE 4 letters/numbers to the left of the BARS.)

7.   Now you should receive an "**Activation**" message indicating that your BlackBerry has now been successfully **registered on the Wireless Network**. You should now be able to send and receive email and browse the web.

8.   Go to the e-mail inbox on the BlackBerry, very shortly you should see a message similar to this:

> **FROM: Activation Server**
> **Subject: Welcome to BlackBerry Internet Service**
>
> **Message: You BlackBerry Internet Service is now Active . . . .**

9.   You can now Send and Receive e-mail from your BlackBerry.

Good Signal but Web Browsing Still Not Working?

If you have tried some of the other methods described in this book for Wireless Troubleshooting (cycle your radio off/on, cycle your power off/on, reset the device) and still nothing works, then try registering the BlackBerry on your network. This is also mentioned above for email connectivity troubleshooting, but it sometimes is required just to get your Web Browser working again.

Try to "Register Now" from your Options Host Routing table as shown:

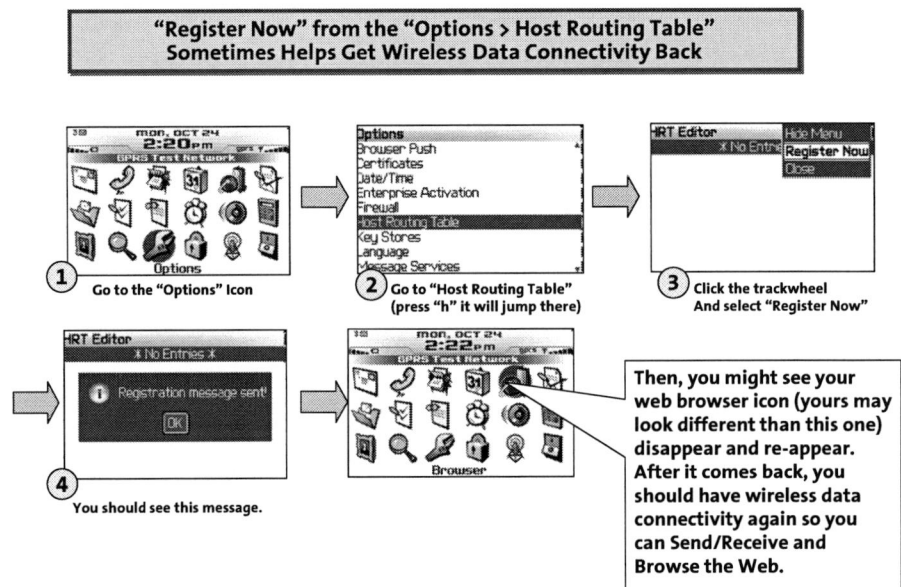

> **"Register Now" from the "Options > Host Routing Table"**
> **Sometimes Helps Get Wireless Data Connectivity Back**

① Go to the "Options" Icon

② Go to "Host Routing Table" (press "h" it will jump there)

③ Click the trackwheel And select "Register Now"

④ You should see this message.

Then, you might see your web browser icon (yours may look different than this one) disappear and re-appear. After it comes back, you should have wireless data connectivity again so you can Send/Receive and Browse the Web.

In a minute or so, your BlackBerry will be re-registered on the Network and you should be able to browse the Internet.

Fixing Your BlackBerry 'Reply-To' E-Mail Address and 'Sent from BlackBerry Handheld' Default Signature

Depending on what type of BlackBerry Internet Service Web Site your Carrier has, you'll need to do this slightly differently.

Open a Web Browser on your PC and Log In to your BlackBerry Internet Service site. You   (See the "BlackBerry Internet Service Web Site List" earlier in this book for the correct link – or click here to jump to the list if you are reading the electronic version of this book)

Do you have a "Separate" or "Imbedded" BlackBerry Internet Service site? See how to tell the answer earlier in this book.

> If your carrier has an "Imbedded" type site, then please go to this area in the "Imbedded" Type Email section:
> (Check the table of contents for the exact page number or click here if you are reading the electronic version to jump there)
>
> If your carrier has a "Separate" type site, then please go to these two sections in the "Separate" Type Email section:
> Fixing your "Sent From" Email Address
> Fixing your Email Signature
> (Check the table of contents for the exact page number or click on the title above if you are reading the electronic version to jump there)

Testing Your BlackBerry Email Setup

Here are a few routines to help you get familiar with your new BlackBerry email setup. Mix and match these and maybe have some friends try sending you email or replying to yours. One thing is certain, if you do these tests, you will get a good feel for how your BlackBerry email works, looks and how long it takes to receive and send emails from it with your configuration.

Test 1: Do you receive email on your BlackBerry?

Send yourself an email from your PC to your newly configured email account...
Does it arrive on your BlackBerry?
How long did it take?
Try it again a few more times – does it take the same amount of time?

Using BlackBerry Internet Service and want to speed it up? (Try a server forwarding rule – learn more earlier in the "Speed Up Email by 95%" section earlier in this book)

Test 2: Can you "Reply" from your BlackBerry?

"Reply To" one of the messages you received...
When you receive the reply on your email account
Are the "Reply To" and "Friendly Name" correct? (If not, log into your BlackBerry Internet Service web site and change them. Remember that you may need to configure these things for each email account.)
How long did it take to receive the Reply? (Is it consistent if you try again?)

See the section above on fixing Signature and Reply To addresses if you need to fix either one.

Test 3: Compose Send a new message on your BlackBerry to yourself.

Does it arrive?
Are the "Reply To" and "Friendly Name" correct?
How long did it take?
Try it again a few more times – does it take the same amount of time?

Contacts   Calendar

Tasks   Memo Pad

Putting Your Stuff on the BlackBerry the First Time

Putting Your Names and Addresses on the BlackBerry

What's an electronic organizer without all your important names and addresses? And your calendar?

In this section we'll cover the basics of how to get your contact names, calendars and other information onto the BlackBerry.

As the same concepts apply no matter what personal information manager (PIM) you use on your computer, in this e-book we'll demonstrate syncing the BlackBerry to the most common of all personal information managers - Outlook. (Look for our other e-books on syncing BlackBerries to other contact managers such as ACT!)

To sync, or transfer, contact names, calendar items, memos and tasks, between your BlackBerry and computer, follow these steps:

See the VIDEO of how to install Desktop Manager!

Check out the free sample video clip on our web site here:
 http://www.blackberrymadesimple.com/videos/videos.htm

> **Tip!**
>
> Many times the BlackBerry Desktop Manager on the CD that came with your BlackBerry is OUT-OF-DATE when you receive it – visit the link on this page to download the latest version!

> **Tip!**
>
> **BULK ERASE:** If you need to delete your entire BlackBerry Address Book, Calendar, Task List or Memo Pad, then check out our "Quickly Clearing Addresses, Calendar and other Data From Your BlackBerry" section.

> **CAUTION**
>
> If your BlackBerry was issued by your company, please check with your IT department for the right version of Blackberry Desktop Manager.

1. Ensure BlackBerry Desktop Manager is installed.

This is the software that came on the CD when you purchased your BlackBerry.

TIP: Many times, the CD is out-of-date when it ships. If you are not sure if you have the latest version of your Desktop Manager Software, please go to this screen and click on your carrier name and follow the directions to download the latest software!

Finding The Latest Desktop Manager Software

1. Try your carrier's web page
2. Try this link from BlackBerry's web site:
   http://www.blackberry.com/support/downloads/index.shtml

Click the "Download" link

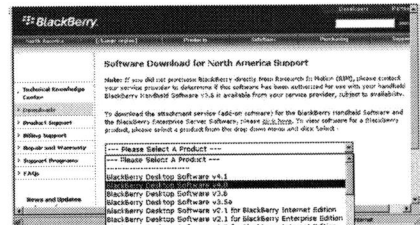

Select the appropriate version of BlackBerry Desktop Manager for your organization.

Then follow the instructions to download the software (you'll have to supply contact information and agree to the legal terms.)

2. After you have installed and opened your BlackBerry Desktop Manager, connect your BlackBerry to your computer and ensure it says **Connected**

3. Next, double-click on the Intellisync Icon

4. Click → Configure PIM

5. Wait for Desktop Manager to 'Setup the Intellisync User'

Your BlackBerry Screen should look like this:

6. Check the Address Book Row and click → Choose

7. Highlight MS Outlook (or your preferred address book application). Leave the default "**Synchronize**" Select the → **Browse** button if necessary to find your address book (usually Desktop Manager can find the address book if located in the default Outlook directory) → **Choose the Synchronize** radio button, then click → **OK.**

8. If you wish to do any advanced configuration, such as set Field Mapping (defining what fields in Outlook sync to fields on the BlackBerry), choose the **Configure** → **Advanced Settings** button in the lower right corner of the screen.

9. Configure your Calendar, Memo Pad and Tasks in the same fashion, by checking their rows and choosing the applications to sync them to.

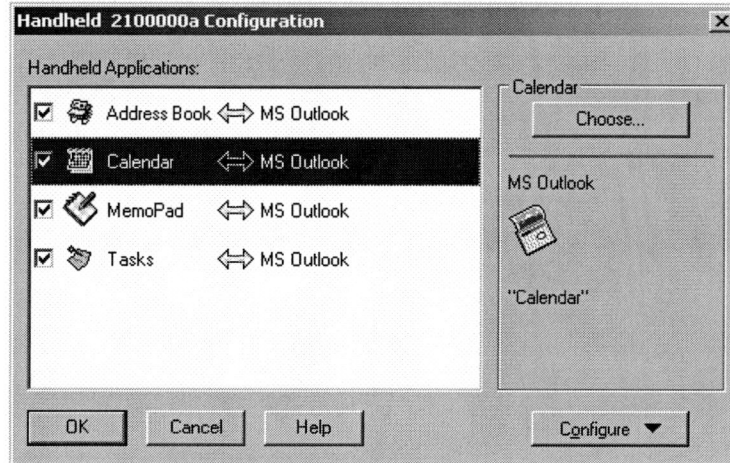

10. Once all applications are configured click → **OK** to get out of the configuration screen.

11. Next, → **Click OK**

12. Finally, on this screen, click **"Synchronize now"**

13. Depending on how many contacts, calendar items, memos and tasks you have to synchronize, this process could take a few minutes to 10 or more.

Quickly Clearing or Restoring Addresses, Calendar and other Data from your BlackBerry ("Bulk Delete or Restore")

Thanks to an inquisitive reader R. Luke from Albany, New York we bring you this useful tip.

Have you ever wanted to simply clear out the entire BlackBerry address book and start fresh? Did you want to do the same for the Calendar, Task List or Memo Pad? This tip will help you do just that.

You will need to be sitting at your computer with BlackBerry Desktop Manager installed. (see the section on installing this if you need help).

1. Connect your BlackBerry to your computer with the USB cable. You should see the "Connected" message on the bottom of the Desktop Manager window as shown, then click on "Backup and Restore"

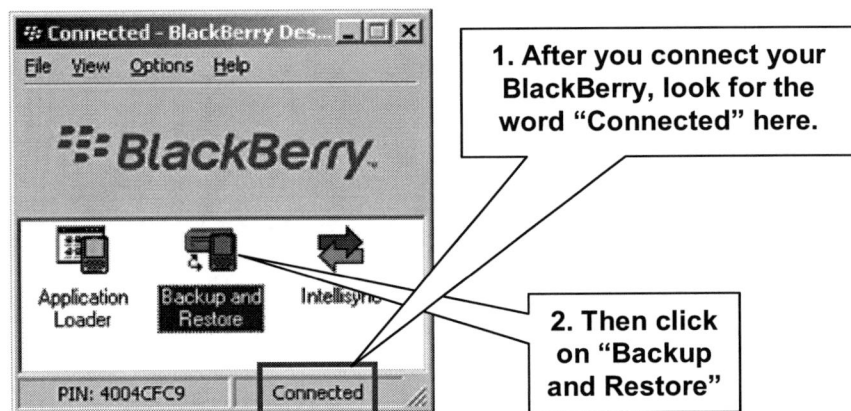

1. After you connect your BlackBerry, look for the word "Connected" here.

2. Then click on "Backup and Restore"

2. Note: Before you do this deletion, you may want to fully Backup your BlackBerry using the Backup button on this screen. Then, after your Backup is complete, click "Advanced..."

Backup and Restore

Backup/Restore Now

Save the databases currently stored on the handheld to a desktop backup file.   **Backup...**

> 1. We recommend you click "Backup..." to backup all your BlackBerry data prior to doing a "Bulk Delete"

Replace handheld databases with the corresponding databases saved in an existing desktop backup file.   **Restore...**

Perform selective backup, modification and restoration of handheld databases.   **Advanced...**

> 2. Click on "Advanced..."

Configuration

Select options to control the automatic backup of databases when the handheld is connected to your computer.   **Options...**

Close   **Help**

3. Now you will see this screen with two windows and a list of items on the right or "Handheld" window. This represents all the information you have on your BlackBerry at this time.

<table>
<tr><td rowspan="2">

Tip!

Selective Restore

You can use this same procedure to selectively restore just one icon's data (e.g. Address Book, but leave the Calendar alone). This would be useful if your address book was corrupted, but your calendar was fine.

</td></tr>
</table>

Backup-(2005-10-18) - Backup/Restore

File

Desktop File Databases
| Name | Entries | Bytes |

Handheld Databases [2.32M free]

Name	Entries	Bytes
Address Book	4393	
Address Book Options		
Alarm Options		
Attachment Data		
Attachment Options		
AutoText	108	
Browser Bookmarks	3	
Browser Channels		
Browser Data Cache		
Browser Folders	2	
Browser Messages		
Browser Options		
Browser Push Options		
Calendar	54	

> 1. To clear the Address Book, click on this row.

> 2. Then click on "Clear"

IMPORTANT: If you clicked on this arrow before you "Clear" you would backup your Address Book to your computer.

Similarly, after you created the backup, you could use this arrow to "Restore" selectively the Address Book, Calendar, Tasks, etc.

Clear   **Refresh**

Close   **Help**

After you click Clear, you will see this screen:

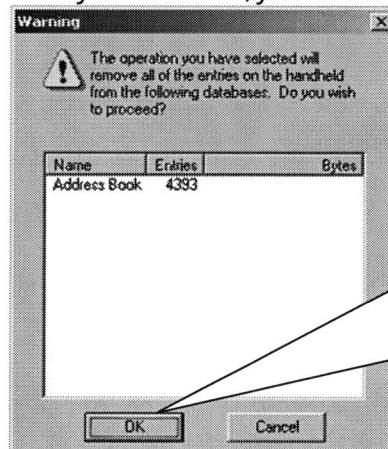

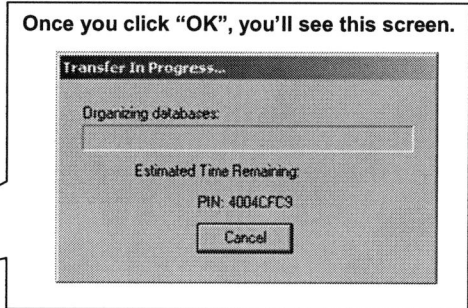

Warning

⚠ The operation you have selected will remove all of the entries on the handheld from the following databases. Do you wish to proceed?

Name	Entries	Bytes
Address Book	4393	

OK   **Cancel**

> **Once you click "OK", you'll see this screen.**
>
> **Transfer In Progress...**
>
> Organizing databases:
>
> Estimated Time Remaining:
>
> PIN: 4004CFC9
>
> **Cancel**

As shown above, this same process can be used to selectively "Restore" data to your BlackBerry. It can be useful if your address book gets corrupted, but your calendar is fine. Then you would restore just your Address Book.

4. If you wanted to erase your Calendar, you would follow the same procedure, just highlight the Calendar row and click "Clear"

TIP: You can select multiple databases at once by holding the "Ctrl" key on your computer and clicking on each row – so you could delete the Address Book and Calendar at the same time, just highlight both rows in the right hand window prior to clicking "Clear"

SETTINGS:

Setting Correct Date and Time Zone

If your BlackBerry is new or you have had to remove the battery, you will notice the time zone is Casablanca (GMT) – Greenwich Mean Time, BlackBerries default setting.

Follow these steps to adjust your Time zone:
1. Go to the Settings Icon (Color: wrench icon or Monochrome: Swiss army knife)

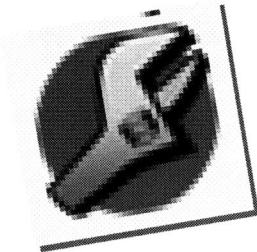

2. Select → "Date/Time" and click the → trackwheel

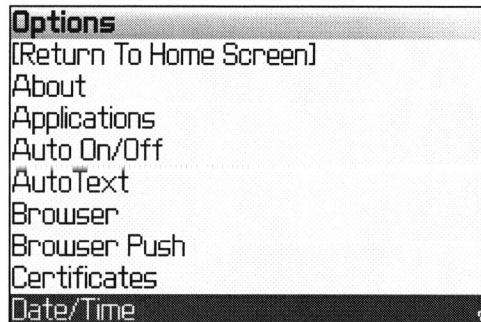

3. The Time Zone field will be highlighted –

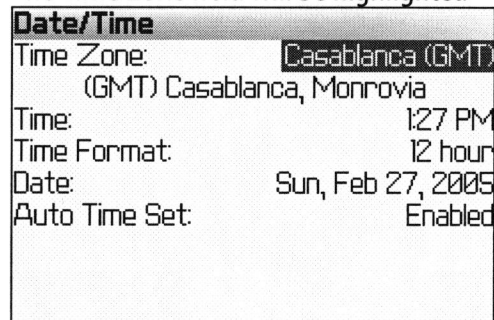

4. Adjust the time zone by either selecting "Change Option" and choosing the correct one or by holding the ALT and rolling the trackwheel as shown:

Date/Time	
Time Zone:	Indiana (-5)
(GMT) Cas	**Eastern Time (-5)**
	Caracas (-4)
Time:	Santiago (-4)
Time Format:	Atlantic Time (-4)
Date:	Newfoundland (-3.5)
Auto Time Set:	Buenos Aires (-3)
	Brasilia (-3)
	Greenland (-3)
	Mid-Atlantic (-2

5. Once you've selected the correct time zone, click the trackwheel and select "Save"

    WARNING: If you don't click "Save" but instead hit the Escape key, then you'll see this warning message:

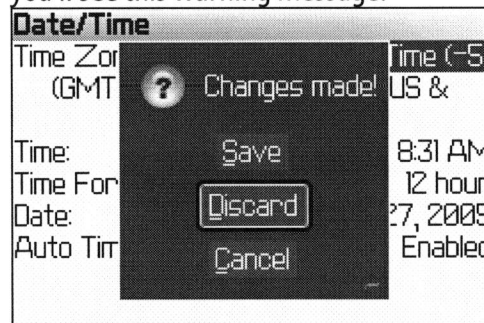

Date/Time		
Time Zor		ime (-5)
(GMT	? Changes made!	US &
	Save	
Time:		8:31 AM
Time For	[Discard]	12 hour
Date:		27, 2005
Auto Tim	Cancel	Enabled

    Just make sure you roll up with the trackwheel and click "Save" so you can save your settings.

Checking Your BlackBerry System Software Version

Running the latest version of System Software available for your BlackBerry will allow you to take advantage of all the latest new features. In order to check which version you are running on your BlackBerry, follow the steps below.

Checking Your Version of BlackBerry System Software

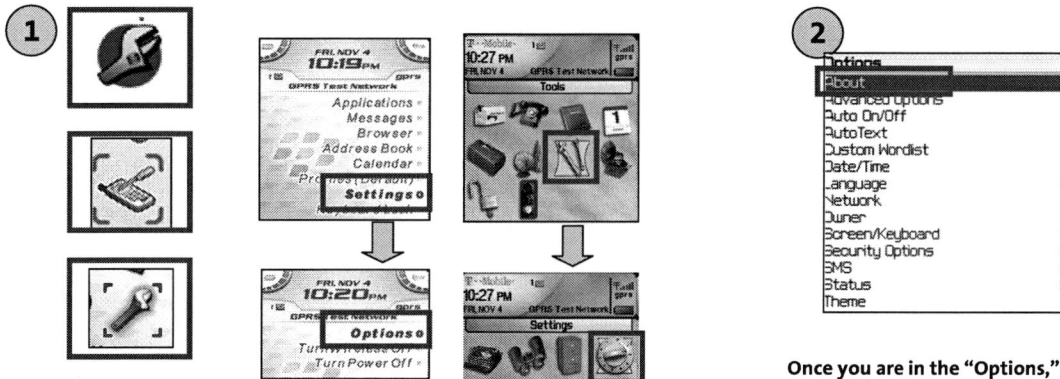

Go to the "Options" Icon, it may look slightly different than these, or be under the "Settings" icon/menu item. Look for the word "Options" on the top/bottom of the screen.

Once you are in the "Options," click on the "About" item at the top of the list.

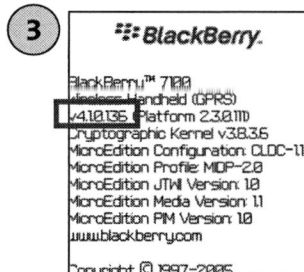

Look under the words "Wireless Handheld" for the version number. (This one shows version v4.1.0.136)

What is the Latest Software for my BlackBerry?

Running the latest version of System Software available for your BlackBerry will allow you to take advantage of all the latest new features. In order to check if you are running the latest version, please visit your carrier web page (e.g. www.t-mobile.com or www.nextel.com).

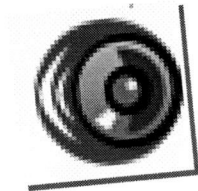

How to make your Calendar Alarms Vibrate!

(Even when your BlackBerry is sitting on the table!)

Most new BlackBerries sold today are set with the Default profile to VIBRATE for Emails ("Messages") and Calendar scheduled alarms In the Holster and DO NOTHING (no vibrate or tone) when the BlackBerry is out of the holster.

If you're like most BlackBerry users, you sometimes pull your BlackBerry out of the holster and leave it on your desk after you read an email. With the default setting, it will Do Nothing when an alarm should be ringing for an appointment! So we recommend at least changing the Profile for the "Calendar" so it Rings or "tones" when out of the holster.

Changing BlackBerry Profiles:

1. Open Profiles form the home screen

2. Select Default (On) profile, or any other profile you may have "On" and choose →Edit

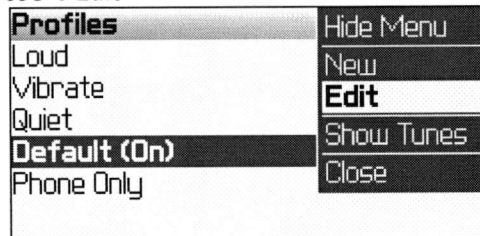

Profiles	Hide Menu
Loud	New
Vibrate	**Edit**
Quiet	Show Tunes
Default (On)	Close
Phone Only	

3. Locate the "Calendar" and click "Edit" from the menu

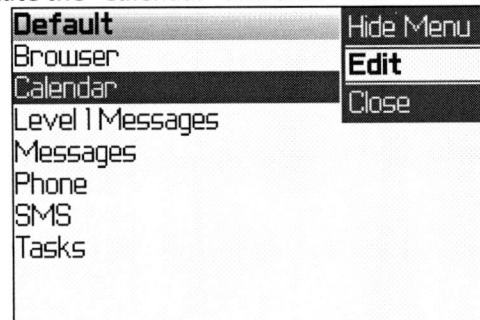

Default	Hide Menu
Browser	**Edit**
Calendar	Close
Level 1 Messages	
Messages	
Phone	
SMS	
Tasks	

4. Change the "Out of Holster" from None to either "Tone" or "Vibrate + Tone" so that it will alert you when you have a ringing calendar appointment alarm.

Calendar in Default	
Out of Holster:	None
Tune:	Tone
Volume:	Vibrate
Number of Beeps:	Vibrate+Tone
Repeat Notification:	LED Flashing
In Holster:	Vibrate
Tune:	BlackBerry 2
Volume:	Mute
Number of Beeps:	

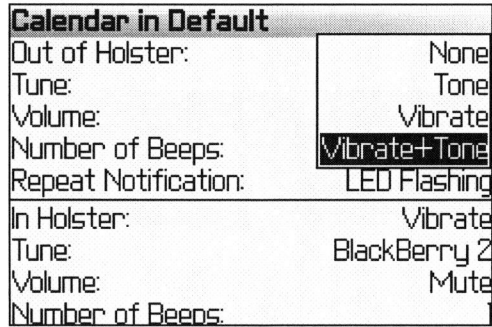

5. Save and Close two times to get back to the Home screen.

    Now, whenever you have a ringing calendar alarm, you're covered –
    whether you have you BlackBerry on your desk, in your car's cup holder or
    in the holster!

How to show phone call logs in your Inbox

By default, the BlackBerry System Software version 4.0 and higher does not show you the incoming, missed and outgoing phone calls in your Inbox. If you are used to seeing this on your older model BlackBerry, or just like the idea of seeing a comprehensive log of all communication, whether voice or email, then you should follow these steps to turn on CALL LOGGING in your INBOX.

1. Go into the Phone on your BlackBerry by:
Pressing the Phone Button on the top of your BlackBerry or Click on the Phone Icon:

Phone Key
(or Walkie-Talkie
feature some models)

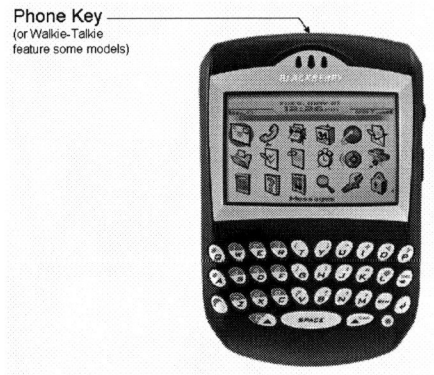

2. Click the trackwheel and select "Options"

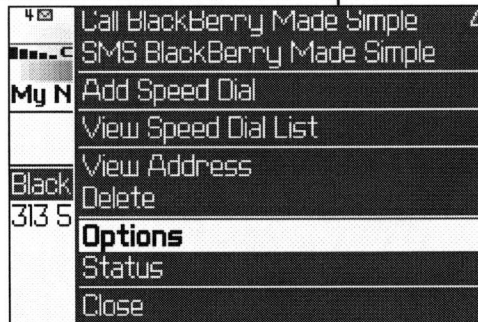

Call BlackBerry Made Simple
SMS BlackBerry Made Simple
Add Speed Dial
View Speed Dial List
View Address
Delete
Options
Status
Close

3. Select "Call Logging" and press the trackwheel:

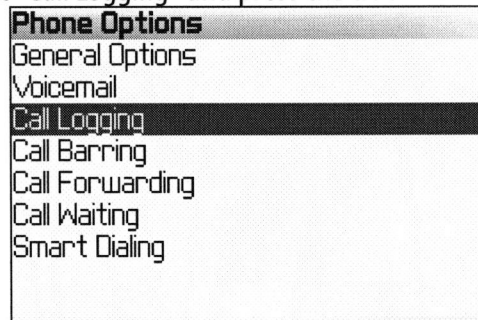

Phone Options
General Options
Voicemail
Call Logging
Call Barring
Call Forwarding
Call Waiting
Smart Dialing

4. Select "All Calls" by rolling the trackwheel and pressing the space bar to highlight the radio button next to "All Calls" then "Save"

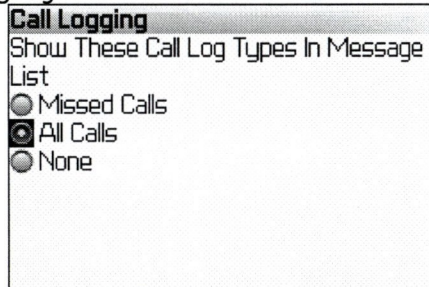

5. Hit "Esc" back to the home screen, now all your incoming, missed and outgoing calls will be logged in your Inbox "Messages" screen like this:

Great Time Saving Tip: ALT + Trackwheel

The best shortcut to know on the BlackBerry is understanding when to use the ALT key and Trackwheel together. This is a universal key combination that can save you many keystrokes and steps in many places on the BlackBerry

ALT + Trackwheel to edit text

When editing text anywhere on the BlackBerry, use ALT+Trackwheel to scroll left/right one character at a time.

Tip!

Move one character at a time with ALT-Trackwheel.

Select from drop-down list with: ALT+Trackwheel

Trackwheel

ALT Key

Hold while pressing Trackwheel

Roll while pressing ALT to select from Drop-down list

ALT+Trackwheel when selecting from a drop down list

Use ALT+Trackwheel in a drop down list, to scroll through the list of items WITHOUT having to select "Change Option".

Tip!

A real time saver is the ALT-Trackwheel to select a drop down item.

Move left/right one character at a time: ALT+Trackwheel

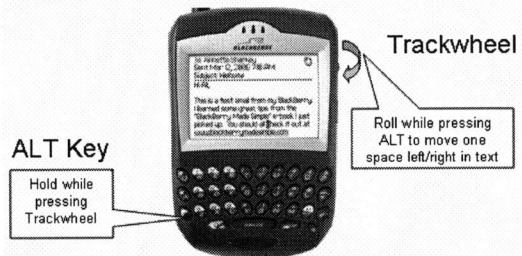

Trackwheel

ALT Key

Hold while pressing Trackwheel

Roll while pressing ALT to move one space left/right in text

ALT+Trackwheel on the Home Screen

When you're on the BlackBerry home screen (in Icon View), using ALT + Trackwheel moves the cursor up and down one icon at a time.

To set quickly set an appointment time:

1.   Highlight the Start field
2.   Scroll over to the minutes (":30") as shown.
3.   Hold the ALT key
4.   Roll the trackwheel to scroll up/down in the highlighted field – in this example – it scrolls up/down in 15 MINUTE increments.
5.   You can also use the SPACE key to move down to the next item in a dropdown list.

Tip!

Did you know that pressing the "SPACE" key will also move you down one item in a drop down list. For example, if you highlighted the 30 in 12:30 and pressed STAR, then you would now be at 12:45

New Appointment
Subject: Lunch Meeting
Location: Bernie's Resturant
☐ All Day Event
Start: Mon, Feb 28, 2005 5:30 PM
End: Mon, Feb 28, 2005 6:00 PM
Duration: 1 Hour 0 Mins
Time Zone: Eastern Time (-5)
Reminder: 15 Min.
Recurrence: None

Multi-Tasking with your BlackBerry "ALT-ESC"

One of the most useful but least known tricks on your BlackBerry is the ALT-Escape trick, also known as multi-tasking. It's similar to "ALT-Tab" in Windows. Here are some of our multi-tasking favorites:

- Compose an email while on the phone
- Pull up an email from your Inbox while on the phone
- Take notes in your Memo Pad while on a phone
- Jump to your calendar while in the middle of composing an email or on a phone call
- Quickly copy and paste text between application while leaving them both open
- The list goes on....

To multi-task on your BlackBerry, follow these steps:

1. From within any application on the BlackBerry
2. Hold down the ALT key
3. While still holding down ALT, → press the Escape key (don't let go of the ALT key)

Multi-Tasking with ALT+ESC

ESC Key
Press this ESC while holding the ALT key to switch between applications

ALT Key
Hold while pressing the ESC key

4. You will see a "mini-ribbon" of applications running or of icons (depending on which Theme you are in – "List" or "Icon")

5. While still holding down ALT, roll the trackwheel to the application you want to jump-to and release all keys.

Following the steps above you can instantly jump between open applications on the BlackBerry.

Simplify your Life - Hide or Move Icons

Working With Icons

To save time and scrolling, your most frequently used icons, should be at the top of your BlackBerry home screen. You can easily move and hide BlackBerry icons.

Hide a BlackBerry Icon:
(May not be available on all models)

1. Go to the BlackBerry home screen
2. → Scroll to select the icon you want to move or hide. In this example we will hide the "Enterprise Activation" icon.
3. Hold down the → ALT key and click the → trackwheel and → select Hide Application.

Move a BlackBerry Icon:
It's also easy to move BlackBerry icons. In this example we'll move the Task List icon.

1. Scroll to the Tasks icon:

MemoPad

2. Hold the →ALT key
3. Click the → track wheel
4. Select → Move Application

Tasks

5. → Roll the trackwheel to move the application

Moving Application

6. Click the → trackwheel again to place the icon where you would like it.

Tasks

Retrieving Hidden Icons

Don't worry if you accidentally an important icon such as email, they are easy to retrieve.

1. Go to the BlackBerry home screen
2. → Click and hold the ALT key, then →click the trackwheel
3. On the menu, click the → Show All option.

4. The homescreen will now show all previously hidden icons with an "X" through them

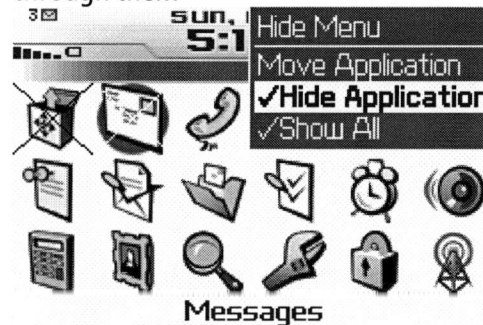

5. Select the icon you want to show again (in this example it is the email icon)

6. Click → ALT+trackwheel again and → select/uncheck Hide Application to "unhide" the email icon.

7. To re-hide your other hidden icons again, click → ALT+Trackwheel and
    → select/uncheck "Show All"

Note: You can't hide the Wrench (Options), Lock and Radio Tower icons.

BlackBerry Keyboard Tricks:

Typing Symbols

You can get basic symbols, numbers and other characters by holding down the ALT key and pressing the appropriate key.

To get additional symbol characters such as $ and %, follow these steps:

1. Go anywhere on the BlackBerry that text can be entered, (e.g. email, adding a memo item or adding a calendar event or task item)

2. In a text field, press the "SYM" key to get this screen:

Symbol Key

Press this to bring up the Symbol Menu

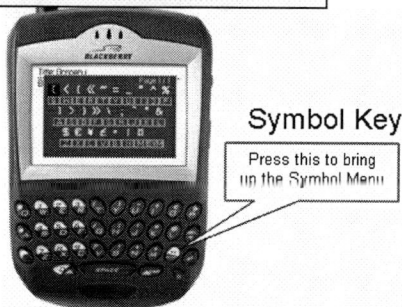

3. Roll the trackwheel to the desired symbol and click the trackwheel (Or press the key underneath the symbol to select it. For example press 'Z' to get the dollar sign).

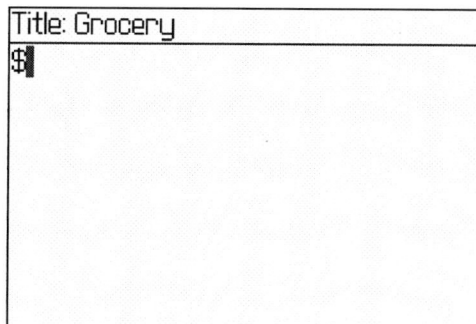

Font Size: Making Text LARGER or smaller

Adjusting the font size on the BlackBerry is simple to do and can let you see significantly more text on a screen, or enlarge the text so it's easy to read at arms length.

To adjust font size, follow these steps:

1. Click the Options (wrench) icon from the BlackBerry homescreen
2. Select Screen/Keyboard

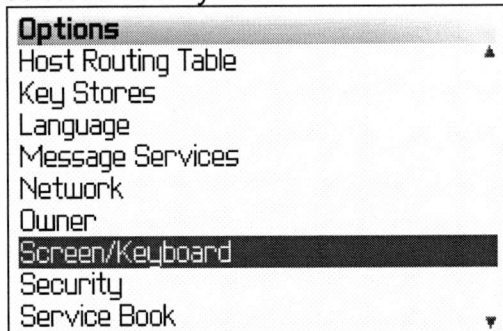

```
Options
Host Routing Table          ▲
Key Stores
Language
Message Services
Network
Owner
Screen/Keyboard
Security
Service Book                ▼
```

3. Highlight the Font Family line, and change the selection by holding the ALT key and rolling the trackwheel.

As you change the Font Family, you will notice the sample text (The quick brown fox...) changes, reflecting the Font Family you choose.

```
Screen/Keyboard              BBCapitals
                             BBCasual
Font Family:                 BBCondensed
Font Size:                   BBMillbank
Font Style:                  BBMillbankTall
Antialias mode:              BBSansSerif
The quick brow|  BBSansSerifSquare
over the lazy d|             BBSerif
Backlight Timeout:           BBSerifFixed
Key Tone:                    System
```

```
Screen/Keyboard
Standby Screen               Enabled
Standby Timeout              10 Min.
          Preview
Font Family:                 System
Font Size:                   7
The quick brown fox jumps over the lazy
dog.
Backlight Timeout:           45 Sec.
Key Tone:                    Off
Key Rate:                    Fast
```

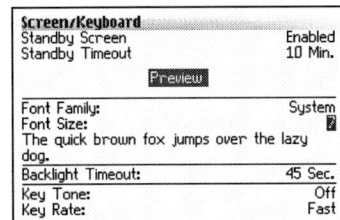

4. Change the Font Size
5. Click in the trackwheel and select → Save

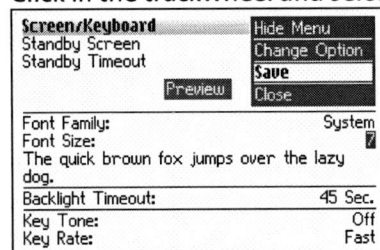

```
Screen/Keyboard      Hide Menu
Standby Screen       Change Option
Standby Timeout      Save
          Preview    Close
Font Family:                 System
Font Size:                   7
The quick brown fox jumps over the lazy
dog.
Backlight Timeout:           45 Sec.
Key Tone:                    Off
Key Rate:                    Fast
```

6. By changing the Font Size you can see significantly more text on a single BlackBerry screen.

Tip!

Keep your BlackBerry FRESH!

Just change your Font from time-to-time

With Small Font

From: BlackBerry▌
Subject: Welcome!
_____
If you have not done so, refer to the
printed documentation that accompanied your
handheld for important setup instructions.

After setup, use the handheld's keyboard,
symbols library, and AutoText feature to
compose messages. Use the trackwheel to
scroll through message text.

The address book is your source for contact
information. The calendar, task list, and ▾

With Large Fo

From: BlackBerry▌
Subject: Welcome!
_____
If you have not done so, refer to the
printed documentation that accompanied
your handheld for important setup
instructions.

After setup, use the handheld's keyboard, ▾

How Do I Set the Programmable Keys on the 8700c?

The Convenience Keys (8700c)

To program this key:
1. Go to Options
2. Screen / Keyboard
3. Set the keys to start
any program (Icon)

**Side
User-Definable
Key
(Programmable)**

**Front
User-Definable
Key
(Programmable)**

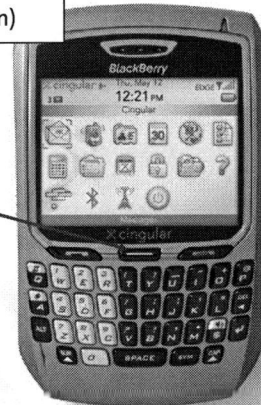

Left Side

Can my BlackBerry 7520 accept voice commands?

Yes, the 7520 model can accept voice commands with a software add-on.
Check out the voice recognition software here:
http://www.mobilevoicecontrol.com/. This software works with the
"Direct Connect" (2-Way Radio) key to transform voice commands into
many functions:

- Start a phone call "Call Mary on Mobile"
- Compose an email by speaking "Email" Mary "Subject" Hello
  "Body" It was great to see you today. Regards Martin.
- You can even add a new calendar event by speaking it!

EMAIL Tips

Moving Around in BlackBerry Messages – Fast!

Here are a few tips to help you navigate your BlackBerry inbox.

Navigate Days worth of Email Messages, Phone Logs or SMS Logs in your Inbox

When in the BlackBerry email inbox the following keys to quickly navigate between days.

- Press "N" (Next Day) to instantly navigate to the Next Day
- Press "P" (Previous Day) key – to go to "previous" days
- Press "T" (Top) to go to the top of your inbox
- Press "B" (Bottom) to go to the bottom of your inbox
- Press "SPACE" to go down a page in your inbox or while reading a message.

- Highlight a Date Row in your Inbox and press ENTER – to instantly compose a new email message.

Deleting Email Messages – Fast!

Follow these steps to delete a large number of email messages quickly from the BlackBerry:

1. Go into the BlackBerry Message icon (email)
2. Highlight a date in the past,
3. Click in the trackwheel to see this menu

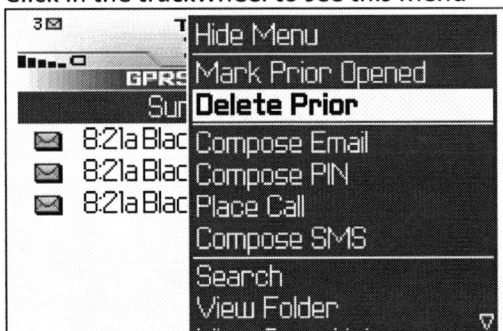

Choose → **Delete Prior** to easily delete all prior emails. (This command will not delete items from your inbox even if you have wireless email reconciliation turned on.) The only way to delete items from both places is when you delete an individual email or a group using the SHIFT-TRACKWHEEL combination to select a series of emails in a row then you "Delete Messages"

Tip!

FAST COMPOSING:

Highlight a DATE separator row in your Inbox and Press Enter to COMPOSE a new message.

Fast Cleanup!

Clean up your inbox quickly with the DELETE PRIOR command!

Delete a few messages in a Row!

Click on the first message to delete, then hold the shift key to the right of the space bar and roll the trackwheel up/down to select (highlight) multiple messages, then click the trackwheel and select "Delete Messages" (You could also "Save Messages" using the same technique)

Wireless Email Reconciliation

This feature is pretty cool, but only works in very specific email environments – it allows you to sync up exactly what you do on your Blackberry Inbox with your regular Email Inbox, so you don't have to remember what email you "read" on your BlackBerry or delete the same email message in both places. Delete the message once on your BlackBerry and it also deletes back in your regular inbox! (Same thing works the other way – delete a message on your regular inbox and it will be deleted from your BlackBerry.)

It's a great feature that was originally designed only to work with the Desktop Redirector (leave your PC running 24x7 connected to the Internet) or BlackBerry Enterprise Server environments (usually only found in large organizations). But now, with the newest BlackBerry Internet service, almost every individual with web-based email has the possibility of getting this working – at minimum for deletions and maybe full mailbox synchronization. It depends on the finer points of your email setup and the capabilities of your email account provider's POP3 server.

Works with POP3 Web-Based Email:

You use BlackBerry Internet Service to forward email to your BlackBerry and your regular Inbox is *only* "Web-Based Email" – you access your email exclusively from a web-browser and you have POP3 access to the server (Paid Yahoo Account, Standard POP3 service, etc.), your email provider allows the email synchronization messages from the Blackberry Internet Service (e.g. delete notifications) to operate on your email Inbox. In other words, if you download your email to your PC with Outlook, Outlook Express or a similar email program, you cannot use wireless email reconciliation.

Works with In-House Email Server and BlackBerry Enterprise Server:

Wireless Email Reconciliation will also work if you have email hosted in-house with a Microsoft Exchange, Lotus Domino or Novell GroupWise mail server and a BlackBerry Enterprise server. *(Usually this is the case when your work at a larger organization)*

Save Time with Wireless Email Reconciliation!

This feature is pretty cool – it allows you to sync up exactly what you do on your Blackberry Inbox with your regular Email Inbox. So you don't have to do things twice – on your BlackBerry and again on your regular Inbox!

Anti-SPAM vs. Wireless Email Reconciliation

You cannot be using a "forwarding anti-SPAM service" (like Spam Arrest) as we recommend above. This is because your Anti-SPAM inbox creates a layer between your BlackBerry and your regular Inbox. *(But if you're filtering SPAM, it's likely you won't need to delete as many emails – so don't worry!*

Wireless Email Reconciliation – Configuring Your BlackBerry
After verifying your Email setup as described above, configure your BlackBerry as follows:

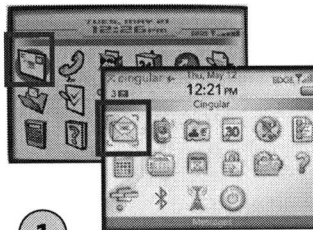

1 Click Trackwheel to select "Messages" (Inbox)

2 Click Trackwheel and select "Options"

3 Select "Email Reconciliation"

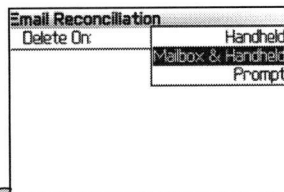

4 Change the "Delete On" to "Mailbox & Handheld"

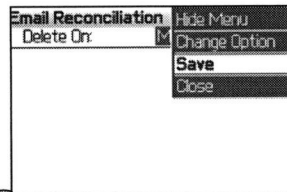

5 Click the trackwheel and "Save" your settings.

6 Now, any email you delete on your BlackBerry or on your Email Inbox should also be deleted on the other place!

Please make sure to read all the email configuration items in this section to make sure you have the correct setup.

BlackBerry Slow?

Sometimes the BlackBerry will really slow down (lots of hour glasses) if you're running low on memory. First try a Soft Reset. If that doesn't help, then do a "Delete Prior" on your email inbox. Finally, you may need to remove some other data from your device. (e.g. Addresses, Calendar, Memo Pad or other third party applications)

Checking BlackBerry Memory with the Quick Help & Status Screen

There is a great status screen on your BlackBerry to show everything from free memory, to batter, to signal strength.

Press ALT+CAP+H for the "Help Me!" Screen as shown:

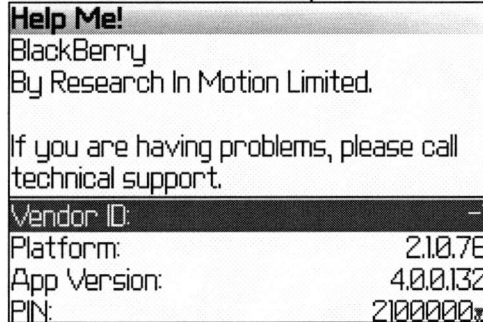

```
Help Me!
BlackBerry
By Research In Motion Limited.

If you are having problems, please call
technical support.
Vendor ID:                        -1
Platform:                    2.10.76
App Version:               4.0.0.132
PIN:                       2100000x
```

Scroll down to see the rest...

```
Help Me!
Platform:                    2.10.76
App Version:               4.0.0.132
PIN:                       2100000a
IMEI:              123456789000000
Uptime:                   6202 secs
Signal Strength:             -40 dBm
Battery Level:                  100%
File Free:            5456068 Bytes
File Total:         15269888 Bytes
```

Taking Notes while on a Call

To take notes on your BlackBerry while on a call, follow these steps:
To take notes on your BlackBerry while on a call, follow these steps:

1. Start a call and click the trackwheel to select the "Notes" menu item.

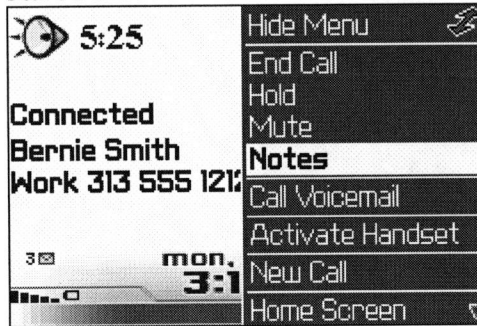

```
-O-> 5:25          Hide Menu       ⟰
                   End Call
                   Hold
Connected          Mute
Bernie Smith       Notes
Work 313 555 121   Call Voicemail
                   Activate Handset
3⌧          mon.   New Call
▮▮..□       3:1    Home Screen     ▽
```

2. Type as many notes as you'd like:

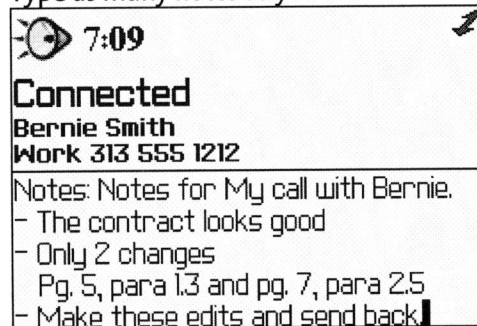

```
-O-> 7:09                          ⟰

Connected
Bernie Smith
Work 313 555 1212

Notes: Notes for My call with Bernie.
- The contract looks good
- Only 2 changes
  Pg. 5, para 1.3 and pg. 7, para 2.5
- Make these edits and send back.▮
```

3. At the end of the call, click in the trackwheel and choose → Save.

4. The Call Log will be saved in your BlackBerry Messages (Inbox):

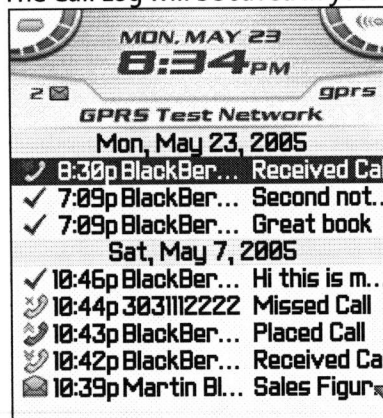

```
         MON, MAY 23
         8:34PM
2⌧                      gprs
     GPRS Test Network
       Mon, May 23, 2005
✓ 8:30p BlackBer... Received Call
✓ 7:09p BlackBer... Second not...
✓ 7:09p BlackBer... Great book
       Sat, May 7, 2005
✓ 10:46p BlackBer... Hi this is m...
⟿ 10:44p 3031112222 Missed Call
⟿ 10:43p BlackBer... Placed Call
⟿ 10:42p BlackBer... Received Call
✉ 10:39p Martin Bl... Sales Figur▽
```

5. Select the Call Log and select "Open" from the menu to view your notes.

6. Now you can see all your notes:

```
View Call Log
Date: May 23, 2005 8:30p
Type: Received Call
Duration: 3:19
BlackBerry Made Simple
Work 3135551212
Notes from my call with BB Made
Simple folks - got great advice!
- Use the ALT-ESC Trick to get
more done with my BlackBerry!!!
```

Tip!

Email the call notes to the person whom you spoke with to confirm understanding of what was discussed!

7. You can even email "FORWARD" the notes to the caller for good record keeping and making sure you and the caller have the same understanding of what was discussed.

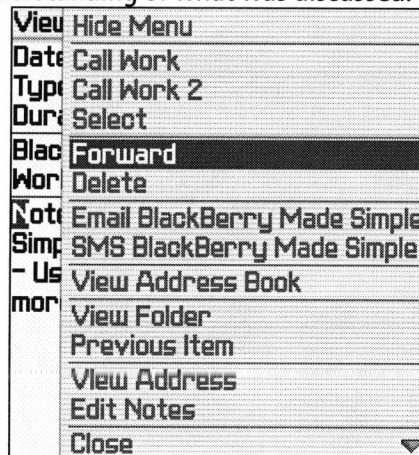

```
View   Hide Menu
Date   Call Work
Type   Call Work 2
Dura   Select
Blac   Forward
Wor    Delete
Note   Email BlackBerry Made Simple
Simp   SMS BlackBerry Made Simple
- Us   View Address Book
mor    View Folder
       Previous Item
       View Address
       Edit Notes
       Close
```

Tip!

Using these steps you can:
- Call a contact
- Take Notes
- Email those notes to the contact to confirm understanding and agreement.

Bottom Line: You've moved the relationship forward!

```
To: BlackBerry Made Simple
Subject: Fw: Call Log
Here are the notes I took of our
call, please confirm you have the
same understanding.
Thanks!
--------------------
Date: 5/23/2005 8:30p
Duration: 3:19
BlackBerry Made Simple (Work)
3135551212
--------------------
Notes from my call with BB Made
Simple folks - got great advice!
- Use the ALT-ESC Trick to get
```

BATTERY: Getting the most o
of your Battery

Here are the best tips to ensuring you get the
out of your BlackBerry Battery

- If you use your BlackBerry as a phone **charge your BlackBerry every night**
- Prolong your battery life by keeping your BlackBerry in its plastic "Holster" – This is because when it's in the holster, the screen is automatically powered down – conserving battery life.
- If your battery level falls below 10%, your radio will automatically turn off (by design). Solution: Plug-in to the wall power or to your computer!

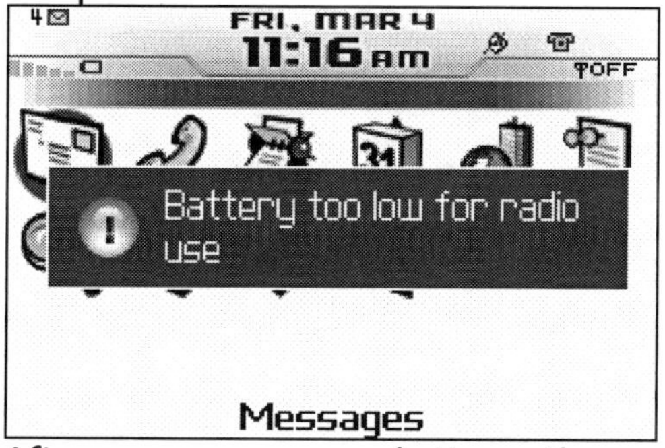

- After you re-power your battery – then you need to MANUALLY turn the radio back on as shown here to continue to send/receive emails, use data applications and browse the web. Do this by highlighting and clicking on the radio tower icon.

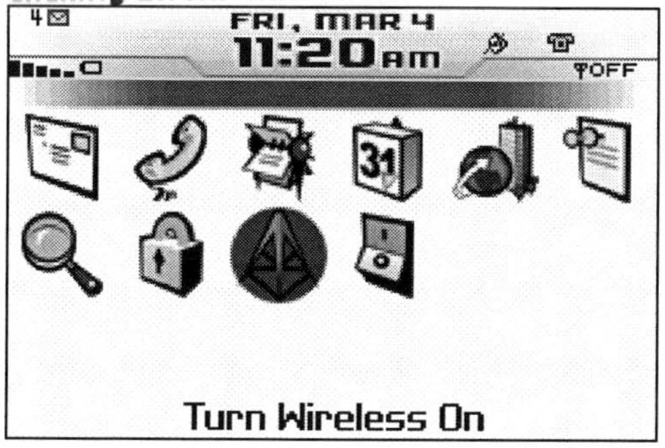

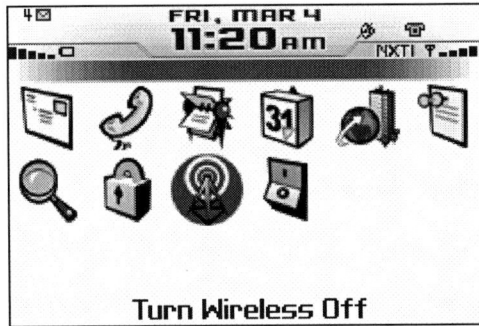

Turn Wireless Off

- Your BlackBerry is designed to shut down if the battery gets too low so that it can preserve all your information (email, addresses, etc.)!

MemoPad

TIP: Did you know that plugging your BlackBerry into your computer (or laptop) with the USB cable will charge it!

AUTOTEXT: Select Any of Multiple E-Mail Signatures Instantly!

Using AutoText – The BlackBerry will type your Signatures for you!

As a Power Email user – you may want to have various email signatures – one for formal business emails, one for informal business, one for family and one for friends. With the AutoText feature of your BlackBerry, you can easily create all of these signatures and select them with just a few keystrokes!

What you do is "teach" the BlackBerry each signature and assign it a separate few "code letters." For example – you might call your business formal signature: "bus1" and your business informal signature "bus2"

In the below example, let's say you wanted to create your formal business signature and call it "bus1"

To use the AutoText feature, follow these steps:

1. Go into the Options Screen:

Tip!

You can easily have and use multiple e-mail signatures with AUTO TEXT!

2. Select AutoText:

```
Options
[Return To Home Screen]
About
Applications
Auto On/Off
AutoText
Browser
Browser Push
Certificates
Date/Time                      ▼
```

3. Select "New" from the trackwheel menu:

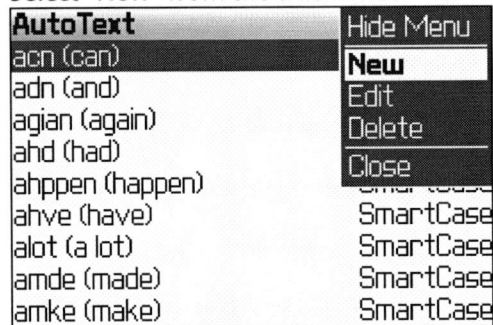

```
AutoText              Hide Menu
acn (can)             New
adn (and)             Edit
agian (again)         Delete
ahd (had)             Close
ahppen (happen)
ahve (have)           SmartCase
alot (a lot)          SmartCase
amde (made)           SmartCase
amke (make)           SmartCase
```

4. In this case we will teach the BlackBerry recognize the letters "bus1" and replace it with your business formal signature
    "Best regards,
    James Smith
    Sales Manager
    Best Products Company
    1325 Main St. Detroit, MI 48305
    Tel: 313-555-1212 Fax: 313-555-3322"

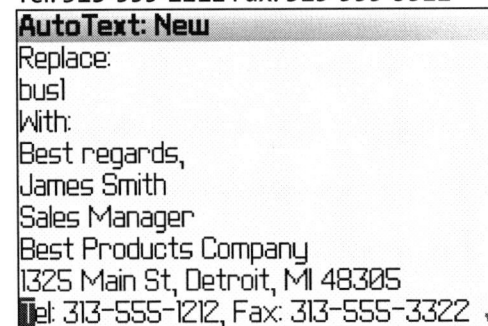

```
AutoText: New
Replace:
bus1
With:
Best regards,
James Smith
Sales Manager
Best Products Company
1325 Main St, Detroit, MI 48305
Tel: 313-555-1212, Fax: 313-555-3322 ▼
```

TIP: "SmartCase" means you don't have to worry about upper/lower case when you type the "bus1"

5. Save the new AutoText

```
┌─────────────────────────────────────────────┐
│ AutoText: New          │ Hide Menu            │
│ Replace:               │ Select               │
│ [us1                   │ Clear Field          │
│ With:                  │ Save                 │
│ Best regards,          │ Show Symbols         │
│ James Smith            │ Close                │
│ Sales Manager          │                      │
│ Best Products Company                         │
│ 1325 Main St, Detroit, MI 48305               │
│ Tel: 313-555-1212, Fax: 313-555-3322          │
└─────────────────────────────────────────────┘
```

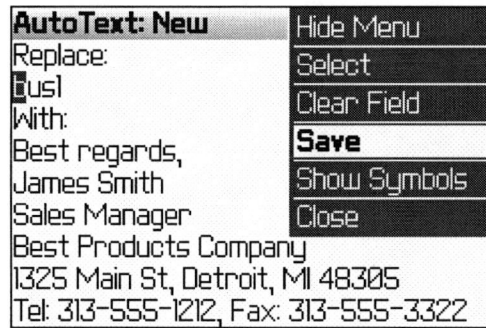

AutoText is a great way to save typing frequently entered information! (Email Signatures, Driving Directions, etc.)

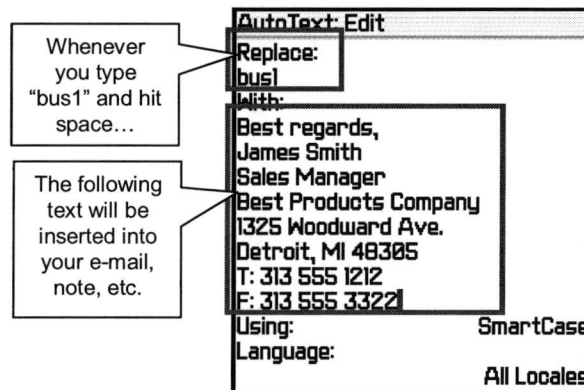

Whenever you type "bus1" and hit space…

```
┌──────────────────────────────────────┐
│ AutoText: Edit                        │
│ Replace:                              │
│ bus1                                  │
│ With:                                 │
│ Best regards,                         │
│ James Smith                           │
│ Sales Manager                         │
│ Best Products Company                 │
│ 1325 Woodward Ave.                    │
│ Detroit, MI 48305                     │
│ T: 313 555 1212                       │
│ F: 313 555 3322                       │
│ Using:              SmartCase         │
│ Language:                             │
│                     All Locales       │
└──────────────────────────────────────┘
```

The following text will be inserted into your e-mail, note, etc.

6. Try it out by starting a new email and type your body of your email then when you're done, just type "bus1" as shown.

```
┌──────────────────────────────────────┐
│ To: Chris Huffman                     │
│ Subject: Testing New Email Signature  │
│ Hi Chris,                             │
│                                       │
│ I'm testing my new email signature.   │
│                                       │
│ Bus                                   │
│                                       │
└──────────────────────────────────────┘
```

7. When you press the SPACE BAR – watch the business formal email signature just appear:

Hi Chris,

I'm testing my new email signature.

Best regards,
James Smith
Sales Manager
Best Products Company
1325 Main St, Detroit, MI 48305
Tel: 313-555-1212, Fax: 313-555-3322

☑ You can also use AutoText for anything else that is long/complex and you need to type multiple times. For example, your company name and address, directions to your home or office location, just about anything you can imagine!

☑ TIP: If you prefer to type all the directions on your house on your regular computer instead of the BlackBerry little keyboard – try this: Type them and email them to yourself! Then you can **copy/paste** the text from the email into the AUTOTEXT feature and you're done in seconds!

☑ Here is an example where we will teach the BlackBerry recognize the letters "**homedir**" and replace it with directions to your house.

AutoText: Edit
Replace:
homedir
With:
1. Take I-95 to Exit #305 Daytona
Beach Hwy #41
2. Exit and go WEST on Hwy #41 for 2.2
miles
3. Turn RIGHT into Chickasaw Crossings
Development

Continue typing directions: (as much as you need!)

AutoText: Edit
3. Turn RIGHT into Chickasaw Crossings
Development
4. Follow main road in complex until you
see lake on left.
5. Turn LEFT after lake and our house
is 3rd on Right hand side.
Home Address:
17 Lake Road, Daytona Beach, FL 33200
Home Tel: 586-555-1212

TIP: "SmartCase" means you don't have to worry about upper/lower case when you type the "homedir"

Then whenever you type homedir and hit SPACE, then you will see the directions to your home instantly "pop" up and be typed for you!

Inserting Date, Time or Other Cool Info with AutoText Macros

The following are the macros you can use with AutoText items:

AutoText: New	AutoText: New
Rep¹ dd With	Rep¹ dd With
Insert macro:	**Insert macro:**
Short date (%d)	Owner name (%o)
Long date (%D)	Owner info (%O)
Short time (%t)	Phone Number (%p)
Long time (%T)	Handheld PIN (%P)
Owner name (%o)	Backspace (%b)
Owner info (%O)	Delete (%B)
Phone Number (%p)	'%' (%%)

For example – if you wanted to insert today's date into an email, you could create an auto text for "dat" and replace with "Today's Date: %D" as shown:

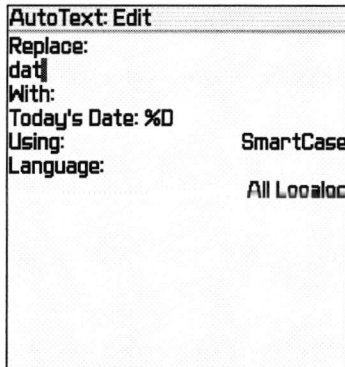

```
AutoText: Edit
Replace:
dat|
With:
Today's Date: %D
Using:                    SmartCase
Language:
                          All Looaloo
```

When you type "dat" in an email message and press space you see:

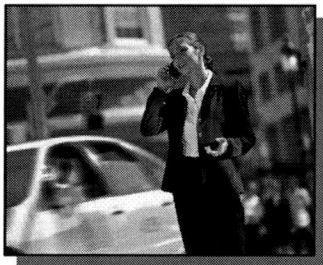

To: BlackBerry Made Simple Subject: Notes	To: BlackBerry Made Simple Subject: Notes
John,	John,
Notes from the meeting: Dat|	Notes from the meeting: Today's Date: Tue, May 24, 2005	

TIP: You can also use AutoText for customized email signatures. For examples, setup "sig1" to be your formal email signature, "sig2" could be your informal signature, and "sig3" could be your signature with full mailing address.

Searching Email Messages

If you're like most BlackBerry users, you probably have 100's of messages (emails, call logs, etc.) in your Messages Inbox folder.

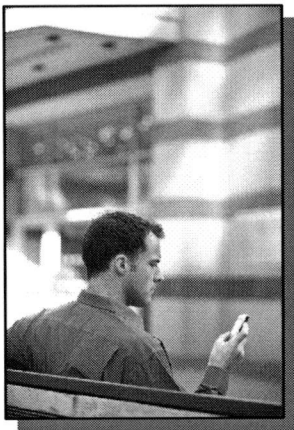

You have three options to Search for email in the BlackBerry Messages application:
1.   Search (General search for Emails, Phone, SMS and Direct Connect - for certain Carriers)
2.   Search Recipient (only visible when you're on an email message)
3.   Search Subject (only visible when you're on an email message)

Searching email

To search email, follow these steps:
1.   Open Message on the BlackBerry
2.   Click the trackwheel and select → Search

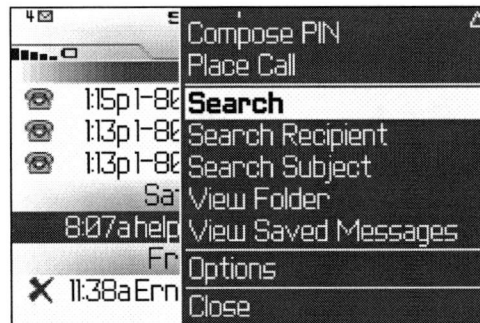

3.   Type in the text to search for and → Select which address field you want to search:

Tip!

WILD CARDS:
Use an asterisk (*) as a wild card – for example to search for email to people with "blackberry" anywhere in their email address, in the "Name:" field enter "blackberry*"

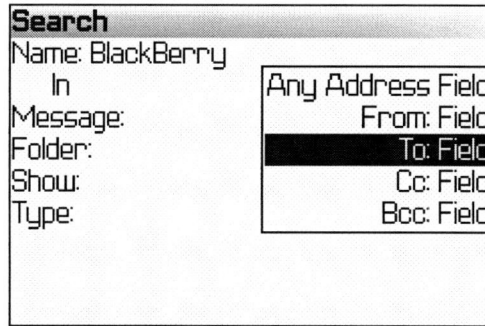

Search
Name: BlackBerry
    In
Message:
Folder:
Show:
Type:

Any Address Field
From: Field
To: Field
Cc: Field
Bcc: Field

4. Select a specific folder or "All Folders"

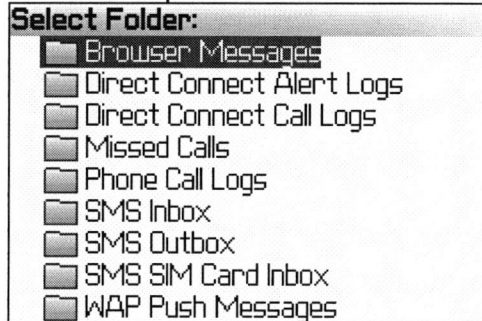

Select Folder:
- Browser Messages
- Direct Connect Alert Logs
- Direct Connect Call Logs
- Missed Calls
- Phone Call Logs
- SMS Inbox
- SMS Outbox
- SMS SIM Card Inbox
- WAP Push Messages

5. If you know it's only SENT items you can select "SENT ONLY" in the Show Field

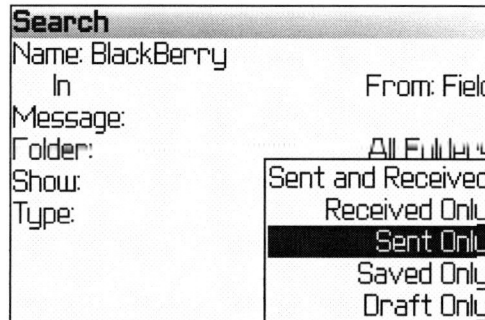

Search
Name: BlackBerry
    In
Message:
Folder:
Show:
Type:

From: Field

All Folders
Sent and Received
Received Only
Sent Only
Saved Only
Draft Only

6. You can also specify if it's only email that you want to search – because you know it's an email message.

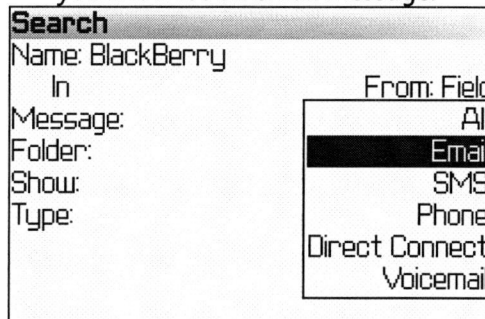

Search
Name: BlackBerry
    In
Message:
Folder:
Show:
Type:

From: Field

All
Email
SMS
Phone
Direct Connect
Voicemail

7. Search Recipient – (you only see this if you are on an email message) will find all email messages sent to that particular email address .

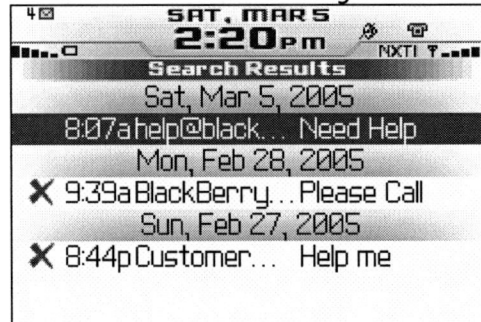

MEMOPAD: Your Mobile Book of Knowledge

Memo pad entries are great because they are virtually unlimited in length (only limited by memory on your BlackBerry), can be searched and can be synced or transferred electronically from your desktop computer.

Finding the Memo Pad Icon

8700 Series

Applications (sub-menu)

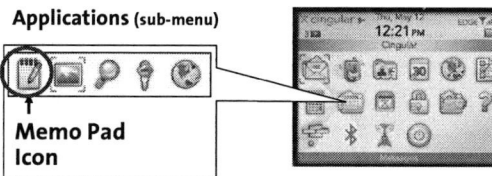

Use the Memo Pad Icon to take notes, write lists, store important information. They are fully searchable and can be organized with "Categories"

Memo Pad Icon

All Other Full Keyboard BlackBerries

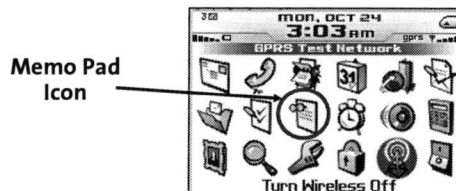

Memo Pad Icon

If you have important procedures for your mobile workers, or just things you want to have with you on the road at all times without a bulky paper manual... use Memo Pad and your BlackBerry Desktop Manager's Intellisync!

If you are a MS Outlook user, just drop your important information into the Notes in Outlook and sync it over using the BlackBerry desktop manager and your sync cable.

TIP: If you don't want to bother with Outlook, you could email yourself the text for the MemoPad item and then use your BlackBerry Copy/Paste function to copy information from the email into your MemoPad!

MEMOPAD: Your Mobile Idea Catcher

Did you ever think up a great idea but didn't have any thing to write it down? Just use your MemoPad and capture it where ever you are!

Did you hear a great song on the radio or a great new book being reviewed on the radio, and don't want to forget the name – just use your BlackBerry and write it on the MemoPad.

WEB: Great Stuff on your BlackBerry Web Bowser!

Your BlackBerry is unbeatable for wireless email but can you browse the web on it? The answer is yes! There is a lot of great stuff you can with your BlackBerry web browser. The trouble people usually run into is that they try to access the same web sites they do on their desktop and quickly get discouraged as they see one image crawl in at a time and 5 minutes later the page is still not loaded. The key is to use sites specifically designed for the BlackBerry or other wireless phones!

Starting Your Web Browser

All other Full Keyboard BlackBerries

8700 Series

Web Browser Icon

Highlight and click in to start your Web Browser

Web Browser Icon

Highlight and click in to start your Web Browser

Convenience Key

You can set this to start your Web Browser

Note:
Your Web Browser Icon may look very different from those above. The key to look for is the word "Browser" at the bottom of the screen here when you roll over the icon.

Google on your BlackBerry Solves that Golf Emergency!

Say you've just arrived at the golf course for your 8:00am tee off time, but the course is closed because they received 4.5 inches of rain yesterday. No problem – you whip out you trusty BlackBerry and go to www.google.com and type in "golf courses ormond beach fl" or "golf courses (your location)". In a few seconds, Google Local will show you all the local golf courses, complete with addresses and phone numbers.   Scroll down to any of the courses, highlight their phone number and click "Call" Within a few minutes, you've located a new course and booked a tee time – the golf outing is saved! And, if you end up liking the course, then just find that number in your recently dialed list on your BlackBerry and click "Add to Address Book", type in the name of the course and your ready to call them back any time.

BlackBerry Web Browsing Tips:

Use the sites your carrier recommends

> Tip!
>
> Check out the "standard" sites that come with your BlackBerry – they are packed with information!

Most wireless carriers have put together a list of the sites that they think work best on their devices. This is usually a good list of mobile information site for news, sport, weather, traffic and more. How you access these resources varies device by device, but the carriers usually prominently display these links the first time you enter their browser. For example on T-Mobile BlackBerries, upon entering you see a list of web links to access mobile editions of CNN, ESPN. Nextel offer the same type of list right when you access their NOL, Nextel Online Browser.

How to enter a web page into your browser:

1. Start your browser (see above for details on how to do this)

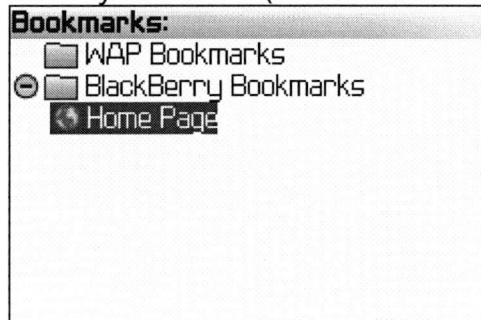

Bookmarks:
- WAP Bookmarks
- BlackBerry Bookmarks
  - Home Page

> Tip!
>
> Check out the "standard" sites that come with your BlackBerry – they are packed with information!

2. Click the trackwheel and select "Go To..."

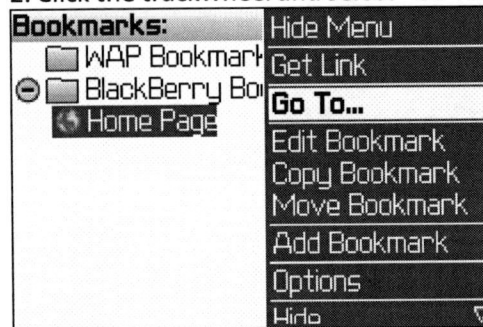

Bookmarks:
- WAP Bookmark
- BlackBerry Bo
  - Home Page

Menu:
- Hide Menu
- Get Link
- **Go To...**
- Edit Bookmark
- Copy Bookmark
- Move Bookmark
- Add Bookmark
- Options
- Hide

3. Type in the web address, you don't need to type the "http://" it's already there!

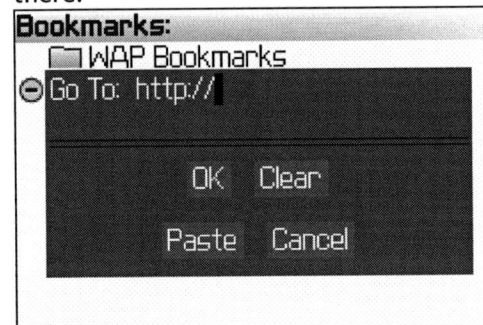

Bookmarks:
WAP Bookmarks
Go To: http://

OK　Clear

Paste　Cancel

4. Once you type your web address, then scroll the trackwheel down to "OK" and click in.

Bookmarks:
Go To: http://www.blackberrymadesimple.com
http://www.blackberrymadesimpl...

OK　Clear

Paste　Cancel　Help

5. Then after seeing this "Loading" screen, you will see your web site.

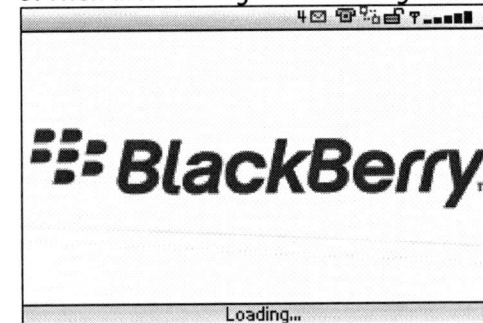

BlackBerry™

Loading...

```
BlackBerry Made Simple... 4⊠ ☎%⊟▚▐▌▐▌
BlackBerry Made
Simple
Home | E-Books | FAQs|
Tell-A-Friend About Us! | Contact
Us | Partner Program
Ebooks / Contact Us
Newsletter Signup
```

BlackBerry Recommended Sites "BlackBerry Home Page

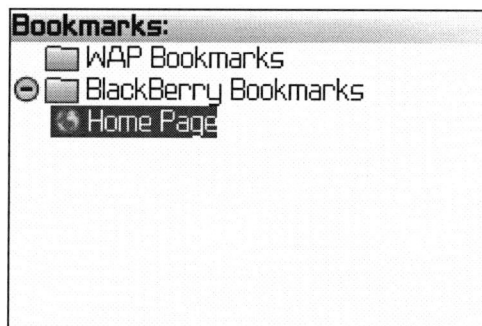

```
Bookmarks:
    ☐ WAP Bookmarks
⊖ ☐ BlackBerry Bookmarks
    ⟲ Home Page
```

The people at BlackBerry have also done a nice job of putting together a list of good sites designed for mobile devices. Point your BlackBerry Browser to http://www.blackberry.net/go/mobile/ to check out their suggestions.

Complete List of BlackBerry Sites – *(Note: This list will probably be somewhat or significantly different on your BlackBerry, but it will give you a sense of what is possible.)*

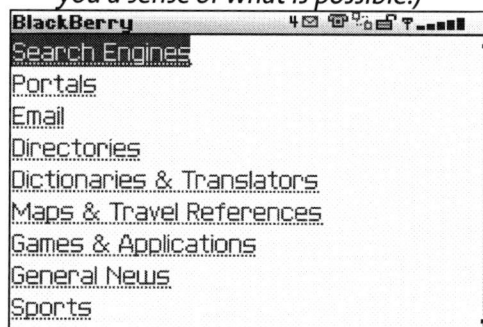

```
BlackBerry            4⊠ ☎%⊟▚▐▌▐▌
Search Engines
Portals
Email
Directories
Dictionaries & Translators
Maps & Travel References
Games & Applications
General News
Sports
```

```
BlackBerry          4⊠ ☎📶🔒📶▁▂▃▅
Weather
Business and Finance
Brokerages
Entertainment
Food
Shopping
Technology
Automotive
Shipping
```

```
BlackBerry          4⊠ ☎📶🔒📶▁▂▃▅
Technology
Automotive
Shipping
Miscellaneous

How to change your home page
_____
Legal Copyright © 2005 Research In
Motion Limited, unless otherwise noted.
```

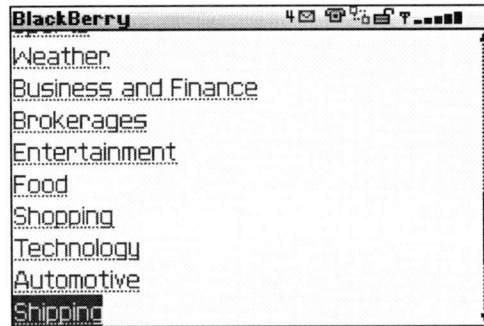

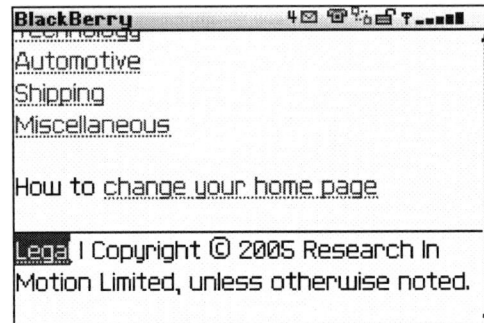

Search Engines:

```
Search Engines      4⊠ ☎📶🔒📶▁▂▃▅
Search Engines

AltaVista Search
AskMeNow
Euroseek
Google Search
Google iMode Search
go2 Search
Yahoo
```

BlackBerry™

Organized?   **Try Portals:**

```
Portals             4⊠ ☎📶🔒📶▁▂▃▅
Portals

Alan's Pocket Portal
Evolution Mobile
Go2
Yahoo! Mobile
MSN mobile
My Lycos
Pawgo
```

Hotmail/Yahoo?   Try Email:

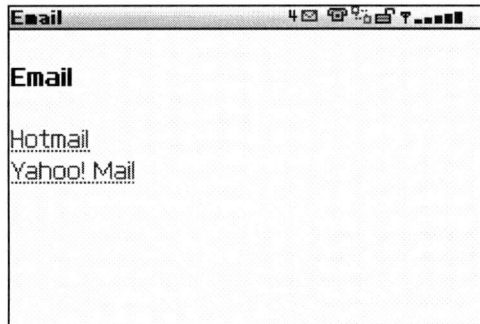

Need Info?   Try Directories:

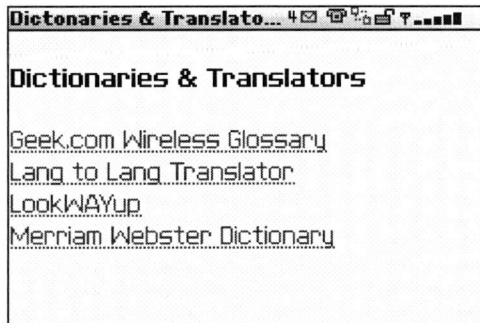

Confused?   Try Dictionaries and Translators:

Tip!

Traveling? Use the BlackBerry translator to figure out how to say "Thank You" in many different languages!

Lost?   Try Maps and Travel References:

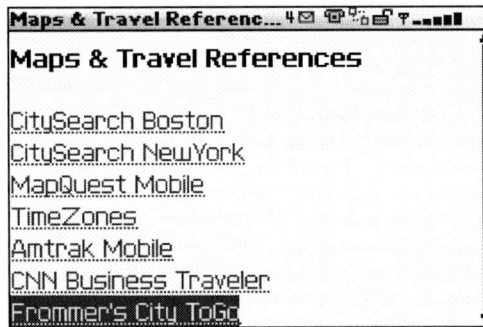

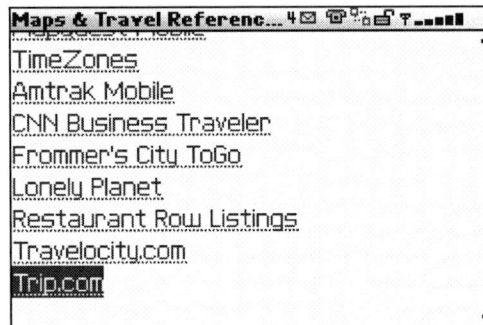

Maps & Travel Referenc... ▫ ☎ ☐ ☐ ☐ ☐

Maps & Travel References

CitySearch Boston
CitySearch NewYork
MapQuest Mobile
TimeZones
Amtrak Mobile
CNN Business Traveler
Frommer's City ToGo

Maps & Travel Referenc... ▫ ☎ ☐ ☐ ☐ ☐

TimeZones
Amtrak Mobile
CNN Business Traveler
Frommer's City ToGo
Lonely Planet
Restaurant Row Listings
Travelocity.com
Trip.com

Bored?   Try Games & Applications:

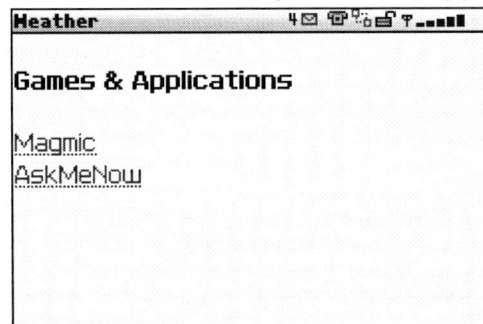

Weather   ▫ ☎ ☐ ☐ ☐ ☐

Games & Applications

Magmic
AskMeNow

Want info?   Try General News

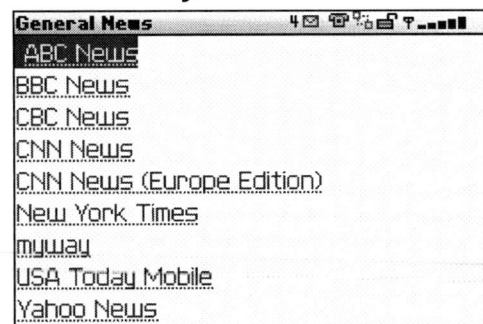

General News   ▫ ☎ ☐ ☐ ☐ ☐
ABC News
BBC News
CBC News
CNN News
CNN News (Europe Edition)
New York Times
myway
USA Today Mobile
Yahoo News

Sports buff?   Try Sports

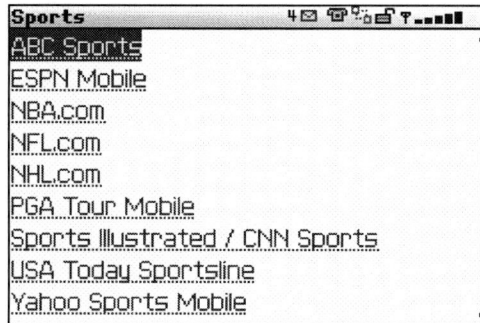

```
Sports                    4⊠ ☎⁰b⚏ ⏚.∎∎∎∎
ABC Sports
ESPN Mobile
NBA.com
NFL.com
NHL.com
PGA Tour Mobile
Sports Illustrated / CNN Sports
USA Today Sportsline
Yahoo Sports Mobile
```

Raining?   Try Weather?

```
Weather                   4⊠ ☎⁰b⚏ ⏚.∎∎∎∎

Weather

AccuWeather
CNN Weather
The Weather Channel
Weather Channel UK
Yahoo Weather
```

Tip!

Book mark your local weather page for instant access!

Business?   Try Business & Finance

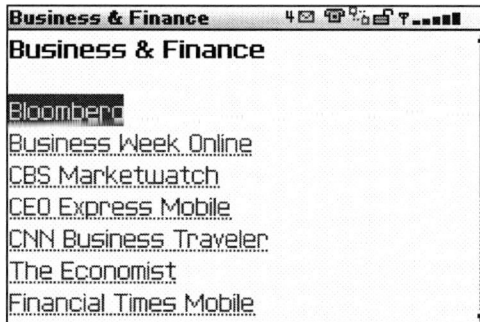

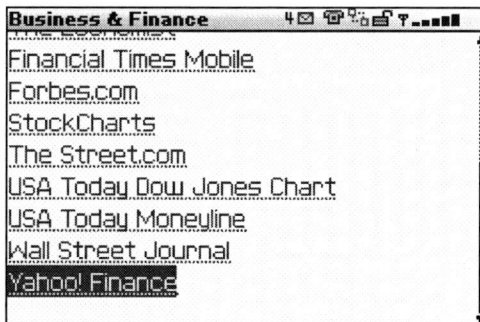

```
Business & Finance   4⊠ ☎⁰b⚏ ⏚.∎∎∎∎
Business & Finance

Bloomberg
Business Week Online
CBS Marketwatch
CEO Express Mobile
CNN Business Traveler
The Economist
Financial Times Mobile
```

```
Business & Finance   4⊠ ☎⁰b⚏ ⏚.∎∎∎∎
The Economist
Financial Times Mobile
Forbes.com
StockCharts
The Street.com
USA Today Dow Jones Chart
USA Today Moneyline
Wall Street Journal
Yahoo! Finance
```

Stocks?   Try Brokerages

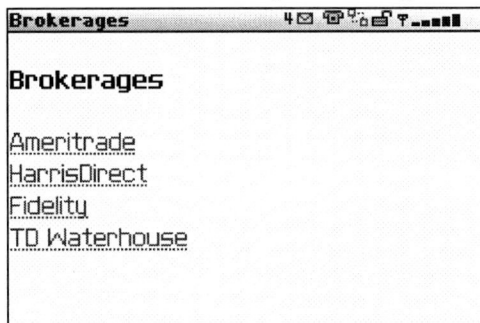

```
Brokerages          4⊠ ☎▯▯◧ ▾▪▪▪▪

Brokerages

Ameritrade
HarrisDirect
Fidelity
TD Waterhouse
```

Like Movies?   Try Entertainment

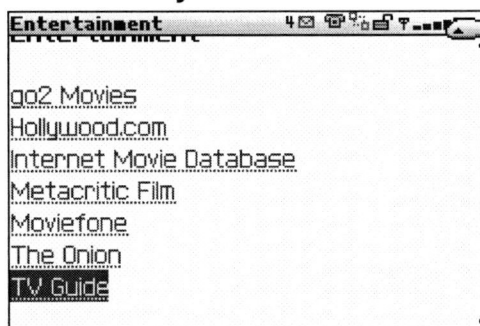

```
Entertainment       4⊠ ☎▯▯◧ ▾▪▪◖

go2 Movies
Hollywood.com
Internet Movie Database
Metacritic Film
Moviefone
The Onion
TV Guide
```

Hungry?   Try Food

```
Food                4⊠ ☎▯▯◧ ▾▪▪▪▪

Food

Cooking Index
Dine Site Restaurant Reviews
Fodor's Hotel and Restaurant Finder
Restaurant Row
Starbucks Locator
Wine Lovers
```

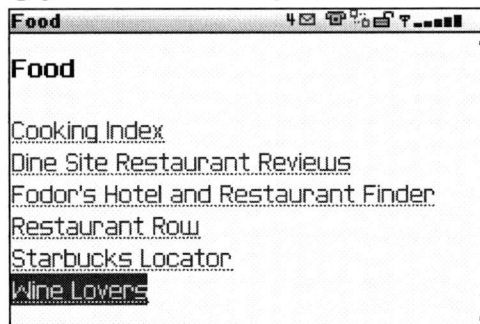

Want to buy? Try Shopping

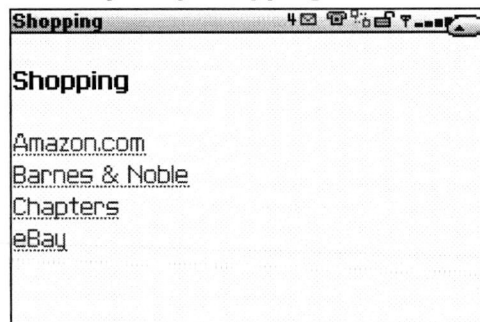

```
Shopping            4⊠ ☎▯▯◧ ▾▪▪◖

Shopping

Amazon.com
Barnes & Noble
Chapters
eBay
```

Techie?   Try Technology

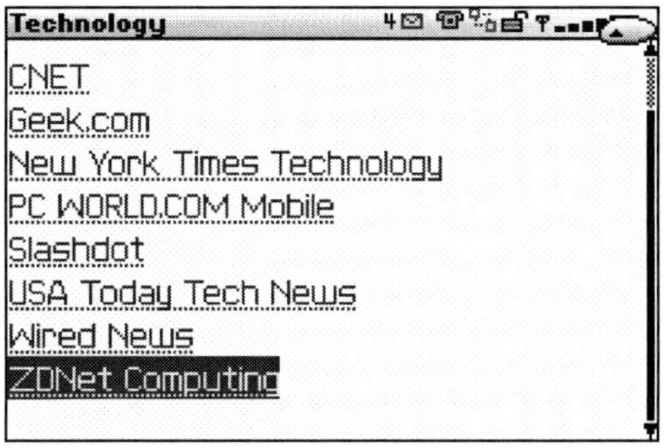

```
Technology              4⊠ ☎ %₀⊟ ▼▪▪▪
CNET
Geek.com
New York Times Technology
PC WORLD.COM Mobile
Slashdot
USA Today Tech News
Wired News
ZDNet Computing
```

Buy/Sell Car? Try Automotive

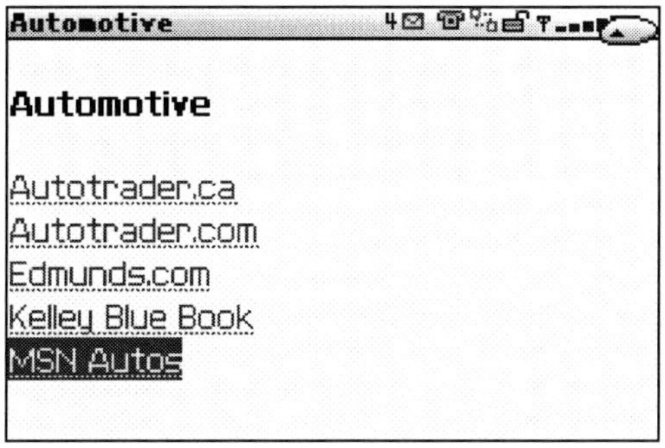

```
Automotive              4⊠ ☎ %₀⊟ ▼▪▪▪

Automotive

Autotrader.ca
Autotrader.com
Edmunds.com
Kelley Blue Book
MSN Autos
```

Tracking shipment?   Try Shipping

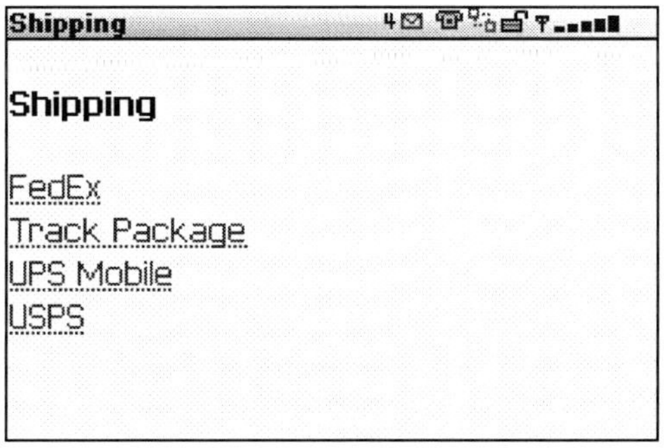

```
Shipping                4⊠ ☎ %₀⊟ ▼▪▪▪▪

Shipping

FedEx
Track Package
UPS Mobile
USPS
```

Curious?   Try Miscellaneous

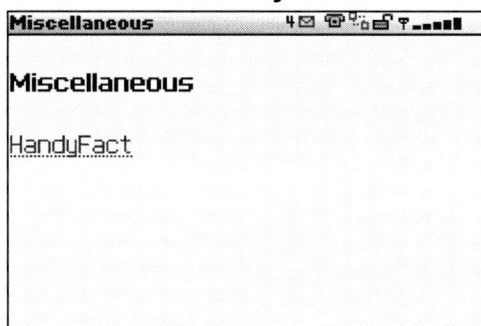

Miscellaneous   4⊠ ☎⬚⬚⬚⬚ ⊤▄▄▄█

Miscellaneous

HandyFact

A few of interesting sites

1. Need a Starbucks – FAST! (Under BlackBerry Home Page / Food)

Starbucks Store Locator 4⊠ ☎⬚⬚⬚⬚ ⊤▄▄█

Starbucks Store Locator

Retail ▼ Store Type:

Address:

City:

–Select a state– ▼ State:

Zipcode: Find

2.   http://mobile.google.com/mobilesearch.html

Google Search   4⊠ ☎⬚⬚⬚⬚ ⊤▄▄█

Google

Search the Web

Google Search
Full Google

3. Amazon.com: (Get to it from the BlackBerry Home page)

Amazon.com
Home | Account | Help | Feedback
amazon.com.

Find
[All Products ▼]
[   ] [Go]
Check out What's Playing Movie Showtimes
Books
Music

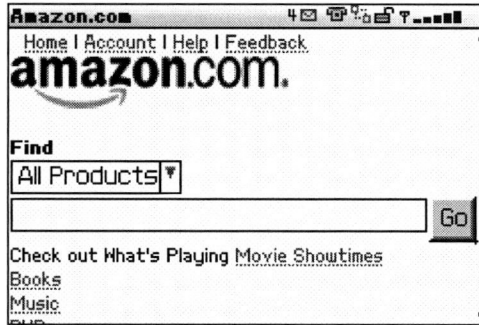

4. Language to Language Translator

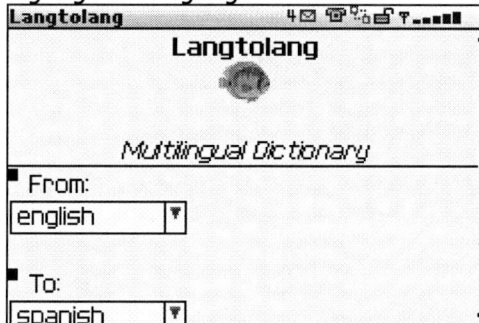

Langtolang
Langtolang

Mutilingual Dictionary

■ From:
[english   ▼]

■ To:
[spanish   ▼]

5. Mapquest Mobile (from BlackBerry Home Page)

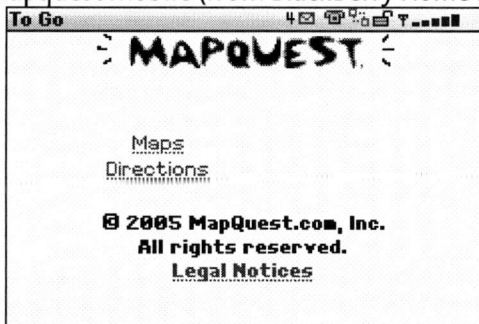

To Go
MAPQUEST

Maps
Directions

© 2005 MapQuest.com, Inc.
All rights reserved.
Legal Notices

6. Go2 Portal (Under BlackBerry Portals section)

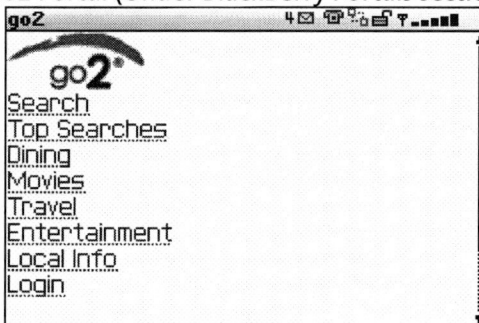

go2
go2®
Search
Top Searches
Dining
Movies
Travel
Entertainment
Local Info
Login

Find a site your like? Bookmark it.

If you spend some time browsing the wireless web, if you find a site you like
bookmark it right away because it may have been painstaking to get
there the first time!

Here's how to bookmark a website on your BlackBerry!

1. Open the Browser on your BlackBerry using your convenience key.
(8700 Series) or Browser Icon.

Starting Your Web Browser

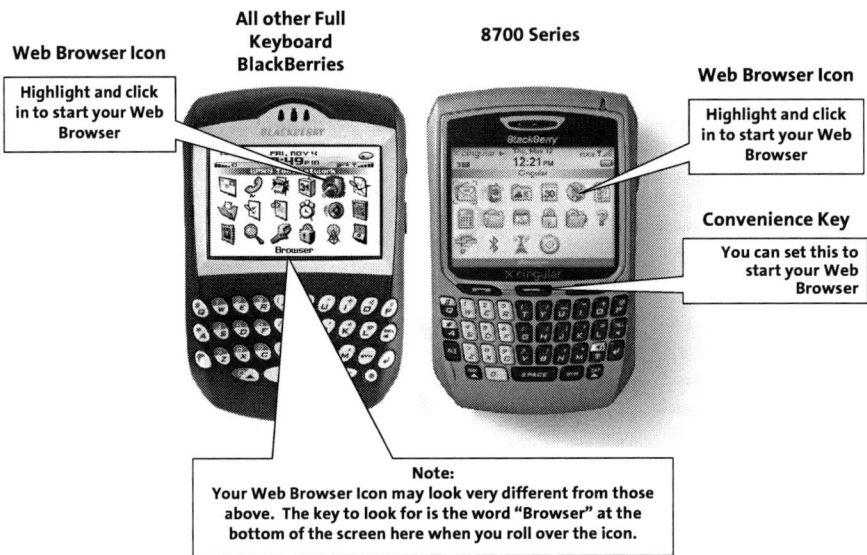

Web Browser Icon

All other Full Keyboard BlackBerries

8700 Series

Web Browser Icon

Highlight and click in to start your Web Browser

Highlight and click in to start your Web Browser

Convenience Key

You can set this to start your Web Browser

Note:
Your Web Browser Icon may look very different from those
above. The key to look for is the word "Browser" at the
bottom of the screen here when you roll over the icon.

2. Navigate to the site you want to bookmark

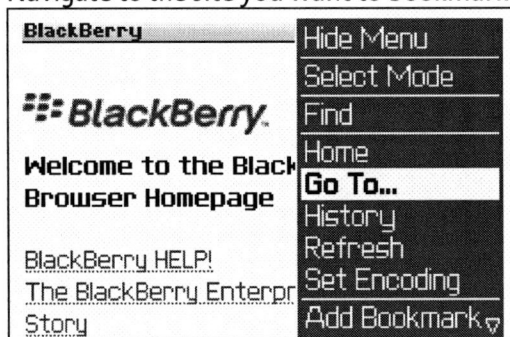

BlackBerry

Welcome to the Black
Browser Homepage

BlackBerry HELP!
The BlackBerry Enterpr
Story

Hide Menu
Select Mode
Find
Home
Go To...
History
Refresh
Set Encoding
Add Bookmark

> **Tip!**
>
> Book marking sites is a great way to save time on your Browser!

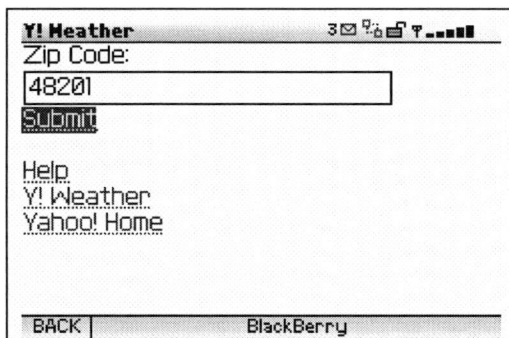

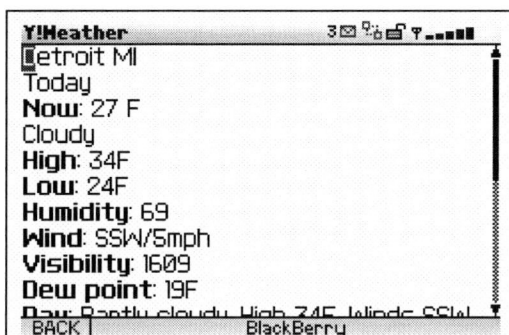

3. Once on the page you want to save, click in the trackwheel and select →
Add Bookmark

4. On the Add Bookmark page, change the page name if necessary, then
roll down and click → **Add.**

5. Now, next time you enter the BlackBerry browser, you can immediately go to your favorite pages.

Bookmarks:
- 📁 WAP Bookmarks
- ⊖ 📁 BlackBerry Bookmarks
  - 🌐 Home Page
  - 🌐 Y!Weather-Detroit

How to see your Current Web Page Address

In order to see what the address of your current page on your BlackBerry browser, click the trackwheel and select the "Page Address" item:

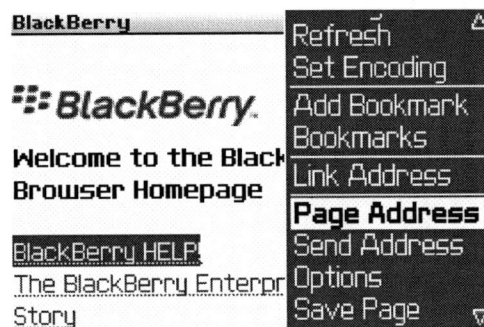

BlackBerry

BlackBerry.

Welcome to the Black
Browser Homepage

BlackBerry HELP!
The BlackBerry Enterpr
Story

Menu:
- Refresh
- Set Encoding
- Add Bookmark
- Bookmarks
- Link Address
- **Page Address**
- Send Address
- Options
- Save Page

Then you'll see this pop-up with the address:

BlackBerry

Title: BlackBerry
Address: http://www.blackberry.net/go/mobile/

[OK]

Copy Address

You can then "Copy Address" – and paste it into anything (a person's contact in your address book, or a memo pad item)

You can also "Send Address" – which will ask you to select a person in your Address book and paste the address right into the email:

```
To: BlackBerry Made Simple
Subject: Web Address
http://www.blackberry.net/go/mobile/
```

Stopping SPAM Before it Gets to your BlackBerry

SPAM has become a big problem for everyone! Now that you have a BlackBerry, it's even more annoying. The only way to stop SPAM from getting to your BlackBerry is to stop it before it gets forwarded or pulled into your BlackBerry's Inbox. For large organizations, with anti-SPAM filters running on the email server, stopping SPAM from getting to BlackBerries is not a problem. Unfortunately, most of the individual SPAM filters that install on your PC filter SPAM after it's already been forwarded to your BlackBerry!

The trick is to get a SPAM filter service that works BEFORE your email is forwarded to your BlackBerry.

Today, you have two options to filter SPAM before it hits your BlackBerry:

Option 1: *(Recommended)* Use an anti-SPAM service like the one from Spam Arrest (Enter this link http://www.spamarrest.com/affl?4004399 in your web browser to sign up for a Free Trial)

Option 2: Use a computer-based SPAM filter to "clean your Inbox" on your computer. Then use BlackBerry Desktop Redirector to forward only the "clean" email to your BlackBerry. The big drawback to this "Option 2" approach is: You will stop getting any email on your BlackBerry as soon as your PC or laptop is turned off, goes into sleep mode, your email program is turned off, or your computer is disconnected from the Internet. So this option ties up your computer and assumes it's running 24x7.

We recommend "Option 1" because it doesn't tie up your computer or force it to be left on all the time. You end up with more reliable SPAM-free email delivery on your BlackBerry.

How to setup Spam Arrest™ Anti-SPAM service:

Below we describe how to setup the "Spam Arrest" service – you can use the same setup steps for services from similar anti-SPAM services.
1. Sign up for Spam Arrest (or similar service) - (Enter this link http://www.spamarrest.com/affl?4004399 in your web browser to sign up for a Free Trial)
2. Configure Spam Arrest to receive up to 5 email accounts (POP3, IMAP).
3. Configure your BlackBerry Internet Service to TURN OFF receiving or pulling email directly from your POP3 email accounts.
4. Configure your BlackBerry Internet Service to TURN ON receiving email from your new Spam Arrest email account – something like: username@spamarrest.com Now you will just receive the "clean" email from your Spam Arrest email address, instead of all that annoying SPAM!

SPAM

Large organizations stop SPAM at the email Server Level, before it's sent to your BlackBerry. Unfortunately, most of the typical PC-based SPAM filters don't work because the SPAM has already been sent to your BlackBerry!

The Trick is to make sure that your SPAM filter works BEFORE email is sent to your BlackBerry.

5. Login periodically – every few days – to check the "UNVERIFIED" folder in Spam Arrest to review/approve senders that have not yet answered their "Challenge/Response Question" email to verify their own status.

Service-Type E-Mail SPAM Filters Work with BlackBerries

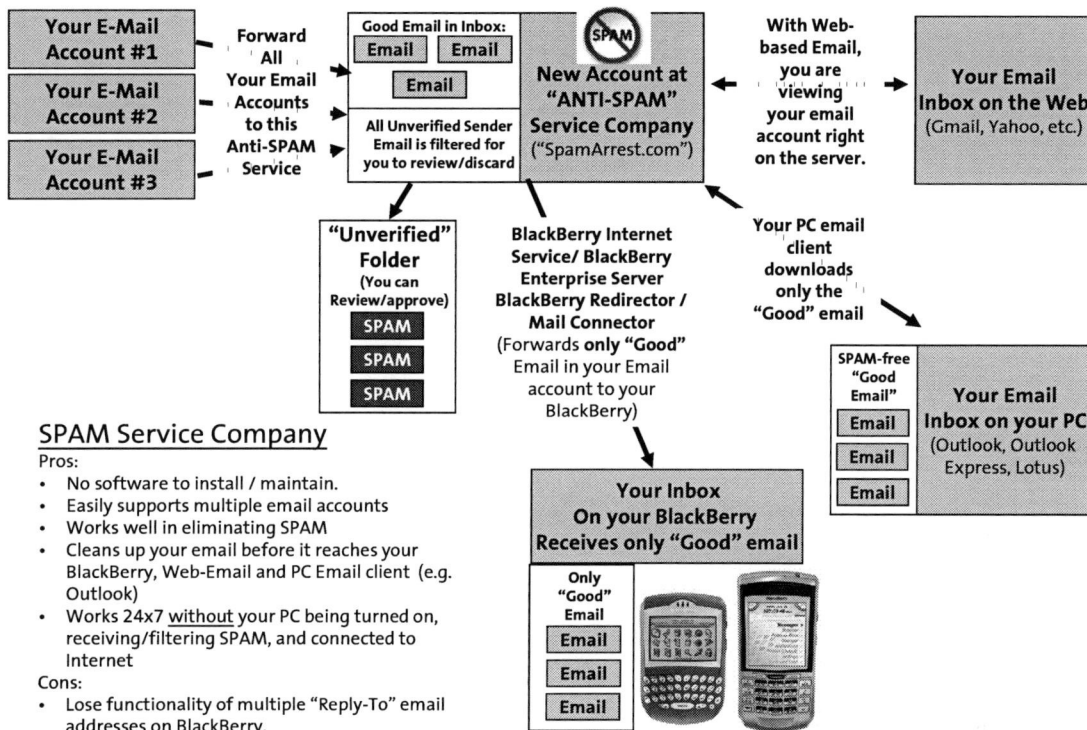

SPAM Service Company
Pros:
- No software to install / maintain.
- Easily supports multiple email accounts
- Works well in eliminating SPAM
- Cleans up your email before it reaches your BlackBerry, Web-Email and PC Email client (e.g. Outlook)
- Works 24x7 without your PC being turned on, receiving/filtering SPAM, and connected to Internet

Cons:
- Lose functionality of multiple "Reply-To" email addresses on BlackBerry.

Spam Arrest™

We recommend the service from Spam Arrest™ to remove SPAM from your BlackBerry.

Enter this link http://www.spamarrest.com/affl?4004399 in your web browser to sign up for a Free Trial of Spam Arrest.

What is Phishing?

Most Anti-SPAM products will also protect against "Phishing Scams" and "E-Mail Fraud." These are the messages that "look legitimate" asking you to "Verify Your Login" information for a Bank, Credit Card, PayPal or other sensitive financial institution. These Phishing emails are trying to steal your login information and ultimately your money!

You need to be very careful about any email asking you to login to a financial institution by clicking on a link in the email. These emails and associated fraudulent web sites that they link to have become VERY real looking – virtually duplicating the entire visual experience of logging into your financial institution so that it looks VERY legitimate.

How to avoid becoming a victim of Phishing:

1. Use one of many anti-SPAM and anti-Phishing products out there to prevent such emails from reaching your inbox and tempting you to click on them.

2. Never click on a link in an email asking you to login to a financial institution.

3. If you need to login to your financial institution, then open a new Internet browser on your computer and type in the correct web address (e.g. www.mybank.com) to make sure you are getting to the authentic web site.

If you Access your Email only on the Web... (e.g. Gmail, Yahoo, etc.)

If you use a hosted email service with only Web Access to your inbox, you will need to subscribe to a SPAM service, since you aren't actually receiving email on your computer.

Again, the same Spam Arrest service we mentioned above will work with all these Web-Only email accounts. Note: You may need to purchase POP3 access on Yahoo or other email services in order for Spam Arrest to work properly.

Enter this link http://www.spamarrest.com/affl?4004399 in your web browser to sign up for a Free Trial of Spam Arrest.

If you receive your email on your computer... (e.g. Outlook® / Outlook Express™)

If you do receive email on your computer using a program like Microsoft Outlook® or Outlook Express™, then you could choose Option 1 or Option 2 mentioned above. We do recommend Option 2 and using Spam Arrest as shown above.

Enter this link http://www.spamarrest.com/affl?4004399 in your web browser to sign up for a Free Trial of Spam Arrest.

Tip!

Electronic fax services will allow you to receive faxes as image attachments (.tif, .pdf, .jpg) which can be easily opened and viewed on your BlackBerry!
Note: You'll probably want to work with a service that supports faxes sent to you in Adobe .PDF format so you can read beyond page 1 of your faxes!

Receiving and Viewing a FAX on Your BlackBerry

You <u>can</u> receive faxes and view them on your BlackBerry for free! In just a few minutes, you can get a free fax number and start receiving faxes. What happens is you sign up for a service that has a bunch of fax servers and get a new fax number. Each fax received to your new fax number is converted to an image file and emailed to you. That email you receive has an image attachment and can therefore be opened by the BlackBerry's attachment viewing software. That gives you the capability to receive and view (and forward or respond via email or phone) to faxes right on your BlackBerry, whether you are across town or across the country from your fax machine.

For the free service, you can use any of a number of electronic fax services – there are many out there. If you do a "Google" search for "electronic fax", you'll find dozens. Almost all of these services will give you a non-local fax number and allow you to receive a limited number of fax pages per month for free. For the purposes of this book, we'll describe the fax service that we happen to use called eFax.

To set up a free eFax account, go to this web page:
https://www.efax.com/en/efax/twa/signupFree?currency=USD

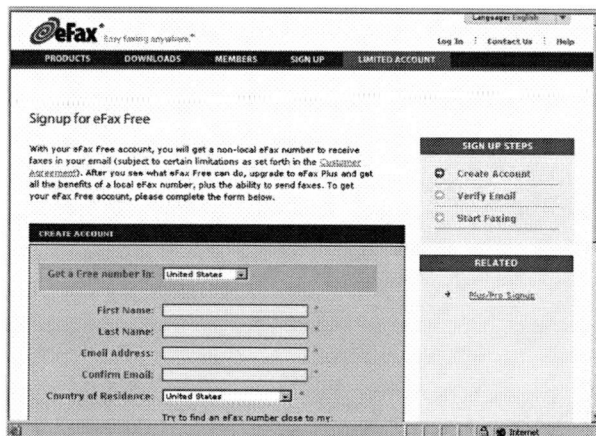

Enter your contact information and email to receive your faxes. The setup is almost instantaneous. Try a test fax and see how it works.

Once you receive your email, then you'll need to highlight the [1 Attachment] in the email, click the trackwheel and use the "Open Attachment" menu item. For more help, please see the " **E-Mail Attachment Viewing**" section of this book.

TIP: If you want to view more than page 1 of the fax, you will need to adjust the fax attached image format to Adobe PDF. If you cannot do it on a settings screen on the fax service, then you can call customer service and ask them to help you. We were able to successfully have eFax Free customer service do this for us.

Sending a FAX from your BlackBerry

In order to send a fax, you'll need to invest about $10 dollars a month in one of the electronic fax services. We have found the service from eFax to work well using attachments in PDF format.

1. To sign up for this service, visit our partners section on our web site: http://www.blackberrymadesimple.com/partners/index.htm

Tip!

Try the service for 30 days for free. Then if you think it will work for you, pay for an annual plan and save over the monthly plan.

Visit: www.blackberrymadesimple.com

Click here

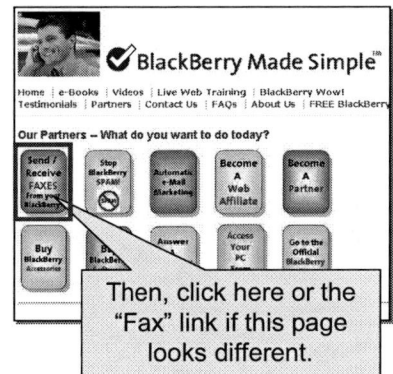

Then, click here or the "Fax" link if this page looks different.

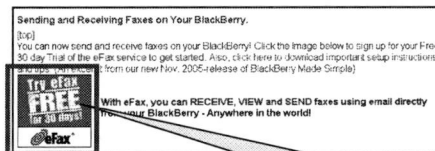

Finally, click on this "Free eFax Trial" Button.

2. Follow the on-screen steps on the eFax web site to sign up providing your contact information and email address for your eFax service.

3. Once you're done, you may be at your settings screens on the eFax web site. If you're not there, then login to the eFax web site using your fax number and PIN (emailed to you after signing up).

4. On the settings screen, you need to click on the "Preferences" link on the right side navigation bar as shown. Then make sure you're on the "Send Options" tab as shown. This screen allows you to add up to 5 email addresses from which you can send email faxes. You need to make sure you have your BlackBerry email address (your "Sent From" / "Reply To") as one of the five for this to work correctly.

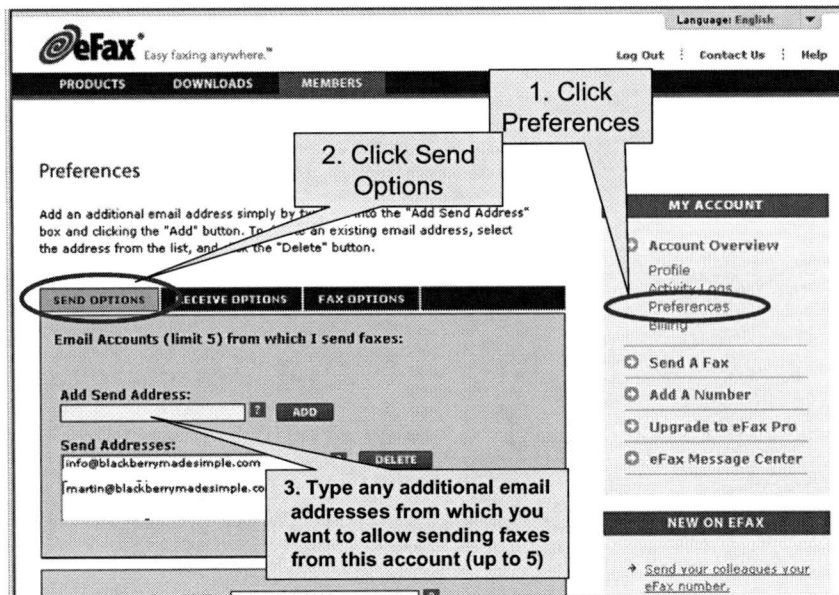

Tip!

If you're traveling away from your office, just use the "send fax" feature to print just about anything on your hotel's (or local office or coffee shop) fax machine.

You're a Consultant: It's 7pm and you just received an email with a 20-page PowerPoint presentation. You need to review it by 9am, but you're in a Hotel with only your BlackBerry.
No problem. Send it from your BlackBerry to the Hotel's Fax machine. Mark it up on paper and use the Hotel's fax to fax it back to your colleague.

5. Now, very important, in order to be able to read multi-page faxes, is to click on the **Fax Options** tab, and set the receive preferences to "PDF" as shown.

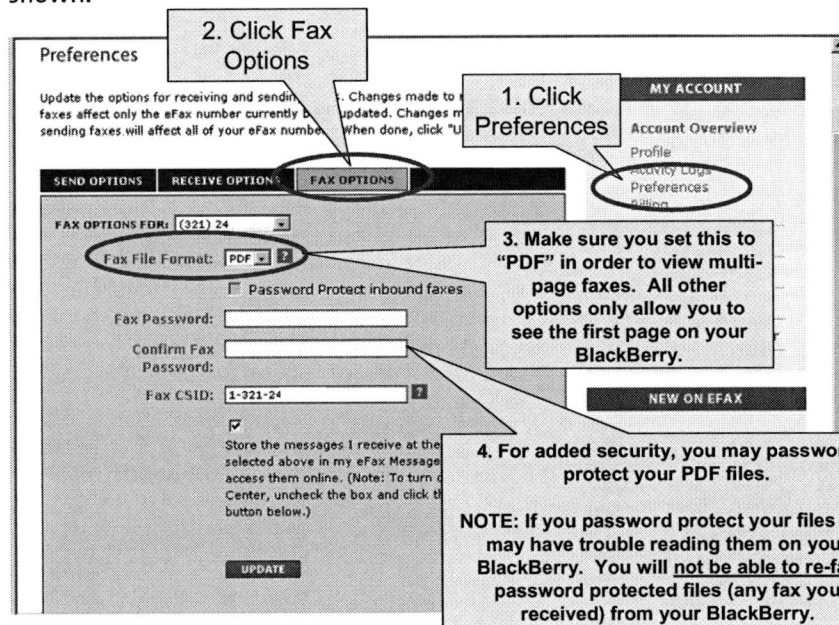

One other note about password protecting your faxes – then you CANNOT send them from your BlackBerry.

6. Receiving faxes works just like described above – you receive the Fax as a PDF attachment to the email message, then you open the attachment.

7. Anything you can compose, send, or forward (with attachments) can be sent as a fax from your BlackBerry. For example, you can send a newly composed email message, you can forward an email message, and most importantly, you can forward an email message with an ATTACHMENT of almost any standard format.

Most file formats you might have as attachments are supported by the eFax service we use. Here is a partial list of the supported Attachment file types as of October 10, 2005:

Word Processing: MS Word, Corel Word Perfect, Lotus Word Pro, RTF, Windows Write, Text
Graphics: Bitmap (BMP), Photoshop, TIF, JPG, GIF, PCX, PNG, PDF, VSD
Spreadsheets: MS Excel, Lotus 1-2-3, Quattro Pro, CSV
Presentations: MS PowerPoint, Corel Presentations Slide Show
Other: MS Publisher, EFX, JFX, HTML

In order to send the fax, you must address it to fax_number@efaxsend.com (e.g. 13865551212@efaxsend.com. For example, if you wanted to fax your email and it's attachment to a fax number at 1-386-555-1212, then you would open the message and select "Forward" then select "[Use Once]" at the top of the address book and type in this email address: 13865551212@efaxsend.com. Then the email, along with its attachment (if any) would be faxed to the number you requested.

Tip!

You're a Realtor:
It's 5pm and you're waiting for two sellers responses on counter offers from your buyers via fax. You're showing houses to a third client when you notice you've received a fax on your BlackBerry. You check it and sure enough the first seller has agreed to the counter offer! You need to get that fax to your first client, but your assistant has gone home for the day. No Problem.

You forward the fax to your first client right from your BlackBerry and also give them a quick call to let them know they got the house and fax to prove it will be there in minutes! All this while you were waiting for your other client to look through a house and after work hours!

Setting Your BlackBerry to Notify you when you receive email from one (or several) Very Important People

Thanks to one of our inquisitive readers, **S. Brennan**, who uses an **O2 BlackBerry** in Ireland, we bring you this new TIP!

The process is fairly involved and takes a few steps on both the BlackBerry Internet Service web site and on your BlackBerry to make it happen. If you're game, here's how to do it:

1. Open a Web Browser on your computer and Log In to your Internet Service site   (Please see the BlackBerry Internet Service Site List earlier in this book)

2. Now, depending on whether or not you have a "Separate" or "Imbedded" type BlackBerry Internet Service, you'll need to follow slightly different directions.

For "Separate" Type BIS:	For "Imbedded" Type BIS:
Click on the "**Filters**" in the top row, then click on the "**New**" button.	Click on the "**Filters**" icon next to your email accounts. Note: If you have more than 1 email address configured, you'll need to set up similar filters for each one.
As shown below, to create your filter for a specific email address, you need to create a filter name (No spaces or special characters), then select "From" and "contains" then put the email address of your Important Person in the last column as shown. Make sure the setting is "Inbox" and that the checkbox is checked next to "Level 1 Notification" then click "Save"	Click the link shown to add your new Filter.

Type a name for the Filter. Remember, you cannot leave any spaces or have special characters.

In this case we just want one condition, if the email is "From" susan@company.com

Leave this as "Inbox"

Make sure to press the button next to "Forward messages to handheld" and check the box next to "Level 1 Notification"

Click here to create your new filter.

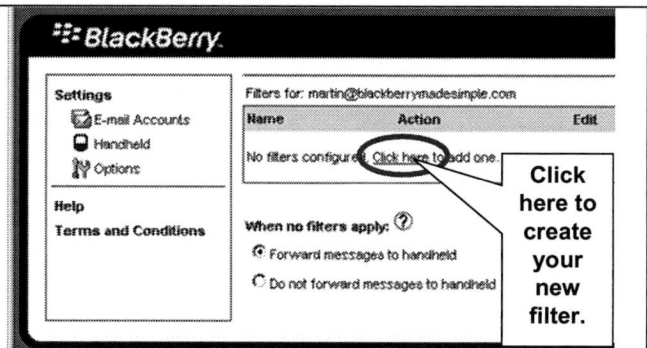

As shown below, to create your filter for one or multiple email address, enter a filter name (No spaces or special characters), then select "'From' field contains" then put the email address(es) of your Important Person(s) in the field as shown. (Separate multiple email addresses with a semi-colon). Make sure the setting is "Forward messages to handheld" and the checkbox is checked next to "Level 1 Notification" then click "Add Filter"

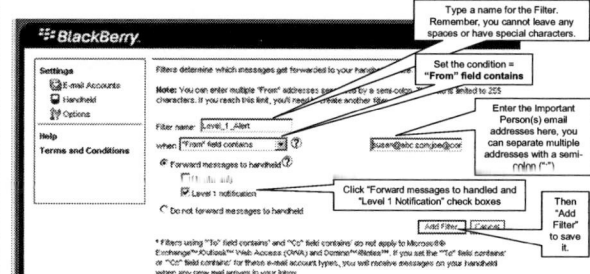

Remember to create the same filter for each email address you have set up to be integrated to your BlackBerry. In the images above, you see two email addresses, the default (user2004@tmo.blackberry.net) and the integrated one (martin@blackberrymadesimple.com). In this example, the same filter would need to be created for each email address on the Blackberry Internet Service.

3.   Now that you've created your filters, each email you receive from your Very Important Person will be sent to your BlackBerry with a "Level 1 Notification" This is important because now you can configure your "Profiles" on your BlackBerry to give you a special ring or loud vibrate or both!

Here's how to set up on your BlackBerry to notify you of that special email:

Depending on your preferences, you can make your BlackBerry notify you with Both a Vibrate and Tone both "Out of Holster" and "In Holster" so that it will alert you whenever you receive that email from a Very Important Person as shown below.

VIP Email Alerts – Configuring Your BlackBerry
After configuring your BlackBerry Internet Service to forward special mails as level 1 alert messaged, configure your BlackBerry as follows:

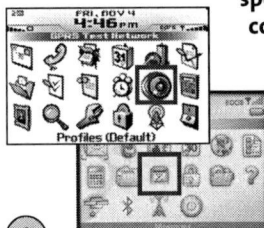

1 Click Trackwheel to select "Profiles"

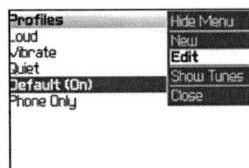

2 Select the profile that's "(On)" and click Edit from the menu.

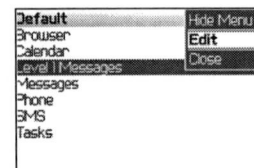

3 Select "Level 1 Messages" and click Edit from the menu.

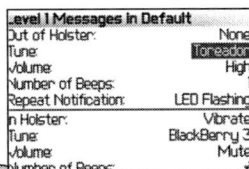

4 Adjust the Tune, Volume and other items depending on your preferences. This will be the way you are notified when you receive your email from your VIP.

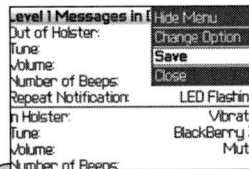

5 Click the trackwheel and "Save" your settings.

6 Now, any email you receive from your VIP (as set up in your BlackBerry Internet Service) will alert you exactly how you have specified on this "Profiles" Icon.

Now, whenever you receive that email from the Important Person, you will have a customized notification (specific ringing and/or vibrating), you're covered – whether you have you BlackBerry on your desk, in your car's cup holder or in your holster!

Speed Email Delivery Up to 95% Faster for BlackBerry Internet Service Users

If you followed our instructions on setting up your BlackBerry to receive email you may notice that it takes <u>at least 15 minutes</u> to receive email

Want to get Email on your BB Faster?
If you have the right access to your email server you can speed email delivery up to your BlackBerry tremendously – from 15 plus minutes, down to seconds.

Read this section for instructions, or have your IT person take a look at it an you will be glad you did!

on the BlackBerry using the BlackBerry Internet Service method which polls your POP/IMAP or other inbox about every 15 minutes. If you have access to your email server settings, or have a good friend in the IT department, here's a trick to speed up email delivery to your BlackBerry.

Instead of having the BlackBerry Internet Service to "poll" your email server every 15 minutes for new messages, set your email server to instantly forward any new message received to the BlackBerry as soon as it's received. What takes up to 15 minutes on a default "polling" setup, only takes 1-2 seconds on the "forwarding" method.

Most Email Servers will allow forwarding while leaving a copy on the server, you should use this functionality.

Here's how, setup a forwarding rule on your email server:

1. Login into your email server via the web.
2. Look for a 'forwarding address' field (usually in "Administration" or "Settings")
3. Enter your BlackBerry Device Address (e.g. johndoe@tmo.blackberry.net) in the forwarding rule field.
4. "Apply" or "Save" your setting.
5. Next, log back into the BlackBerry Internet Service Site and remove the email address you may have configured from the Email Accounts section of the BIS.

This rule you set up will forward a copy of any message received at your address on your mail server to your BlackBerry Device Address.

Using the addresses we used in our examples, our email server forwarding rule in "plain English" would look like this: "forward any message received at test@blackberrymadesimple.com to johndoe@tmo.blackberry.net. "

Anyone with access to your email server should be able to figure out how to setup a forwarding rule as it is a commonly used feature on mail servers.

Tip!

Using a forwarding rule on your web mail account is a great way to receive emails instantly on your BlackBerry – many times faster than on your PC email client!

Note:

If you are using the Spam Service to forward your emails (as described elsewhere in this book), you will not be able to utilize this "Email Forwarding" Tip, because it would bypass your Spam Filter. You have to choose one or the other.

Managing your BlackBerry Internet Service (Separate Format) Mailbox Size

NOTE: This section only applies to the "Separate format" BlackBerry Internet Service. The "Imbedded format" BlackBerry Internet Service does not have a web-based email inbox, therefore cannot get to a point that it's "full."

Most wireless carriers only give you 10 Mega Bytes ("MB" or million bytes) of space in your "Separate format" BlackBerry Internet Service mailbox. Receive a one or two large attachments on your email messages and you quickly reach that 10MB limit!

When you hit that 10MB limit your start receiving confusing **'mailbox full'** messages on your Blackberry and no more messages will be sent to your BlackBerry.

There is nothing worse than being on a business trip with your spiffy new BlackBerry only to find is useless because you are receiving no more email in it!

What to do if you get the 'mailbox full' message on your BlackBerry

NOTE: This section only applies to the "Separate format" BlackBerry Internet Service. The "Imbedded format" BlackBerry Internet Service does not have a web-based email inbox, therefore cannot get to a point that it's "full."

4. Open a Web Browser on your PC and Log In to your Internet Service site (Please see the BlackBerry Internet Service Site List earlier in this book)

5. Click on the "**Inbox**" in the left column.

> **Tip!**
>
> Use the "Auto Aging" rules on your Web Client to keep from getting this message! Check out details later in this book.

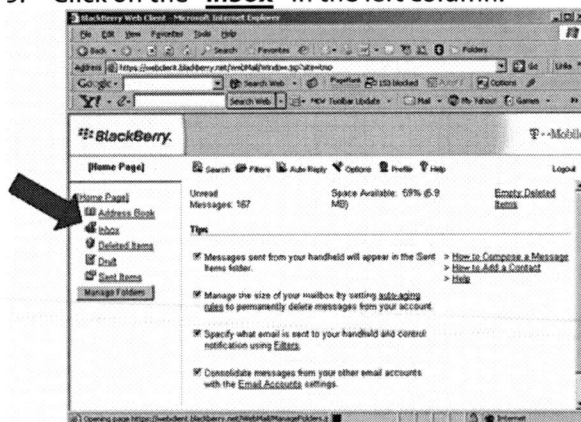

6. Select ALL messages by clicking the top check-box as shown: (see arrow below)

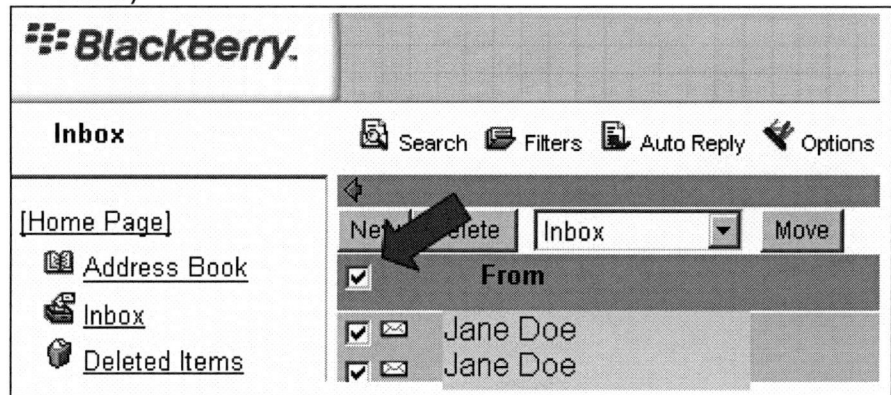

7. Then choose Delete

8. You may have to repeat this several times if you have a lot in your Inbox.

9. Then, go to the BWC and choose the Empty Deleted Items link in the upper right hand corner of the page.

How To Avoid getting the "Mailbox Full" message on your BlackBerry

NOTE: This section only applies to the "Separate format" BlackBerry Internet Service. The "Imbedded format" BlackBerry Internet Service does not have a web-based email inbox, therefore cannot get to a point that it's "full."

1. Open a Web Browser on your computer and Log In to your Web Client site   (Please see the Web Client List earlier in this book)

2. On the BlackBerry homepage, click on the "auto-aging rule" link as shown.

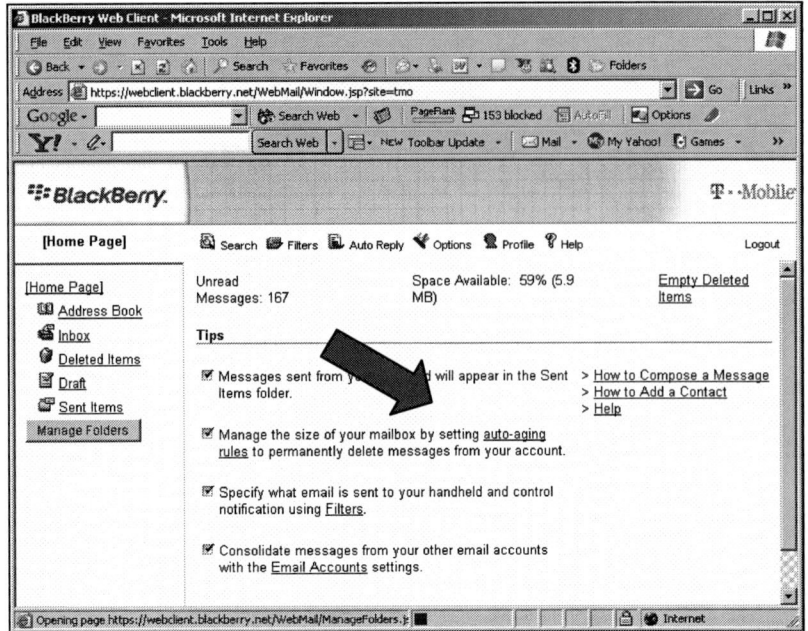

Tip!

"Auto Aging" rules are a great way to avoid getting the "Mailbox Full Message"

3.   Then click on the Inbox folder as shown.

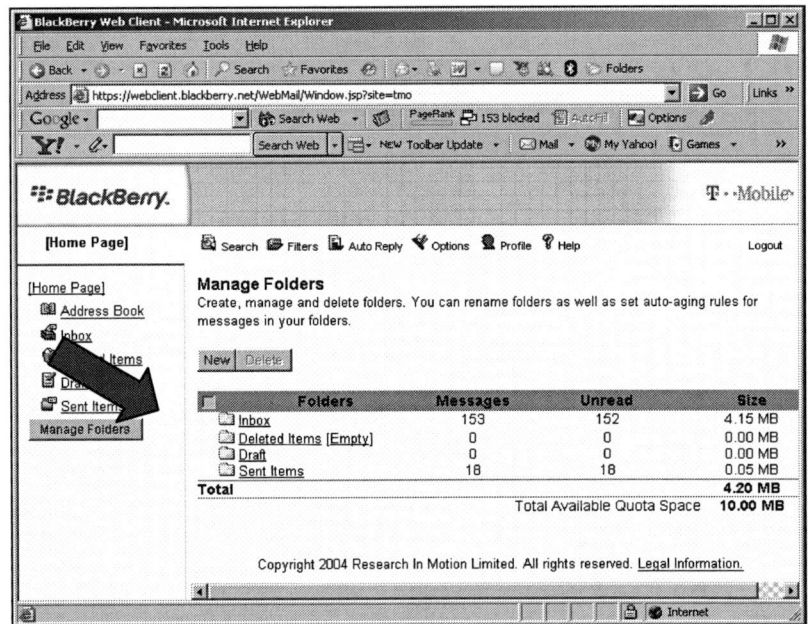

4. Then set your auto-aging preference, or how frequently messages will automatically be deleted from your Web Client inbox (After they have been sent to your BlackBerry). We recommend every 1 day.

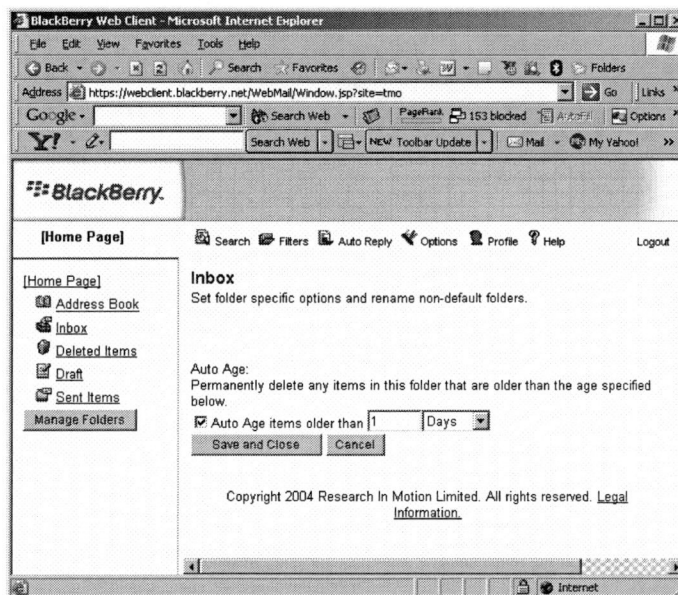

TIP: Remember if you set your Auto-age to delete items older than 1 day, make sure to turn your BlackBerry on everyday so you don't miss receiving any messages.

Managing your BlackBerry Internet Service ("Separate" Type) mail box size from the BlackBerry

If you delete messages from the BlackBerry you can configure deletions on the BlackBerry to also delete the message from your Web Client Account.

To configure your wireless delete options, follow these steps:

1. Open a Web Browser on your computer and Log In to your Web Client site (Please see the Web Client List earlier in this book)

2. Go to the **Profile** Screen

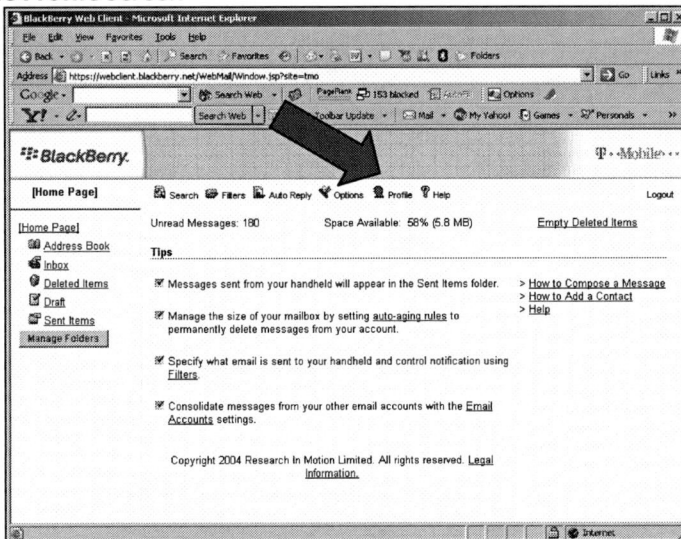

3. Click on the **"wireless delete options"**

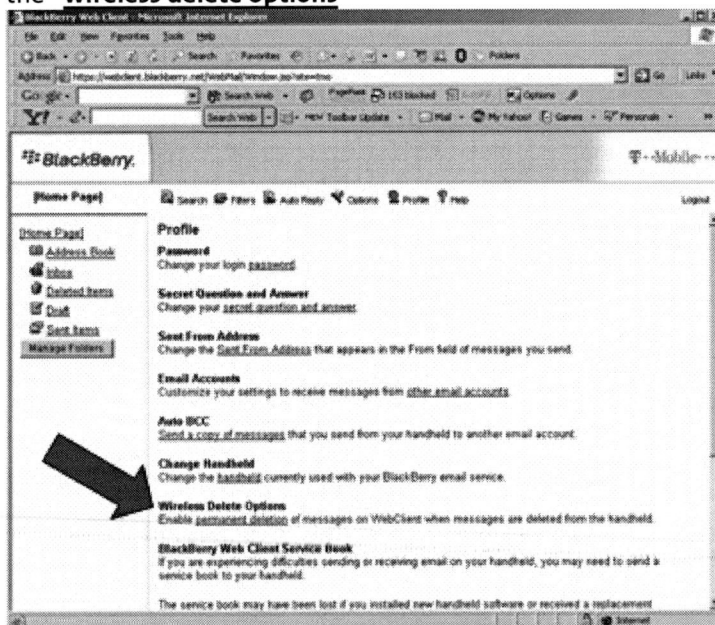

4. On this screen check the box next to "**Enable permanent deletion...**"

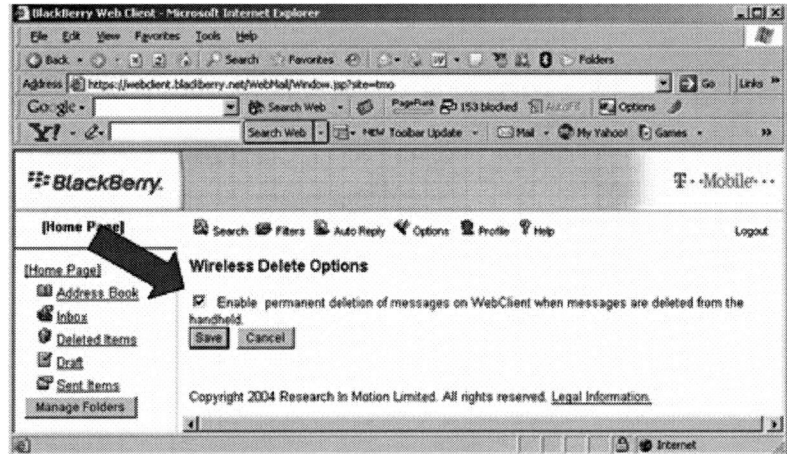

This will permit you to automatically delete the same messages in your Web Client account when you delete them on your BlackBerry.

E-Mail Attachment Viewing

FAXING Tip!

Check out the FAX sections in this book to learn how you can receive, view and even compose and send faxes from your BlackBerry via email!

[1 Attachment] - Whenever you see this text in an email, or the paperclip on the envelope icon, then you know you have an attachment to the email message. Luckily with BlackBerry, you can now open and view most popular attachment types including (Word, Excel, PowerPoint, Adobe PDF, several image types including electronic fax messages). This feature greatly enhances your ability to get work done on the road.

> **KEY NOTE: Thanks to an inquisitive reader D. Given: If you're using BlackBerry Desktop Redirector to forward your email to your BlackBerry, then you cannot view attachments unless you either use a "Server Level Forwarding Rule" or use a "Third Party Attachment Viewing Application."**
>
> To learn about the "**Server-Level Forwarding Rule**" – go to the " Speed Email Delivery Up to 95% Faster for BlackBerry Internet Service Users" section in this book. Using this method, you will not be able to "reconcile" your BlackBerry inbox with your desktop inbox – e.g. if you Read an email on your BlackBerry, it won't reconcile or show as "Read" on your desktop inbox.
>
> If your "standard" BlackBerry Attachment viewing is not working or not enough for you, then please check out our Web Site www.blackberrymadesimple.com/partners for places where you can buy "**BlackBerry Software**" (We may review and compare several of these applications in an upcoming publication.) Some of the current providers all cost between $7 and $10 / month and provide some very good functionality related to attachment viewing.
>> **DataHawk Attachment Service for BlackBerry**
>>
>> **Itrezzo ASP Attachment Viewing**
>>
>> **MetaMessage**
>>
>> **RepliGo Professional for BlackBerry**
>>
>> **Itrezzo Free Attachment Viewing Service**
>>> When you receive an attachment on your Blackberry, forward it to **agent@itrezzo.com**. You should receive a reply in a minute or so with the first 2,500 characters translated into basic text in the body of the email. It does not work for graphics, and I wouldn't use it for anything confidential. But it's a free way to read the text from a word processing, PDF, PowerPoint and related files.

Assuming you are not using BlackBerry Desktop Redirector to receive your email, then to view attachments, please follow these steps: *(Using the free native BlackBerry Attachment Viewing service)*

1. Highlight the [1 Attachment] text at the top of the email or the attachments at the bottom and click the trackwheel.

2. Select "Open Attachment"

3. Scroll down to select "Full Content", click the trackwheel and select "Retrieve"

4. Wait for a few seconds while the attachment is being opened.

NOTE: In a few cases you will not be able to open the attachment and see this error message: "Couldn't receive more"
- If the attachment is of a file or graphics format not supported
- If the message has been deleted from your Web Client or Exchange/Notes Inbox
- If you are out of wireless coverage or your radio is turned off.

5. After you open your attachment, you will need to use the trackwheel (with/without the ALT "half moon" key) and the menu "Zoom, View Cell, etc." to navigate around the document.

TIP: You can forward the Attachment to anyone via email.

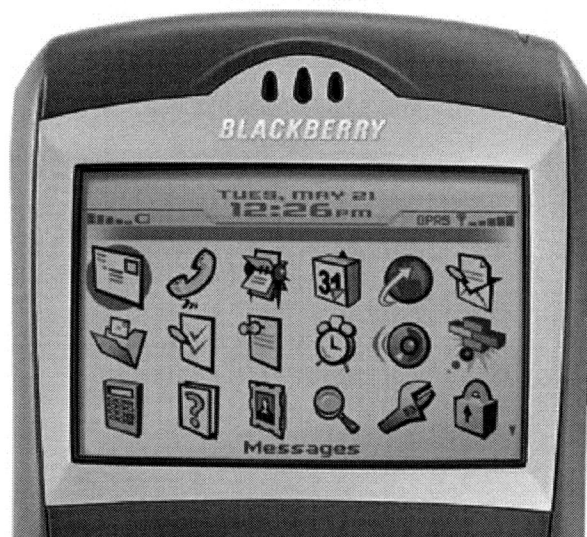

Semi-Automated "e-Mail Merge" From Your BlackBerry

Using the BlackBerry "Save Draft" feature, you can approximate a "mail merge" from your BlackBerry, albeit with more manual steps.

Here's what you do:

1. Compose your email then press the trackwheel and select 'Save Draft'

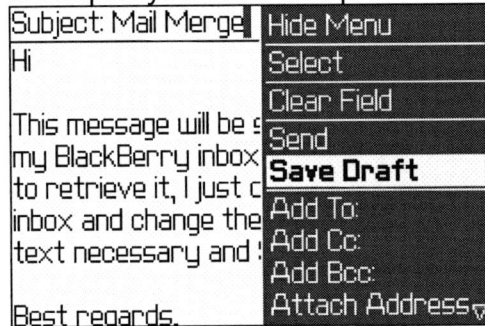

```
Subject: Mail Merge    Hide Menu
Hi                     Select
                       Clear Field
This message will be s Send
my BlackBerry inbox    Save Draft
to retrieve it, I just c Add To:
inbox and change the   Add Cc:
text necessary and '   Add Bcc:
                       Attach Address ▽
Best regards,
```

2. Whenever you want to send this email to anyone, locate it in your inbox and select "Open". The draft email looks sort of like a "note" icon in your inbox.

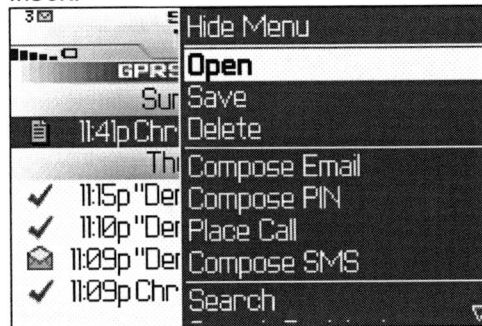

```
3✉                  ⋮ Hide Menu
▮▮▮▮▯◻      GPRS Open
           Sur Save
 📄 11:41p Chr Delete
          Th Compose Email
 ✓ 11:15p "Der Compose PIN
 ✓ 11:10p "Der Place Call
 ✉ 11:09p "Der Compose SMS
 ✓ 11:09p Chr Search
                            ▽
```

3. You can then change the original recipient to a new email address by highlighting the email address in the "To:" line, clicking the trackwheel and selecting "Change Address" from the menu.

To: Chris Huffma
Subject: Mail Me

Hi

This message wil
my BlackBerry i
to retrieve it, I j
inbox and chang
text necessary
Best regards.

Email Chris Huffman
Add To:
Add Cc:
Add Bcc:
Show Address
Change Address
Attach Address
View Contact
Edit AutoText

Select Address
[Use Once]
Chris Huffman
Sarah Jones

Hide Menu
Email Sarah Jones
Filter
New Address
New Group
View
Edit
Delete
SIM Phone Book

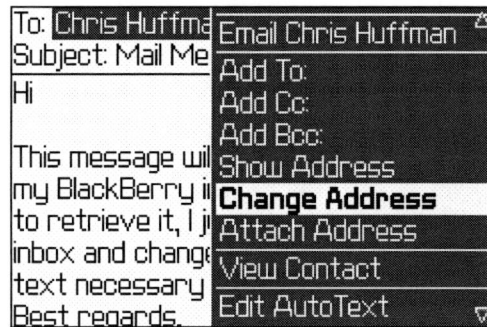

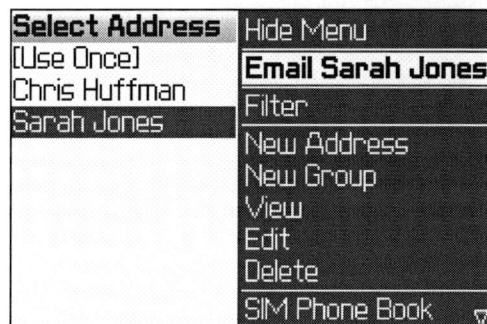

4. Now edit any text necessary to personalize this message, like adding the person's first name:

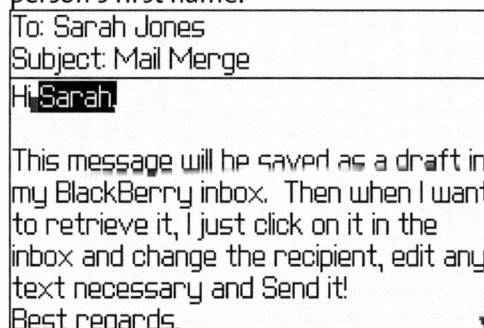

To: Sarah Jones
Subject: Mail Merge

Hi Sarah,

This message will he saved as a draft in my BlackBerry inbox. Then when I want to retrieve it, I just click on it in the inbox and change the recipient, edit any text necessary and Send it!
Best regards.

5. Click "Send" and you're done – you've just sent a (lengthy) personalized mail message with a few clicks of your trackwheel and keys!

TIP: Go wild with the "Save Draft" feature to prepare almost all of your "canned" or typical responses. For example a 3 paragraph thank you letter initial sales call, a follow up call, a proposal presentation trip, (any common event) – could be drafted ahead of time and "Saved Draft" on your BlackBerry for easy access.

TIP: Type the main body text of key "Save Draft" emails on your PC and email them to yourself. Once you receive them, copy the text and paste it into a new email which you will "Save Draft."

How to Impress Contacts by Instantly Emailing Key Literature from your BlackBerry

In many businesses, you have marketing literature that is in electronic or Adobe PDF format which can be emailed to clients and prospects. What better way to be responsive to requests for than to email such literature to yourself and "Save" it on your BlackBerry for later forwarding.

You could even email people from the tradeshow or sales meeting conference table with exactly the material they requested. Imagine the surprise at your responsiveness and great impression you will make by being so responsive!

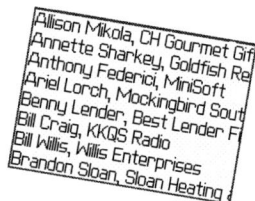

Creating A Mailing List On Your BlackBerry!

You know how much time a mailing list can save you in your desktop email program when you need to mail a group of people many times, now you can create an email list right on your BlackBerry. Most people are not aware of this one – you can actually create a new **Mailing List Group** and send an email to that Group right from your BlackBerry Address Book!

Here's how to do it:

1. Open the Address Book.

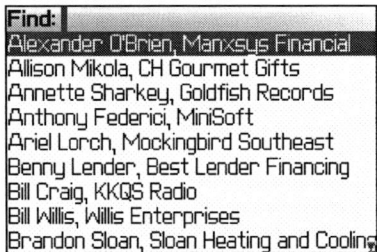

Find:
Alexander O'Brien, Manxsys Financial
Allison Mikola, CH Gourmet Gifts
Annette Sharkey, Goldfish Records
Anthony Federici, MiniSoft
Ariel Lorch, Mockingbird Southeast
Benny Lender, Best Lender Financing
Bill Craig, KKQS Radio
Bill Willis, Willis Enterprises
Brandon Sloan, Sloan Heating and Cooling

2. Click the Trackwheel and select **"New Group"**

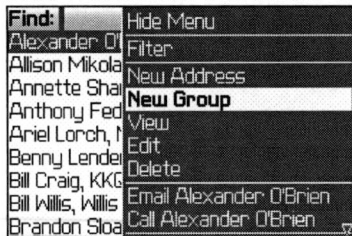

Find:	
Alexander O'	Hide Menu
Allison Mikola	Filter
Annette Sha	New Address
Anthony Fed	**New Group**
Ariel Lorch,	View
Benny Lende	Edit
Bill Craig, KKG	Delete
Bill Willis, Willis	Email Alexander O'Brien
Brandon Sloa	Call Alexander O'Brien

3.   Click the Trackwheel again and select "Add Member"

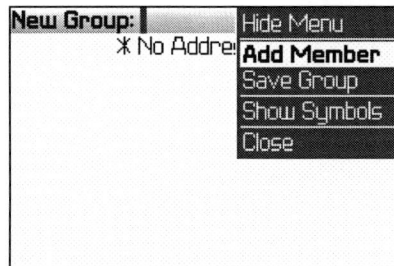

```
New Group:  |        Hide Menu
      ✳ No Addre  Add Member
                   Save Group
                   Show Symbols
                   Close
```

4.   Now select or highlight the first Name (Address) for your group, click the trackwheel and select "Continue":

```
Select Address         Hide Menu
Alexander O'Brien, Man  Continue
Allison Mikola, CH Gourm  Filter
Annette Sharkey, Goldfi  New Address
Anthony Federici, MiniSc  View
Ariel Lorch, Mockingbird  Edit
Benny Lender, Best Len   Options
Bill Craig, KKQS Radio
Bill Willis, Willis Enterprise  Cancel
Brandon Sloan, Sloan Heating and Cooling
```

5.   Then, to add more people, click the Trackwheel and select "Add Member"

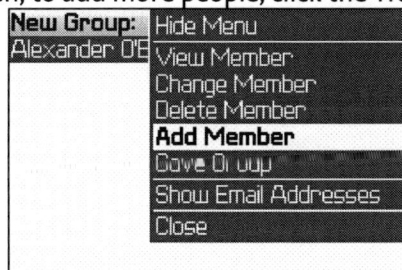

```
New Group:  Hide Menu
Alexander O'E  View Member
              Change Member
              Delete Member
              Add Member
              Save Group
              Show Email Addresses
              Close
```

6.   Repeat the "Continue", "Add Member" Cycle until you have added all the people you need, then "Save Group" as shown

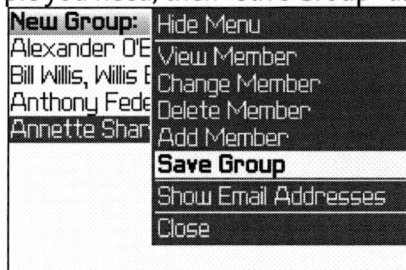

```
New Group:  Hide Menu
Alexander O'E  View Member
Bill Willis, Willis E  Change Member
Anthony Fede  Delete Member
Annette Shar  Add Member
              Save Group
              Show Email Addresses
              Close
```

7.   If you have not entered a group name, then you will be prompted to do it now.

```
New Group: |
Alexander O'Brien, Manxsys Financial
Bill Willis, Willis Enterprises
Anthony Federici, MiniSoft
Ar    ( i )   Please enter a group name.
```

8. Type in your Mailing List Group Name. IMPORTANT: You will use this name to send the email to the group. In this example, we are calling the mailing Group "Project Alpha Team"

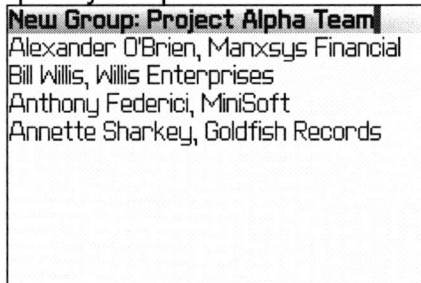

```
New Group: Project Alpha Team|
Alexander O'Brien, Manxsys Financial
Bill Willis, Willis Enterprises
Anthony Federici, MiniSoft
Annette Sharkey, Goldfish Records
```

Sending to a Mailing List Group On Your BlackBerry!

After you have created at new group on your BlackBerry, you want to send everyone a welcome email. You'll notice that "Project Alpha Team" group looks and acts like any other address in your Address Book.

1. Look up the group name in your Address book by typing "Pr A" – it will filter your address book to show only the "Project Alpha Team"

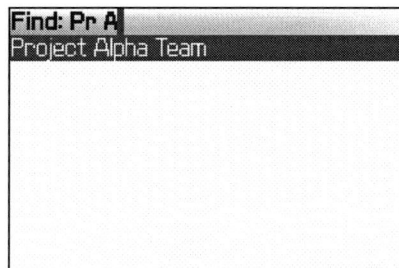

> **Find: Pr A**
> Project Alpha Team

2. Select "Email Project Alpha Team" and compose your email as you would normally:

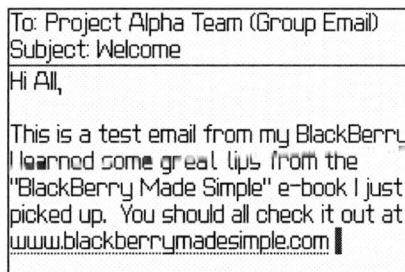

> To: Project Alpha Team (Group Email)
> Subject: Welcome
>
> Hi All,
>
> This is a test email from my BlackBerry. I learned some great tips from the "BlackBerry Made Simple" e-book I just picked up. You should all check it out at www.blackberrymadesimple.com

3. SEND it as you would normally and if you open the email being sent, you will notice that there is a separate "To:" for each member of the group:

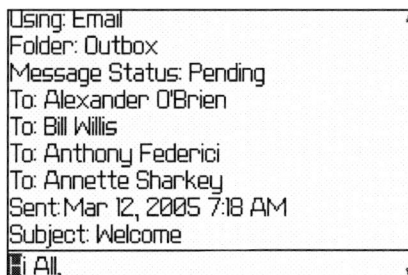

> Using: Email
> Folder: Outbox
> Message Status: Pending
> To: Alexander O'Brien
> To: Bill Willis
> To: Anthony Federici
> To: Annette Sharkey
> Sent: Mar 12, 2005 7:18 AM
> Subject: Welcome
>
> Hi All,

More than Just Email (Phone and SMS Logs)

The BlackBerry Messages icon stores each email you receive and send. This tool also logs each phone call and each SMS "Short Message Service" (Text Message) message sent or received.

Displaying Phone Calls in your Inbox

NOTE: Read the related section on displaying phone call logs in your inbox in order to make this ALT-P (Phone Log) display work correctly!

Showing Only PHONE CALL logs in your Messages "Inbox"

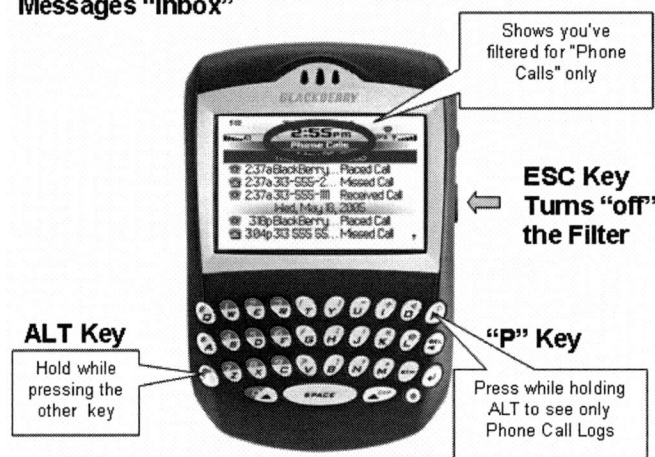

Shows you've filtered for "Phone Calls" only

ESC Key Turns "off" the Filter

ALT Key
Hold while pressing the other key

"P" Key
Press while holding ALT to see only Phone Call Logs

Filtering to display only Phone Calls in your Inbox

To see only incoming/outgoing phone calls in the BlackBerry Messages icon, follow these steps:
1. In BlackBerry messages click → ALT+P (for Phone)
2. That key combination will filter your inbox to display only Phone logs.
3. Click the → Esc key to exit the Phone Log filter

Filtering to display only SMS Messages in your Inbox

To see only incoming/outdoing SMS messages in the BlackBerry Inbox, follow these steps:

1. In your BlackBerry inbox, click → ALT+S (for SMS)

2. That key combination will filter your inbox to display only SMS messages

3. Click the → ESC key to exit the SMS filter

Showing Only SMS MESSAGE logs in your Messages "Inbox"

Shows you've filtered for "SMS Messages" only

"S" Key
Press while holding ALT to see only SMS Message Logs

ALT Key
Hold while pressing the other key

ESC Key Turns "off" the Filter

Tip!

Use your hands free ear bud or speaker phone to take notes while on a phone call - this can be a life saver when you are receiving or making important commitments!

Getting a written record of a conversation!

During any phone call, you can click the trackwheel and select "Notes" to enter notes on what was discussed:

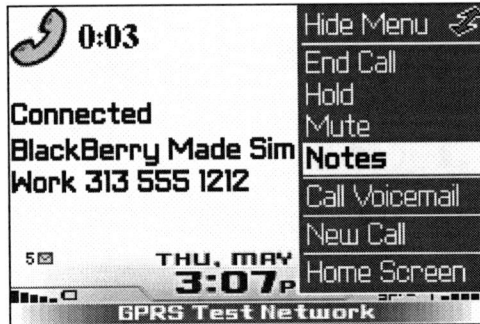

how to take notes on your BlackBerry when you're on a phone call. This section shows you how to email those notes to your colleague after the call.

"Even the faintest of ink is stronger than the loudest of words" -- Anonymous

Email and Calendar Working Together

Have you ever received an email on your BlackBerry with important details that you need to put into your calendar, but don't want to (or can't) re-type information:
- Email Conference call-in details
- Email Directions to an office location
- Email Directions to a restaurant
- A phone number for you to call at a certain time in an email

Transferring (Conference Call #) from email to calendar!

In this example the copy/paste command and the ALT-TAB application switching tool will be used.

Let's sat you receive dial-in details for a conference call in an email and you'll be in the car at the time of the call. This tip will ensure you remember the call and are able to quickly safely dial the number.

1. Copy the details from the email by scrolling the cursor up to the top of the section you need to copy
2. Press the left shift key once

Left SHIFT Key

Press once to start selection of Text to Copy, then roll track wheel to select

3. Roll the trackwheel to highlight the text you want to copy

```
service
To: Ernst Anderson
Sent: Mar 4, 2005 11:38 AM
Subject: Conf. Call Details

Subject: Sales Strategy Call
Date: March 9, 2005
Time: 1:00 - 2:00 pm (Eastern Time)
Dial-in: 1-800-555-1212
Participant Code: 12345
```

4. Click in the trackwheel and →select Copy

Tip!

You really need to put phone numbers right in your calendar events, then you can dial easily immediately after the alarm rings!

Service
To: Ernst Anderson
Sent: Mar 4, 2005 11:
Subject: Conf. Call De
Subject: Sales Strate
Date: March 9, 2005
Time: 1:00 - 2:00 pm
Dial-in: 1-800-555-12
Participant Code: 12:3

Hide Menu
Find
Copy
Cancel Selection
Edit
Save
Resend
Delete
Previous Item

5. ALT-ESC to switch applications to the home screen (or the Calendar directly if it's already running:)

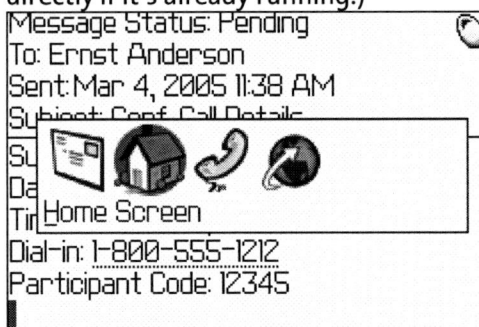

Message Status: Pending
To: Ernst Anderson
Sent: Mar 4, 2005 11:38 AM
Subject: Conf. Call Details
Home Screen
Dial-in: 1-800-555-1212
Participant Code: 12345

Multi-Tasking with ALT+ESC

ESC Key

Press this ESC while holding the ALT key to switch between applications

ALT Key

Hold while pressing the ESC key

6. Open the calendar

FRI, MAR 4
11:39 am
NXT!

Calendar

7. Click in the trackwheel and → go to the correct date, in this case – March 9th.

```
Mar 4, 2005    11:40a ◁ Hide Menu
  9:00a                  Today
 10:00a                  Go to Date...
 11:00a                  Prev Day
 12:00p |                Next Day
  1:00p                  Prev Week
  2:00p                  Next Week
  3:00p                  New
  4:00p                  View Week    ▽
```

8. Since you're already in March, all you need to do is scroll over to the day of the month as shown.

```
Mar 4, 2005    11:40a ◁SMTWTFS▷
  9:00a
 10:00a
 11:00a
 12  Go to Date...
  1              Fri, Mar 4, 2005
  2:00p
  3:00p
  4:00p
```

Tip!

If you only need to go a few days forward in your calendar, hold down the ALT key and roll the trackwheel down – it is the fastest way to scroll forward a day at a time!

9. Change date to the 9th, (do this by pressing the 9 key or simply hold the ALT (half-moon key) and roll the trackwheel down).

```
Mar 4, 2005    11:40a ◁SMTWTFS▷
  9:00a
 10:00a
 11:00a
 12  Go to Date...
  1              Fri, Mar 4, 2005
  2:00p
  3:00p
  4:00p
```

10. Scroll to 1pm

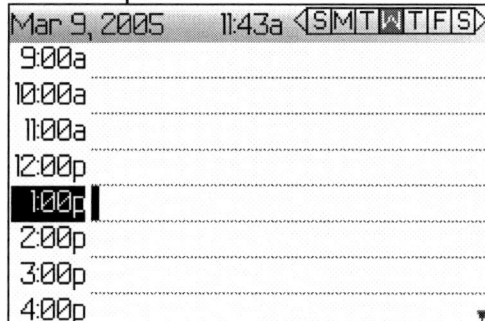

```
Mar 9, 2005    11:43a ◁SMTWTFS▷
  9:00a
 10:00a
 11:00a
 12:00p
  1:00p |
  2:00p
  3:00p
  4:00p            ▼
```

11. Click the trackwheel and select "New"

Mar 9, 2005	11:43a ◁	Hide Menu
9:00a		Today
10:00a		Go to Date...
11:00a		Prev Day
12:00p		Next Day
1:00p		Prev Week
2:00p		Next Week
3:00p		**New**
4:00p		View Week ▽

12. Type in the title for the appointment, scroll to the location and press "Paste"

New Appointment	Hide Menu
Subject: Sales Conf. Cal	**Paste**
Location: ▮	
☐ All Day Event	Save
Start: Wed, Mar	Show Symbols
End: Wed, Mar	Close
Duration:	1 Hour 0 Mins
Time Zone:	Eastern Time (-5)
Reminder:	15 Min.
Recurrence:	None

New Appointment	
Subject: Sales Conf. Call	
Location: Dial-in: 1-800-555-	
1212Participant Code: 12345▮	
☐ All Day Event	
Start: Wed, Mar 9, 2005 1:00 PM	
End: Wed, Mar 9, 2005 2:00 PM	
Duration:	1 Hour 0 Mins
Time Zone:	Eastern Time (-5)
Reminder:	15 Min.▾

13. Notice that there is no space between the Number and the "Participant code" so BlackBerry does not recognize the phone number 1-800 correctly.

14. To make the number valid, turn the participant code into an "EXTENSION" by putting an X and a space between the two numbers as shown.

Tip!

Remember to put an 'X' between the phone number and the extension – this way the BlackBerry will recognize that it is an extension and dial it appropriately!

Appointment Details

Subject: Sales Conf. Call

Location: Dial-in: 1-800-555-1212 x 12345

☐ All Day Event

Start:	Wed, Mar 9, 2005 1:00 PM
End:	Wed, Mar 9, 2005 2:00 PM
Duration:	1 Hour 0 Mins
Time Zone:	Eastern Time (-5)
Reminder:	5 Min

Add the x and the space by scrolling back a few characters (hold ALT key and scroll trackwheel), delete the "Participant Code" and replace with an " x ". Now you see that the phone number has it's underline: 1-800-555-1212 x 12345

15. Now change the reminder appropriately.

Appointment Details

☐ All Day Event

Start:	Wed, Mar 9, 2005 1:00 PM
End:	Wed, Mar 9, 2005 2:00 PM
Duration:	1 Hour 0 Mins
Time Zone:	Eastern Time (-5)
Reminder:	5 Min.
Recurrence:	None

No Recurrence.

☐ Mark as Private

16. Save your appointment

17. Now the calendar is updated and get a reminder 5 minutes before the call.

18. On the call date & time, the reminder will appear!

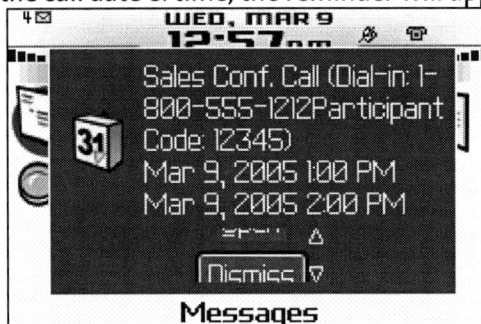

19. Don't Dismiss the alarms, instead, roll up and click on the "Open" option to see the meeting.

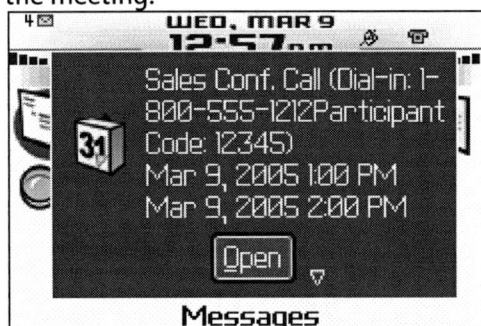

20. Now you can scroll the trackwheel right to the underlined number and dial

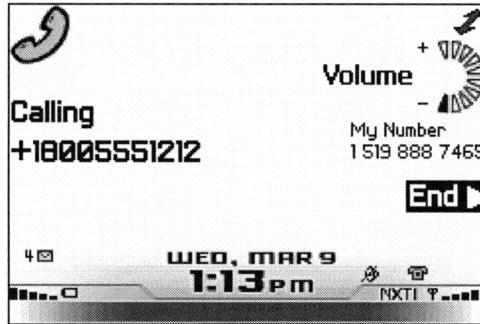

21. In a few seconds the dial extension screen will appear containing the conference call participant code!

You don't need to remember the participant code – your BlackBerry will dial it for you when you select dial at the appropriate time!

22. While you're on the call use ALT-ESC trick to back to the appointment and type notes right in the appointment:

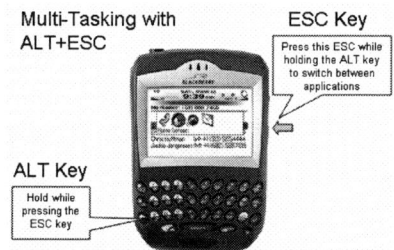

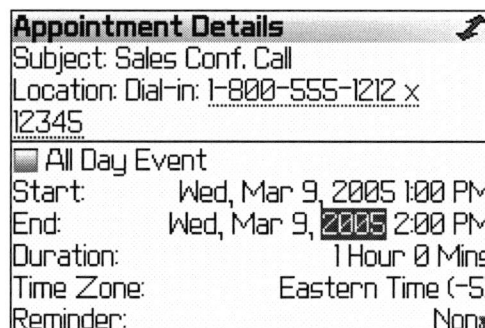

Type as many notes as you want:

Appointment Details
Recurrence.   None
No Recurrence.

☐ Mark as Private

Notes:
Key notes from this call
- Note 1
- Note 2
- Note 3
- Note 4

23. Now you have all your notes right in the meeting – and when you sync from your Blackberry back to your Desktop (Outlook, or some other desktop Personal Information Manger program)!

TIP: If your conference call-in number stays the same (e.g. for a weekly recurring call) then you will be able to just use the recently called list in your phone icon to quickly call the same number and code as shown:

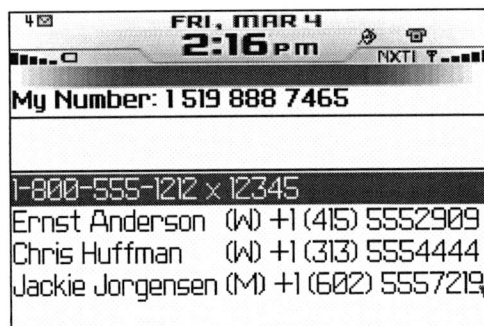

Tip!

Use your frequently dialed (top 20) list if you regularly use the same dial in number frequently for your conference calls!

FRI, MAR 4
2:16 PM
NXTL

My Number: 1 519 888 7465

1-800-555-1212 x 12345
Ernst Anderson   (W) +1 (415) 5552909
Chris Huffman   (W) +1 (313) 5554444
Jackie Jorgensen (M) +1 (602) 5557219

SEARCH: Finding Anything on your BlackBerry

If you have a newer BlackBerry or have upgraded your device to the 4.0 operating system, then you have a great new search tool. While this is not the speediest function, it can be quite useful to find information buried on your BlackBerry.

Tip!

SEARCH is a great tool, but you need to be careful how you enter information. Create a rule and stay consistent.

For example, for Restaurants if you decide to write "restaurant" in one of the address fields, then make sure you always put it in so you can easily look up all your restaurants!

TIP: If you enter information you want to find later in your address book, for instance the name and phone number of a new Indian Restaurant, then make sure you enter some text in the address book entry so you can search for it later. For example, put some key words in addition to the

```
New Address
Title:
First: Indian
Last: Restaurant
Email:
Company: Star of Delhi
Job Title:
Work:
Work 2:
Home:
```

name of the restaurant:

This will allow you to easily search for the information using the BlackBerry Address Book "lookup" feature.

But if you have not (or cannot) use the first name, last name or company name to find something, then you need to go to the "SEARCH" icon and find it there.

Examples of good uses for the SEARCH feature might be:
- I remember Joe sent me his phone number in an email signature last week – but I can't easily find it!
- I remember that the business address was on "Main St." but I can't remember the business name!

The search tools let's you search Messages (email/phone logs), Calendar, Address Book, MemoPad and Tasks.

FLEXIBLE BlackBerry Searching:

Follow these instructions to search on your BlackBerry:
1. Open the search application by going to the Search Icon (varies by model)

Finding the Search Icon

8700 Series

Applications (sub-menu)

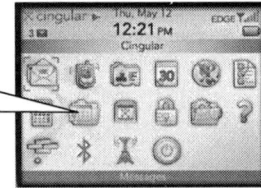

Use the Search Icon to find any text in the Inbox, Address Book, Calendar, Memo Pad or Task List

Search Icon

All Other Full Keyboard BlackBerries

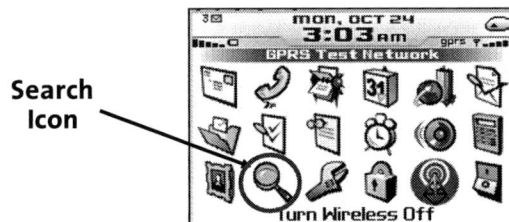

Search Icon

2. You will see this search screen.

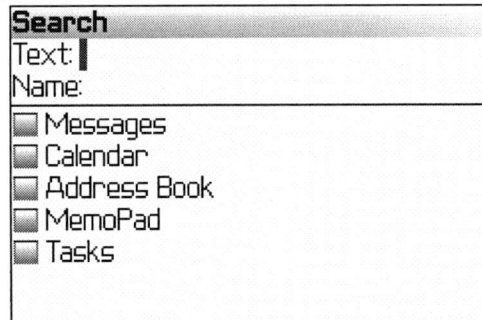

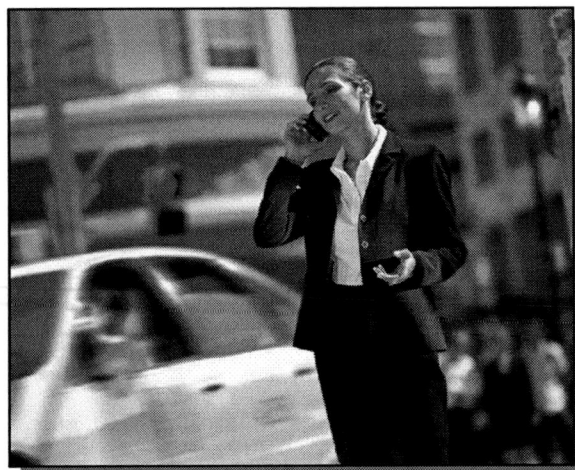

> **Search**
> Text:
> Name:
> ☐ Messages
> ☐ Calendar
> ☐ Address Book
> ☐ MemoPad
> ☐ Tasks

3. Enter the text your want to search for, and select which applications you would like to search for by rolling to the applications and clicking the → spacebar the select applications.

   The below example will find all references to the company name "Verde Mountain Software Inc." in Messages and Addresses.

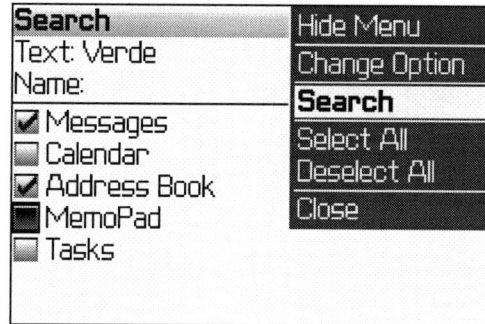

Search	Hide Menu
Text: Verde	Change Option
Name:	**Search**
☑ Messages	Select All
☐ Calendar	Deselect All
☑ Address Book	Close
■ MemoPad	
☐ Tasks	

4. After clicking search, the results are shown:

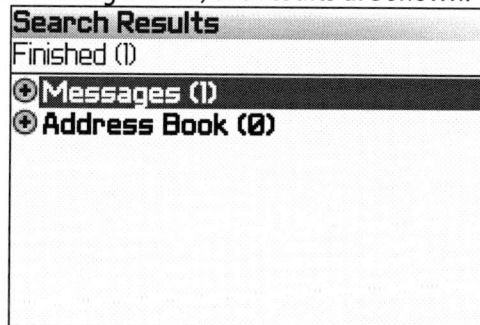

   Search Results
   Finished (1)
   ⊕ Messages (1)
   ⊕ Address Book (0)

5. Click on the area you want to see more detail for choose → Expand

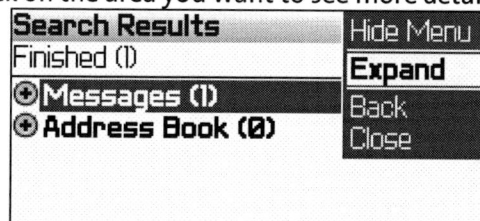

Search Results	Hide Menu
Finished (1)	**Expand**
⊕ Messages (1)	Back
⊕ Address Book (0)	Close

6. Then you can select items and view or open them:

Search Results
Finished (1)
⊖ **Messages (1)**
        Sat, Mar 5, 2005
    8:07a help@black... Need Help

⊕ **Address Book (0)**

Search Results   Hide Menu
Finished (1)
⊖ **Messages (1)**   **Open**
    Sat, Mar 5, 200   Save
  8:07a help@black... Ne   Resend
                Delete

⊕ **Address Book (0)**   Collapse
                Back
                Close

Folder: Outbox
Message Status: Failed to contact
service
To: help@blackberrymadesimple.com
Sent: Mar 5, 2005 8:07 AM
Subject: Need Help

Hi,

I work at Verde Mountain Software,
Inc.

PHONE Tips

Here are a few tips to help you get the most out of your BlackBerry phone.

Dialing by Name

After you have manually entered or synced names into your BlackBerry Address book, you can now dial by name, instead of remembering and typing in the phone number each time.

To dial by name follow these steps:
1. From either the Phone Icon (scroll down first to the area where the names are located) or the Address Book Icon.
2. Find the name you want by typing a few letters of the first name
3. hit the spacebar
4. Then type the first few letters of the last name

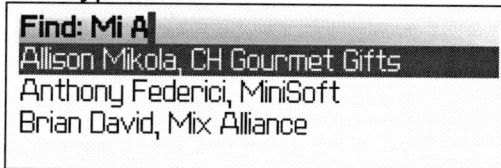

> Find: Mi A
> Allison Mikola, CH Gourmet Gifts
> Anthony Federici, MiniSoft
> Brian David, Mix Alliance

5. Scroll to the correct name and click "Call"

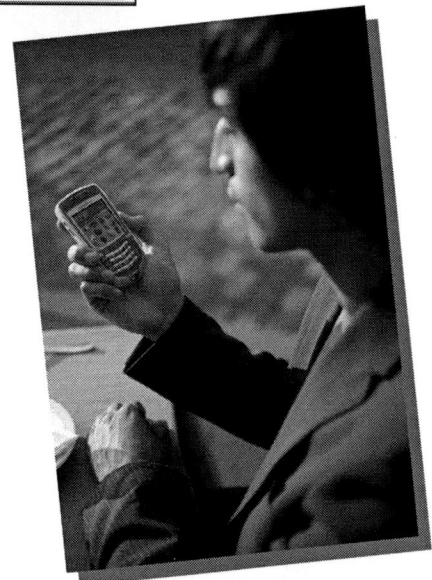

> Find: Mi A
> Allison Mikola, CH | New Group
> Anthony Federici, | View
> Brian David, Mix / | Edit
> Delete
> Email Allison Mikola
> **Call Allison Mikola**
> SMS Allison Mikola
> SIM Phone Book
> Options

Dial from Anywhere! 313-555-1212

On a BlackBerry, you can dial any phone number that is in a "Standard Format" recognized by your BlackBerry. Here are a few examples:

Dial from an E-Mail or Memo Pad item:

If someone sends you an email asking you to call them, → highlight the number and click the → trackwheel and call:

You can dial any phone number that is "Recognized" by the BlackBerry and underlined – even phone numbers in email signatures or conference call email requests:

```
Folder: Outbox  | Hide Menu
Message Statu   | Find
To: BlackBerry  | Copy
Sent: Feb 28, 2 | Select
Subject: Please |
Hi,             | Edit
                | Save
Please give me  | Resend
at 800 222 22   | Delete
                | Call 800 222 2222
```

Remember that people often include their phone number in their email signatures. That's another area you can scroll down to, highlight the number, and click "Call"

Dial from an Email Address:

If you receive an email from someone already included in your address book, you can highlight an email address and call them by following these steps:

1. In the open email, scroll up to the contact's name in email header fields

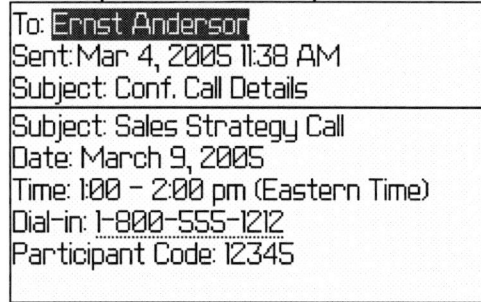

```
To: Ernst Anderson
Sent: Mar 4, 2005 11:38 AM
Subject: Conf. Call Details

Subject: Sales Strategy Call
Date: March 9, 2005
Time: 1:00 - 2:00 pm (Eastern Time)
Dial-in: 1-800-555-1212
Participant Code: 12345
```

2. → Click on their name → scroll down and click "Call"

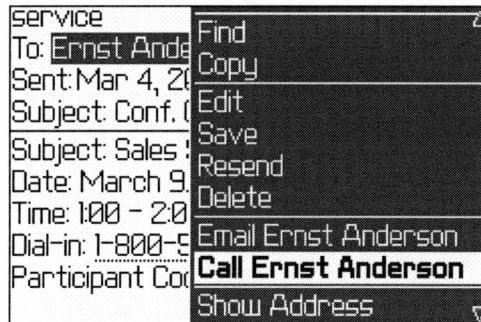

```
service
To: Ernst Ande          Find
Sent: Mar 4, 2(         Copy
Subject: Conf. (        Edit
                        Save
Subject: Sales :        Resend
Date: March 9,          Delete
Time: 1:00 - 2:0        Email Ernst Anderson
Dial-in: 1-800-5        Call Ernst Anderson
Participant Co          Show Address
```

3. Select the appropriate number to call.

```
service
To: Ernst Anderson
Sent:
Subje    Call which number for
         Ernst Anderson?
Subje
Date:    +1 (415) 5552909 (Work)
Time:
Dial-ir  415-555-2910 (Fax)
Participant Code: 12345
```

4. Click the trackwheel and you're calling!

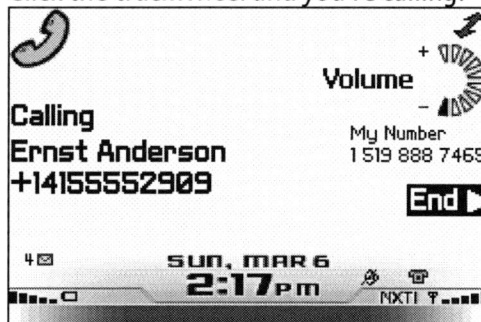

```
Volume
Calling          My Number
Ernst Anderson   1 519 888 7465
+14155552909     End ▶
4 ✉   SUN, MAR 6
      2:17 PM   NXTI
```

BlackBerry as a Speaker Phone

Many BlackBerry models (but not all) have a very nice speakerphone built-in, here's how to use it.

1. Start a phone call.

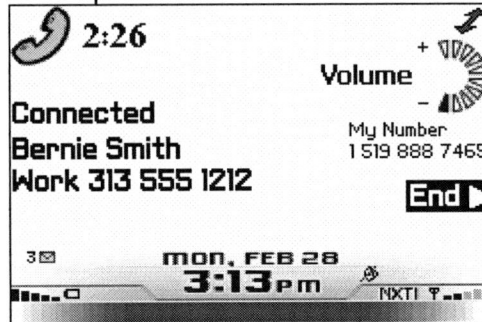

   📞 2:26
   Volume
   Connected
   Bernie Smith   My Number
   Work 313 555 1212   1 519 888 7465
                         End ▶
   3✉   mon, FEB 28
                      3:13 pm
   ▮▮▪▪ ▫   NXTI ☿

2. Click the trackwheel and look for an option that says "Activate Speakerphone":

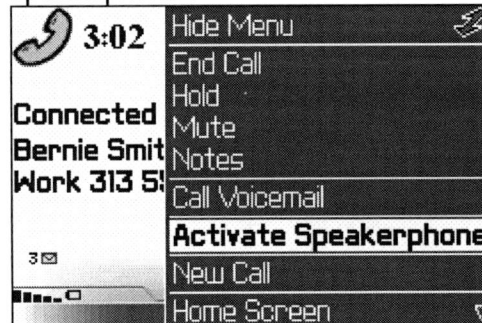

   📞 3:02   Hide Menu
                End Call
                Hold
   Connected   Mute
   Bernie Smit Notes
   Work 313 5! ──────────
                Call Voicemail
   3✉   **Activate Speakerphone**
   ▮▮▪▪ ▫   New Call
                Home Screen   ▽

3. To turn off the speakerphone, just click the trackwheel again and select "Activate Handset":

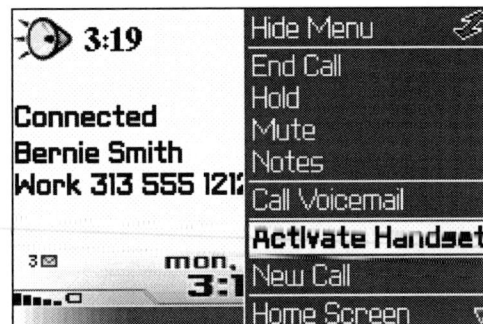

   📢 3:19   Hide Menu
                End Call
                Hold
   Connected   Mute
   Bernie Smith Notes
   Work 313 555 121 Call Voicemail
                Activate Handset
   3✉   mon, New Call
      3:1   Home Screen   ▽
   ▮▮▪▪ ▫

Emailing Your Phone Call Notes

After taking notes during a call, follow these steps:

1. Go to your "Messages" (Inbox) icon.

2. Look for and highlight the call log for your phone call:

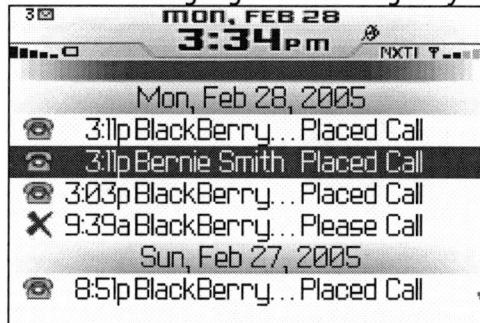

3. Click the trackwheel and select "Forward" as shown:

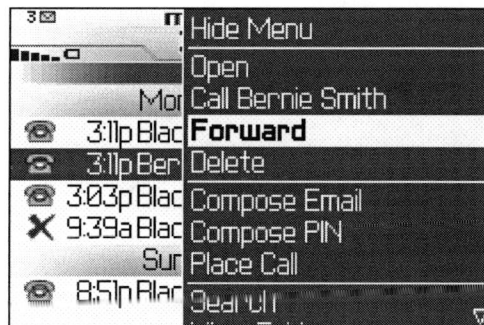

4. Edit the log or add additional information for the email

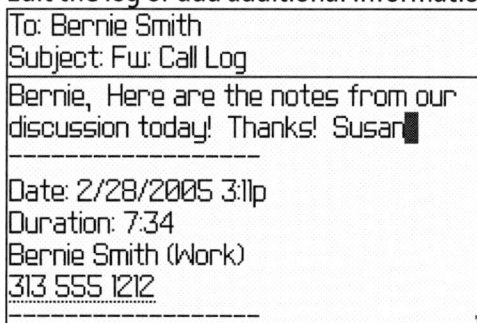

5. Click in the trackwheel and choose send.

```
Date: 2/28/2005 3:11  Hide Menu
Duration: 7:34        Copy
Bernie Smith (Work)   Cut
313 555 1212
                      Cancel Selection
_____
                      Send
Notes for My call wi  Save Draft
- The contract looks
- Only 2 changes      Add To:
  Pg. 5, para 1.3 and Add Cc:
- Make these edits    Add Bcc:
```

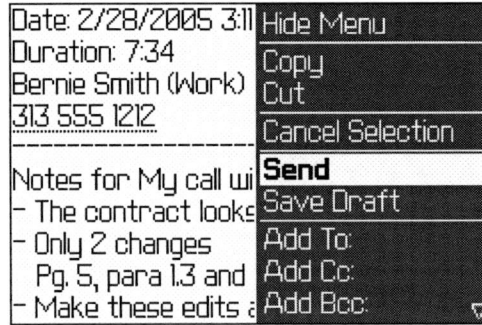

By following the above steps you can:
✓   Call a contact
✓   Take notes
✓   E-mail those notes to the contact
All at the same time.

Bottom Line: You got meaningful work done right on your BlackBerry!

BlackBerry as Portable Conference Call

On most, but not all BlackBerries today, you can use the BlackBerry as a "Portable Conference Call Center". To do this, you need to:

Tip!

You can use your BlackBerry to easily conference together multiple parties – learn more here.

3.   Go to the Phone icon.

4.   Start a phone call either from your address book, by typing in a number or from your recently called list (displayed). In this example will use the call list.

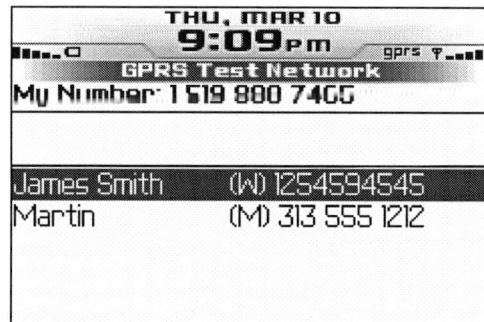

5.   Now call the first party – in this case James Smith, by highlighting his name and clicking on the trackwheel – "Call"

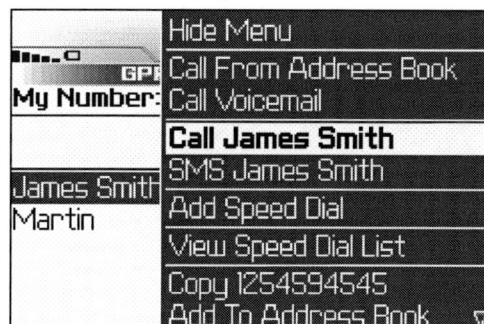

6. Once the call is connected, then put the first caller on hold.

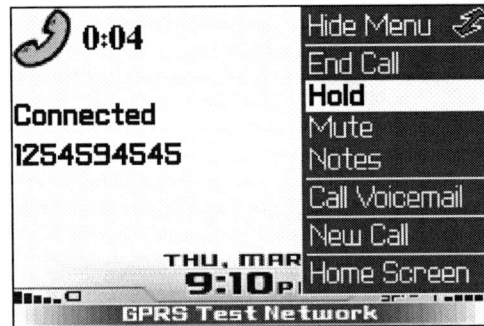

```
 ✆ 0:04            Hide Menu
                    End Call
                    Hold
Connected           Mute
1254594545          Notes
                    Call Voicemail
                    New Call
       THU, MAR     Home Screen
       9:10 P
   GPRS Test Network
```

Then click the trackwheel again and select "**New Call**" to see this screen.

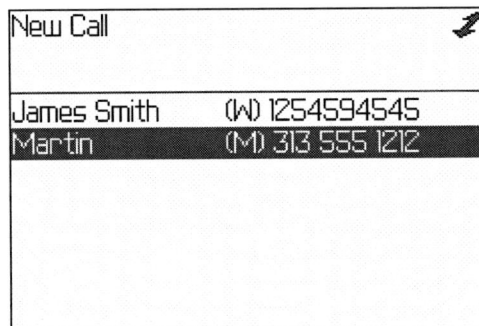

```
New Call

James Smith      (W) 1254594545
Martin           (M) 313 555 1212
```

7. Now select the other name to call from the screen or address book, in this case, Martin

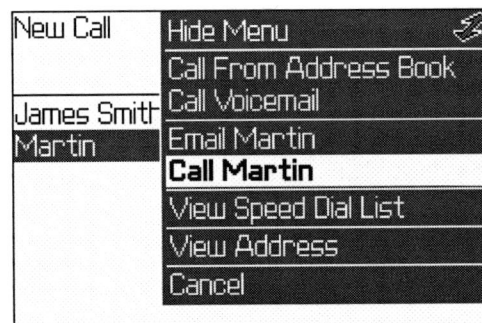

```
New Call    Hide Menu
            Call From Address Book
James Smith Call Voicemail
Martin      Email Martin
            Call Martin
            View Speed Dial List
            View Address
            Cancel
```

8. Now you will see a screen like this showing James Smith "On Hold" and Martin "Connected"

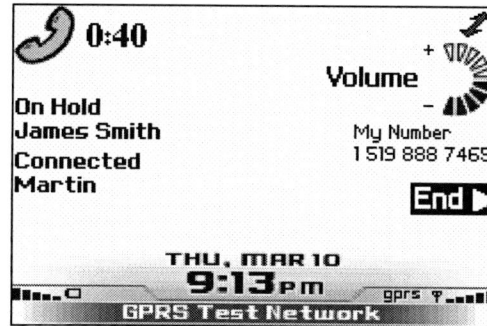

9. Click the trackwheel to see this menu:

10. Select **Join**.

Now you see you are on conference with two people:

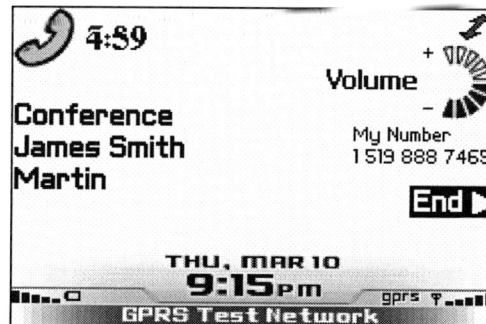

11. You could add additional people to the call by repeating steps 4-9.
12. You can also selectively "DROP" or "SPLIT" participants by using the trackwheel as shown:

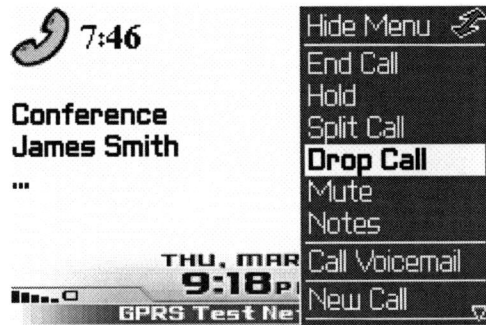

13.   Then you select the caller to drop as shown:

Speed Dial from your Home Screen

It's very easy to set speed dial numbers on your BlackBerry, here's how:

Setting Speed Dial Numbers

1. Go into your phone icon and look at your recently called list:

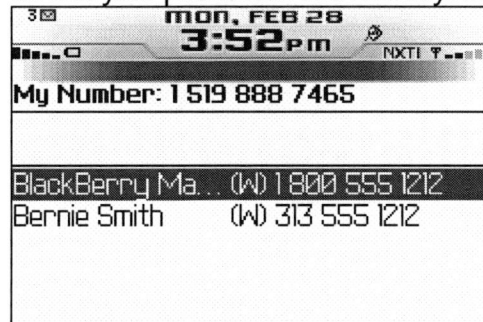

2. Highlight the number you want to add to the speed dial list
3. Choose the letter on the keyboard you want to assign to that number
4. Press and hold that key.

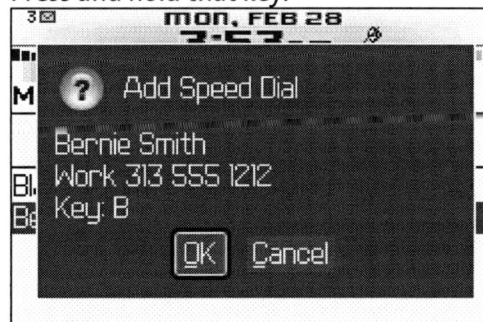

5. Select OK and you're done!

Now you can call Bernie from your Home Screen by pressing and holding the "B" key as shown:

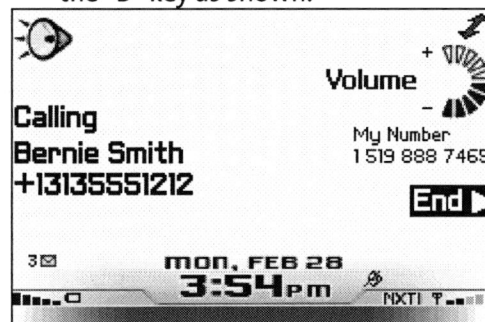

You can assign a phone number to each of the 26 letters of the alphabet.

Viewing Speed Dial List

To look at all your speed dial numbers, go into the phone and select "View Speed Dial List":

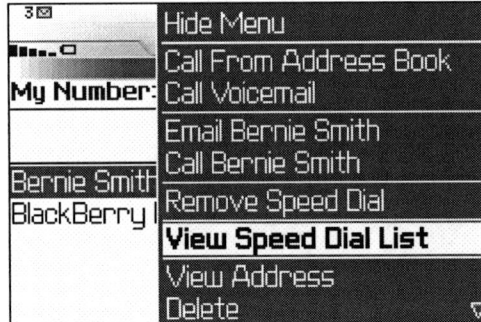

You'll see this screen:

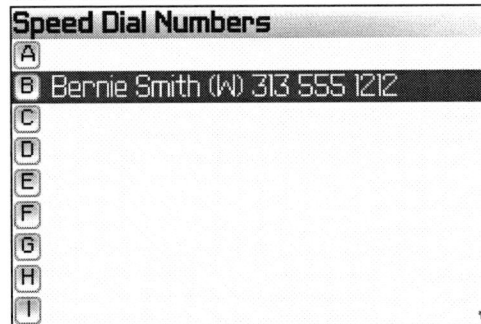

Scroll down to see all the letters:

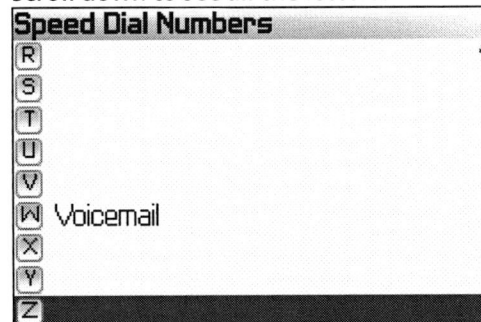

Notice in this case, the "W" key is set to Voicemail.

Dialing Voicemail in One Key with Speed Dial

For most BlackBerry models, if you call your BlackBerry phone number from your BlackBerry, you will be routed to Voicemail. Check with your wireless carrier or view your speed dial list to see what speed dial number is configured to access voice mail.

Change your Voice Mail Speed Dial Number
It's easy to change your voice mail access speed dial number, here's how:

1. In the example below, the default voicemail on this BlackBerry is "W".

2. To change the assigned letter to "V" for Voicemail, → highlight "W" and click → "Move":

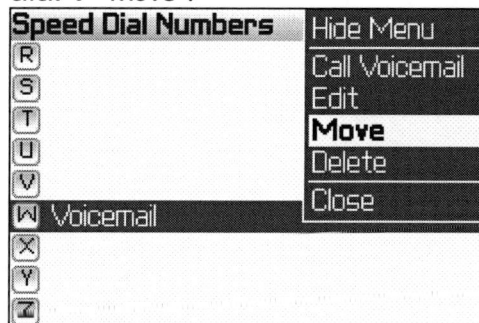

3. → Roll the trackwheel to →move it up to "V" and click the trackwheel to → assign V

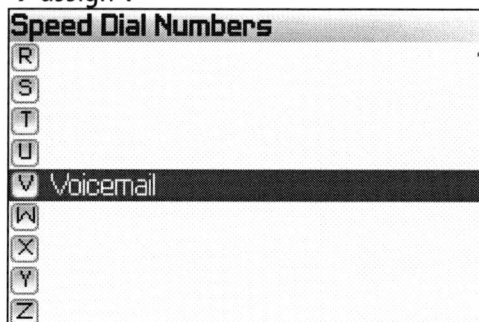

Getting The BlackBerry Phone To Vibrate or Ring!

Most new BlackBerries sold today are set with the Default profile to "TONE" or RING for Phone Calls both In or Out of the Holster. You may want to adjust this according to your location or your needs.

If you're like most BlackBerry users, you sometimes pull your BlackBerry out of the holster and leave it on your desk after you read an email. With the default setting, it makes a phone ringing noise on your desk out of its holster. Some people might prefer that it vibrates out of its holster. Here's how to change that setting and any other setting you might want in profiles.

Changing BlackBerry Profiles:

1.   Open Profiles form the home screen   (For 8700c:)

2.   Select Default (On) profile, or any other profile you may have "On" and choose →Edit

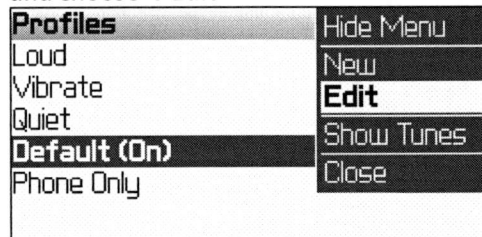

Profiles	Hide Menu
Loud	New
Vibrate	**Edit**
Quiet	Show Tunes
Default (On)	Close
Phone Only	

3.   Locate the "Phone" and click "Edit" from the menu

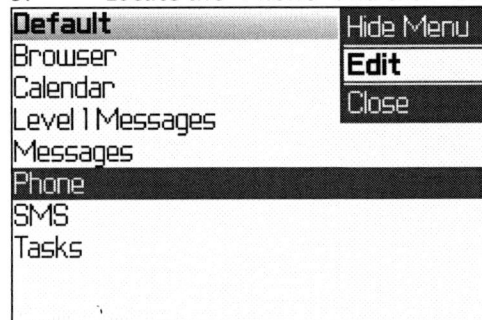

Default	Hide Menu
Browser	**Edit**
Calendar	Close
Level 1 Messages	
Messages	
Phone	
SMS	
Tasks	

4.   Change the "Out of Holster" from Tone to either "Vibrate" so that it will vibrate to alert you when you have a ringing phone call.

Phone in Default	None
Out of Holster:	Tone
Tune:	Vibrate
Volume:	Vibrate+Tone
Number of Beeps:	
Repeat Notification:	None
In Holster:	Vibrate+Tone
Tune:	Ring 6
Volume:	High
Number of Beeps:	

5.   Save and Close two times to get back to the Home screen.

Instantly Schedule New Calendar Items 'Quick Entry'

Follow these steps to ensure quick entry is enabled so you can schedule events instantly.

1. In your Calendar / Options screen, make sure your "Enable Quick Entry"

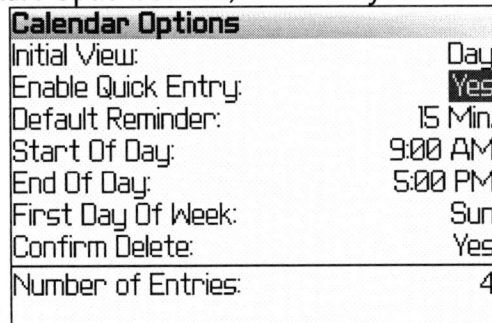

Calendar Options	
Initial View:	Day
Enable Quick Entry:	Yes
Default Reminder:	15 Min.
Start Of Day:	9:00 AM
End Of Day:	5:00 PM
First Day Of Week:	Sun
Confirm Delete:	Yes
Number of Entries:	4

    is set to "Yes".

2. On the calendar, just roll the cursor to the time you want to schedule an activity for and just start typing!

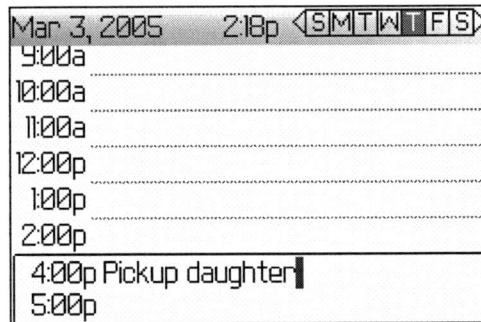

Mar 3, 2005	2:18p ‹S M T W T F S›
9:00a	
10:00a	
11:00a	
12:00p	
1:00p	
2:00p	
4:00p	Pickup daughter
5:00p	

3. If the schedule time should at 4:15 instead, just hold the "CAP" key and roll the trackwheel to change the START TIME:

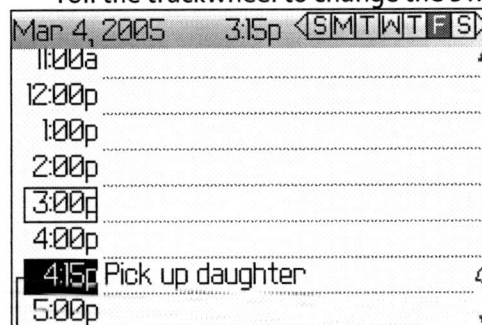

Mar 4, 2005	3:15p ‹S M T W T F S›
11:00a	
12:00p	
1:00p	
2:00p	
3:00p	
4:00p	
4:15p	Pick up daughter
5:00p	

4. The change the end time without changing the start time, roll the trackwheel without holding the CAP key

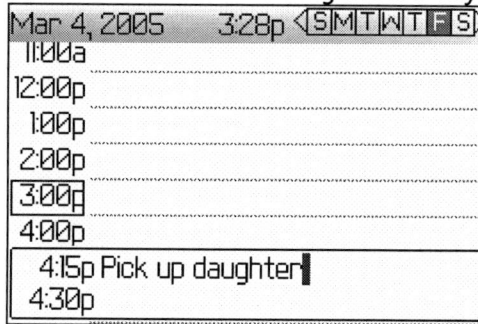

```
Mar 4, 2005    3:28p ‹S M T W T F S›
11:00a
12:00p
  1:00p
  2:00p
  3:00p
  4:00p

   4:15p Pick up daughter
  4:30p
```

Just in a few key clicks – you have scheduled a new meeting at the correct time – AND your BlackBerry will notify you with an alarm.

Quickly Finding a Specific Day or Date (Day View)

To quickly navigate to a specific date in Day View, follow these instructions:

Tip!

You can also click in the Trackwheel on any calendar view screen and select – "Go To Date..." to find a specific date.

1. Open up to Calendar Day view:

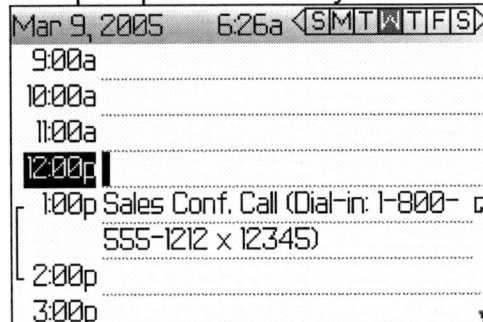

```
Mar 9, 2005    6:26a  ‹S M T W T F S›
  9:00a
 10:00a
 11:00a
 12:00p
  1:00p  Sales Conf. Call (Dial-in: 1-800-
          555-1212 x 12345)
  2:00p
  3:00p
```

2. Scroll the trackwheel UP beyond 9am, you will see the cursor in the days of the week:

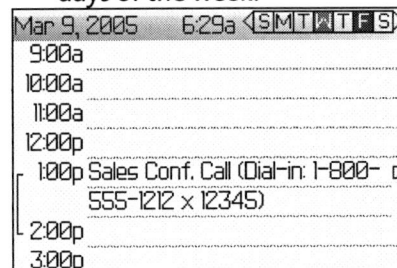

```
Mar 9, 2005    6:29a  ‹S M T W T F S›
  9:00a
 10:00a
 11:00a
 12:00p
  1:00p  Sales Conf. Call (Dial-in: 1-800-
          555-1212 x 12345)
  2:00p
  3:00p
```

Trackwheel

Roll Up/Down

Select Date at top of Calendar Day View by rolling Trackwheel

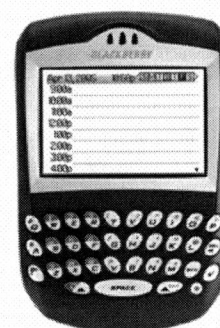

Click "In" to select

3. Now, if you clicked on a day of the week, you would immediately go to that day! For example, click on "F" to go to Friday:

```
Mar 11, 2005    6:30a  ◁SMTWTFS▷
 9:00a
10:00a
11:00a
12:00p
 1:00p
 2:00p
 3:00p
 4:00p
```

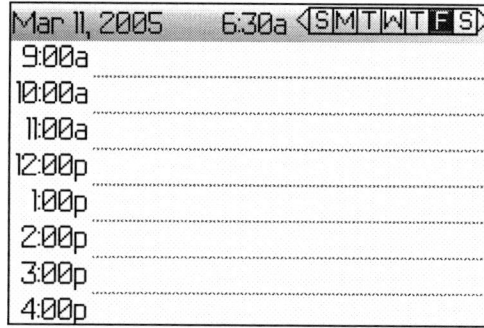

4. If you then keep scrolling up, you will get to the Date at the top of the screen. When you get there you will see that you are highlighting the Month, Day, and Year as you scroll over it.

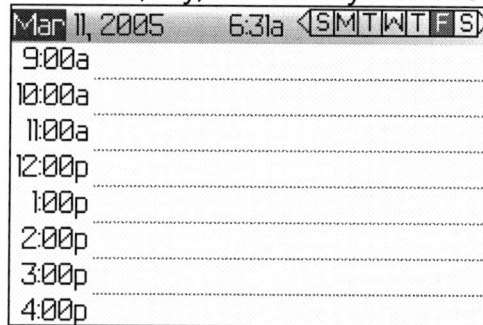

```
Mar 11, 2005    6:31a  ◁SMTWTFS▷
 9:00a
10:00a
11:00a
12:00p
 1:00p
 2:00p
 3:00p
 4:00p
```

5. If you wanted to quickly check out April 15, you would change first the month to "Apr" with the ALT + Trackwheel:

Select Date at top of Calendar Day View Pressing ALT & rolling Trackwheel

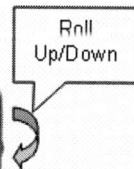

Roll Up/Down

Trackwheel

ALT Key

Hold while pressing Trackwheel

Tip!

You can also click in the Trackwheel on any calendar view screen and select – "Go To Date..." to find a specific date.

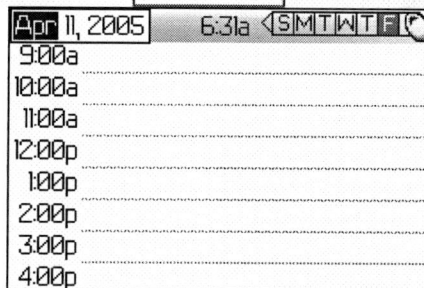

```
Apr 11, 2005    6:31a  ◁SMTWTF◯
 9:00a
10:00a
11:00a
12:00p
 1:00p
 2:00p
 3:00p
 4:00p
```

6. Then scroll over to the 11th and change it to the 15th as shown:

```
Apr 15, 2005    6:32a ◁SMTWTF S▷
 9:00a
10:00a
11:00a
12:00p
 1:00p
 2:00p
 3:00p
 4:00p
```

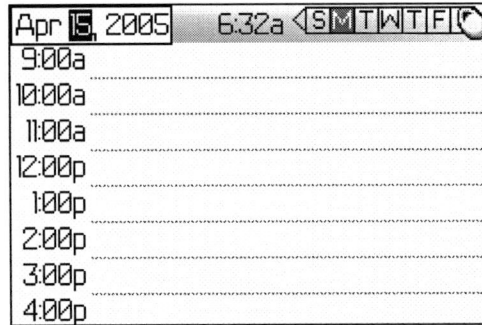

Now you can instantly find a specific day or date right from the calendar view in just a few movements of the trackwheel.

Quickly Scheduling Day / Week View Appointments

If you're in Day or Week view, you can quickly schedule appointments by following these steps:

1. In the calendar day view, hold the SHIFT key while scrolling the trackwheel to highlight the start/end time of an appointment

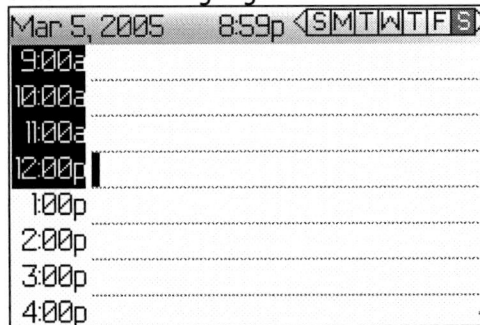

```
Mar 5, 2005    8:59p ◁SMTWTF S▷
 9:00a
10:00a
11:00a
12:00p
 1:00p
 2:00p
 3:00p
 4:00p
```

Tip!

Remember that you can always get back to today's date by either (1) exiting the calendar and re-entering it or (2) click in the Trackwheel on any calendar view screen and select – "Today".

2. With the duration properly selected, just start typing as shown.

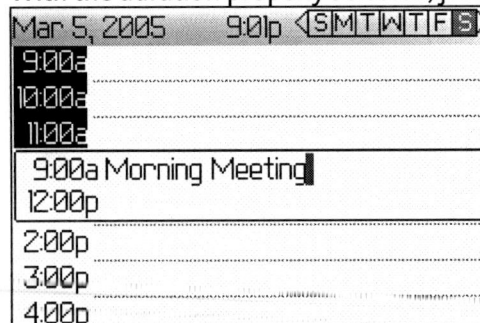

```
Mar 5, 2005    9:01p ◁SMTWTF S▷
 9:00a
10:00a
11:00a
 9:00a Morning Meeting
12:00p
 2:00p
 3:00p
 4:00p
```

3. After starting to type text, to change START TIME, hold the SHIFT + Trackwheel

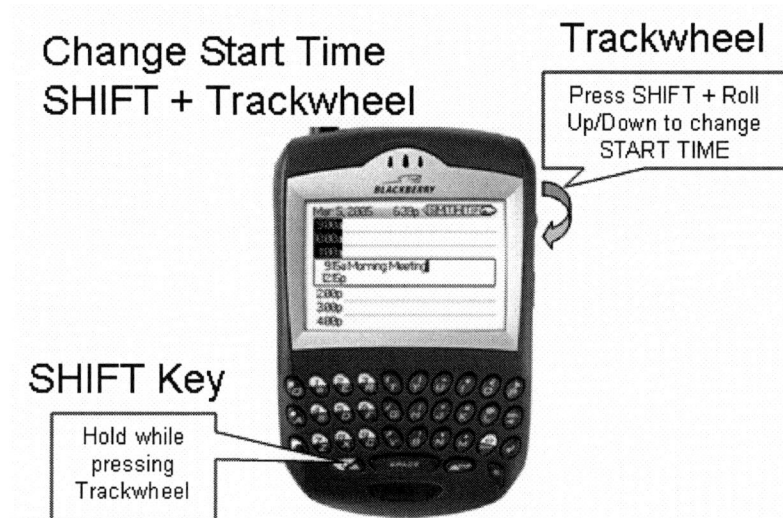

Change Start Time
SHIFT + Trackwheel

Trackwheel

Press SHIFT + Roll
Up/Down to change
START TIME

SHIFT Key

Hold while
pressing
Trackwheel

4. To change the END TIME, roll the trackwheel alone

Trackwheel

Roll Up/Down
To Change END Time

Tip!

Remember that you can always scroll a day or a week at a time when you hold the "ALT" key down and roll the trackwheel in day or week view.

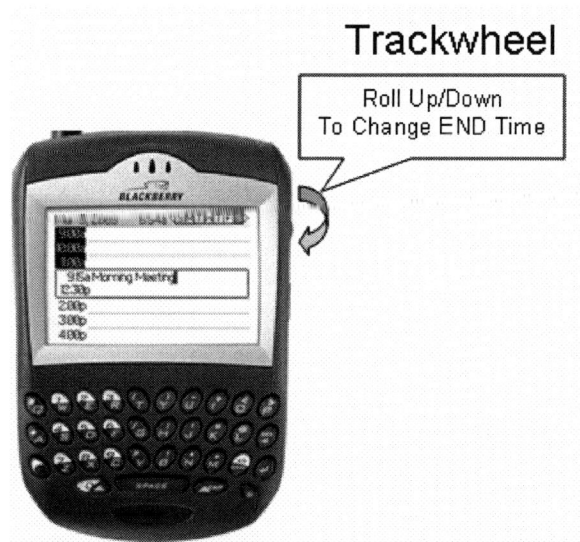

5. To save the meeting hit the Enter key or click the trackwheel and choose Save

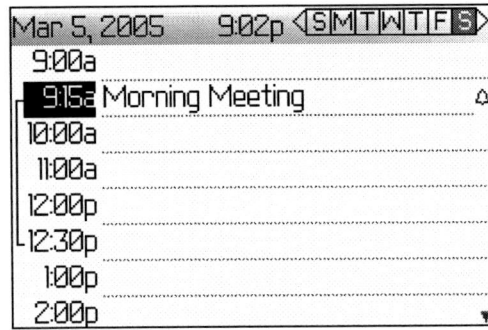

Quickly Scrolling to A Day-At-A-Time

For a day-at-a-time calendar navigation in Day View, follow these instructions:

1. In the calendar day view, hold the ALT key and roll the trackwheel down to advance one day. (You can also use the **SPACE BAR**)

2. Hold the ALT key and roll the trackwheel up to go back one-day-at-a-time.

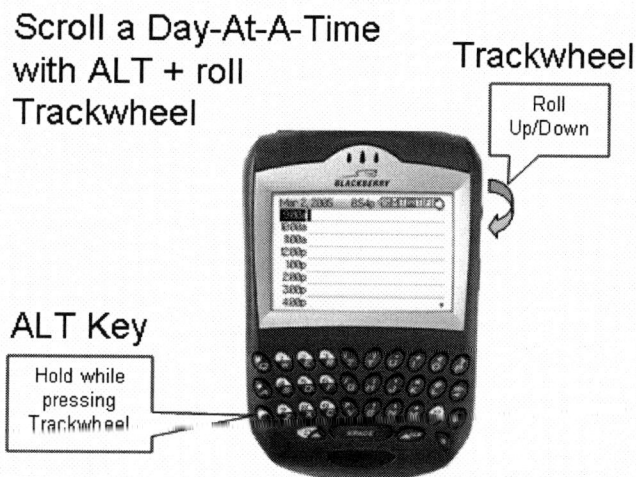

Scroll a Day-At-A-Time with ALT + roll Trackwheel

Trackwheel — Roll Up/Down

ALT Key — Hold while pressing Trackwheel

Check the Calendar while on the Phone "ALT-ESC"

To multi-task on your BlackBerry, follow these steps:
1. From within any application on the BlackBerry
2. Hold down the ALT key

3. While still holding down ALT, → press the Escape key (don't let go of the

Multi-Tasking with ALT+ESC

ESC Key

Press this ESC while holding the ALT key to switch between applications

ALT Key

Hold while pressing the ESC key

ALT key)

4. You will see a "list" of applications or a "mini-ribbon" of icons

5. While still holding down ALT, roll the trackwheel to the application you want to jump-to and release all keys.

Following the steps above you can instantly jump between open applications on the BlackBerry.

Email and Calendar Working Together

Many times, you schedule appointments and modify your calendar based on email you receive. Here is a tip, using the example of driving directions, on how you can include important text from an email on a calendar event.

Copying Email Text (Driving Directions) into a Calendar Event

1. Open the email you want to copy
2. Select the text by pressing the left shift key once and rolling the trackwheel
3. With the text you want to copy selected, click in the trackwheel and select Copy

```
To: info@blackberrymadesim  Hide Menu
Subject: Directions to meetin  Copy
Hello,                          Cut
                                Paste
I look forward to our meet     Cancel Selection
Here are direction to our n    Send
- North on I-75                Save Draft
- Get off at exit 55, turn le  Add To:
- Go through 2 lights          Add Cc:
- Turn right at ABD Drive      Add Bcc:
- We are in first building on  Attach Address
Thanks, John                   Edit AutoText
```

4. Now use the ALT + Escape Trick to jump to the BlackBerry home screen then open the calendar.

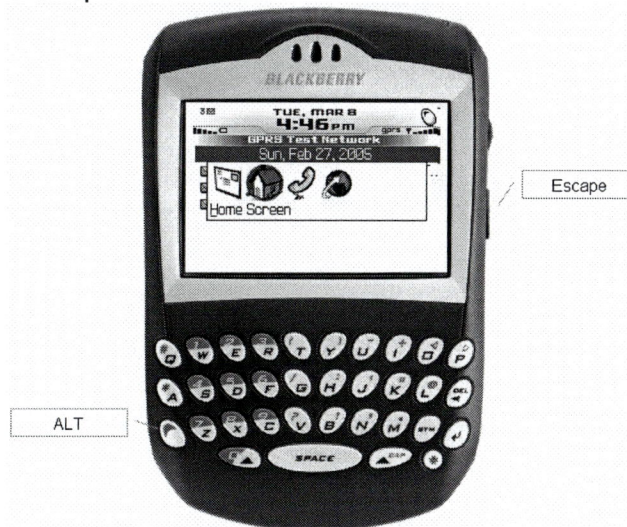

Escape

ALT

5. Go to the appropriate date and create a New activity

6. Place the cursor in the Locations field and click in the trackwheel to Paste the directions

```
New Appointment          Hide Menu
Subject: Meeting with John Doe Paste
Location: █
                          Save
☐ All Day Event           Show Symbols
Start:            Mon, Mar 14 Close
End:              Mon, Mar 14
Duration:               0 Hours 30 Mins
Time Zone:           Eastern Time (-5)
Reminder:                     15 Min.

Recurrence:                      None
No Recurrence.

☐ Mark as Private
```

7. Now you see the directions you pasted into the meeting – ready to be viewed the INSTANT the alarm rings! (no more searching for those directions – they appear exactly when you need them!)

```
New Appointment
Subject: Meeting with John Doe
Location: Here are direction to our new
office:- North on I-75- Get off at exit 55,
turn left- Go through 2 lights- Turn right at
ABD Drive- We are in first building on right█
☐ All Day Event
Start:         Mon, Mar 14, 2005 8:30 AM
End:           Mon, Mar 14, 2005 9:00 AM
Duration:             0 Hours 30 Mins
Time Zone:         Eastern Time (-5)
Reminder:                   15 Min.
Recurrence:                    None
```

8. Click in the trackwheel to Save the appointment

```
New Appointment          Hide Menu
Subject: Meeting with John Doe Paste
Location: Here are direction t Select
office:- North on I-75- Get off Clear Field
turn left- Go through 2 lights-
ABD Drive- We are in first buil Save
☐ All Day Event           Show Symbols
Start:            Mon, Mar 14 Close
End:              Mon, Mar 14, 2005 9:00 AM
Duration:               0 Hours 30 Mins
Time Zone:           Eastern Time (-5)
Reminder:                     15 Min.
Recurrence:                      None
```

9. Then, on the day of the appointment, an alarm is triggered allowing you to instantly see the directions from the email and jump to the activity

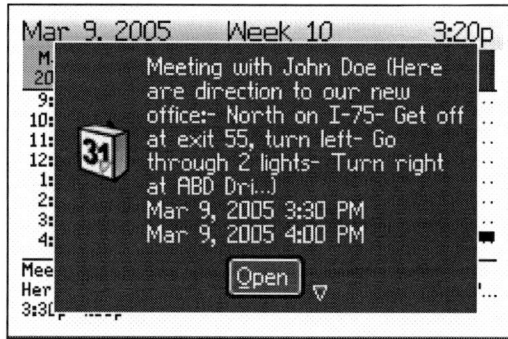

```
Mar 9, 2005      Week 10        3:20p
M.      Meeting with John Doe (Here
20      are direction to our new
9:      office:- North on I-75- Get off
10:     at exit 55, turn left- Go
11:     through 2 lights- Turn right
12:     at ABD Dri...)
1:      Mar 9, 2005 3:30 PM
2:      Mar 9, 2005 4:00 PM
3:
4:
Mee     [ Open ]
Her
3:3C
```

10. "Open" the activity to see the full driving directions – no more hunting for paper or old emails!!

Customizing your Calendar Display Options

The BlackBerry calendar has different display options letting you customize it to meet your needs.

Most of Your Meetings are in the Evening – How do you change your Calendar End time from 5pm (default) to 11pm?

To change your calendar display options, follow these steps:
1. Open the BlackBerry Calendar
2. Click in the trackwheel and select → Options

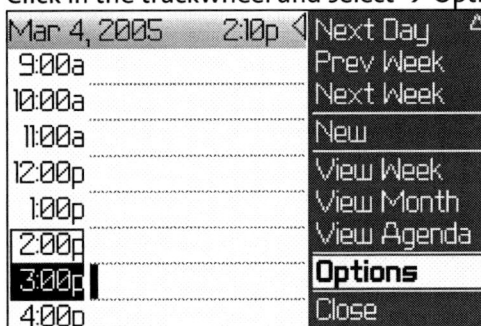

```
Mar 4, 2005    2:10p  │ Next Day
 9:00a                  Prev Week
10:00a                  Next Week
11:00a                  New
12:00p                  View Week
 1:00p                  View Month
 2:00p                  View Agenda
 3:00p                  Options
 4:00p                  Close
```

3. The screen shown below will appear

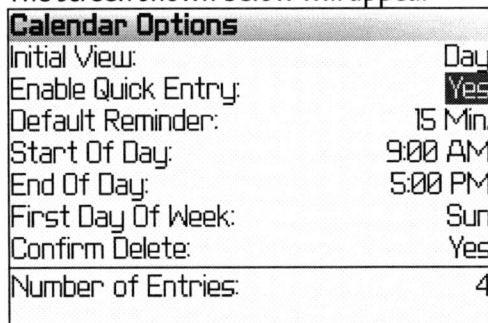

```
Calendar Options
Initial View:              Day
Enable Quick Entry:        Yes
Default Reminder:          15 Min.
Start Of Day:              9:00 AM
End Of Day:                5:00 PM
First Day Of Week:         Sun
Confirm Delete:            Yes
Number of Entries:         4
```

4. If you regularly schedule events before 9am or after 5pm, change the Day View start and end times. If you have a lot of evening / dinner meetings, you might change your "End of Day" to 11pm.

```
Calendar Options                    ◯
Initial View:                     Day
Enable Quick Entry:               Yes
Default Reminder:              15 Min.
Start Of Day:                 9:00 AM
End Of Day:                  [11]:00 PM
First Day Of Week:                Sun
Confirm Delete:                   Yes
Number of Entries:                  4
```

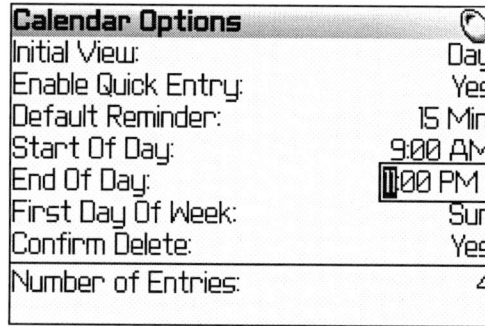

5. Save your settings and go back to day view to see that your view now goes to 11PM

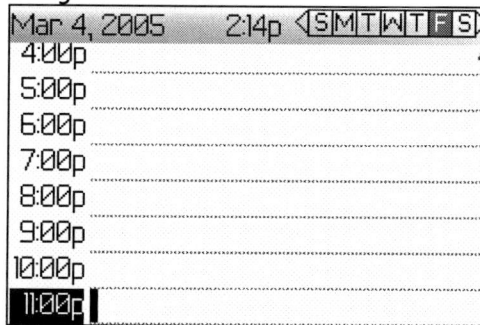

```
Mar 4, 2005     2:14p  ‹SMTWTFS›
 4:00p                             ▲
 5:00p
 6:00p
 7:00p
 8:00p
 9:00p
10:00p
[11:00p]
```

Likewise, you can adjust the day **start time** or first day of the week in the OPTIONS screen.

Choosing The Default Calendar View

To set your BlackBerry calendar to your favorite default view (day, week, agenda, month or "last" view), follow these steps:

1. Open the calendar and select Options

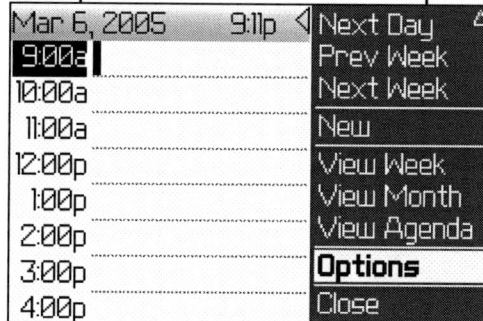

```
Mar 6, 2005     9:11p  ‹  Next Day      △
[9:00a]                    Prev Week
10:00a                     Next Week
11:00a                     New
12:00p                     View Week
 1:00p                     View Month
 2:00p                     View Agenda
 3:00p                     Options
 4:00p                     Close
```

2. Select Initial View and change it to your desired layout

```
┌────────────────────────────────────┐
│ Calendar Options                    │
│ Initial View:              │ Day  │ │
│ Enable Quick Entry:        │ Week │ │
│ Default Reminder:          │ Month│ │
│ Start Of Day:             9│Agenda│ │
│ End Of Day:                │ Last │ │
│ First Day Of Week:          Sun    │
│ Confirm Delete:             Yes    │
│ Number of Entries:          10     │
└────────────────────────────────────┘
```

3. "Last" means whatever view the calendar was on last time it was closed. It will open again in that view.

4. "Agenda" shows you all appointments for that week separated by day, as shown below.

Here's the Agenda View:

```
┌────────────────────────────────────┐
│ Mar 4, 2005                  9:12p  │
│ ████ Fri, Mar 4, 2005 ████████  △  │
│ 4:15p Pick up daughter          △  │
│          Sat, Mar 5, 2005          │
│ 9:15a Morning Meeting           △  │
│          Wed, Mar 9, 2005          │
│ 1:00p Sales Conf. Call (Dial-in: 1-800-  ▯ │
│          555-1212 x 12345)         │
│          Thu, Mar 10, 2005      ▼  │
└────────────────────────────────────┘
```

You Can View Scheduled Tasks on Your Calendar!

With the v4.1 or higher of BlackBerry System software, you can now put your scheduled tasks (those that have a specific due date) on your Calendar so you can see your entire schedule and tasks all in one place.

Note: This feature requires BlackBerry System Software v4.1 and above. *(How do I check my BlackBerry System Software version? – Check the FAQ pages or Table of Contents for help on doing this.)*

To do this, follow the directions below:

Displaying Scheduled Tasks in Your Calendar
(This only works with BlackBerry Software v4.1 and above)

1. Go to the "Calendar" Icon

2. Click the trackwheel and Select "Options" (near the bottom) Tip, hit the letter "O" to jump down to Options

3. Change "Show Tasks" to "Yes" as shown. Tip: Either hit the SPACE Key or hold the "ALT" key down and roll the track wheel to change this.

4. Click Save, then Exit out of The Calendar, by hitting The Escape key.

5. Now, go into Tasks to Create a new "Scheduled" task That has a "Due Date" as shown.

6. Now, go back into calendar To see this task right on your Daily Calendar screen!

This clock icon shows that it is a Scheduled TASK.

Getting the Most out Week View

You can get a lot more out of the BlackBerry calendar week view with a few simple tips.

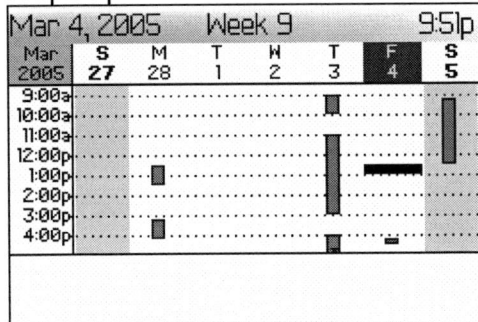

Week View Tips

- To move a Week at a time use the "P" key to go one week "previous" and the "N" key to go to the "next" week.
- Holding the ALT key, while rolling the trackwheel will move you sideways – back or forth - one day at a time.

Scheduling from the Week View

To Schedule an Appointment from the week view, follow these steps:

1. Roll to the correct time

2. Hold the SHIFT key and roll the trackwheel. This will highlight a section of the calendar as shown, then select → New.

3. Enter the information and save it

New Appointment	Hide Menu
Subject: Dinner Meeting	Paste
Location: Hotel	Select
This appointment occur	Clear Field
☐ All Day Event	**Save**
Start: Tue, Mar	Show Symbols
End: Tue, Mar	Close
Duration:	
Time Zone: Eastern Time (-5)	
Reminder: 15 Min	

4. The meeting will be displayed as shown below.

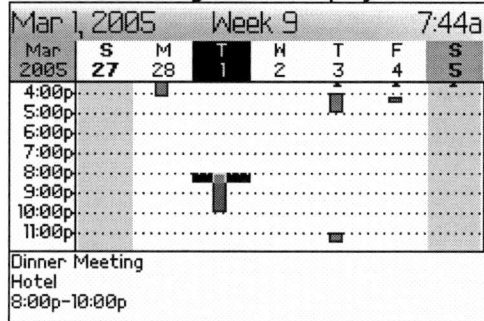

In just a few key and trackwheel clicks you've checked your calendar and scheduled a new meeting!

Tip!

Setup Groups for sending "mass" emails right from your BlackBerry – just like a "mail merge" so you don't have to individually email everyone on your team!

So You're having a Baby ... Announce from the Hospital Room!

In order to create your mailing list for your Baby Announcement, please see the section earlier in this book: Creating A Mailing List On Your BlackBerry! (click here to jump to this section in the electronic version of this book)

You will be creating a "Group" in your BlackBerry Address Book – call the new group anything, for example "Baby Announcement" – then add any name from your address book to the list! Once you're in the hospital, you can send an email right after the baby is born with the details to EVERYONE you need.

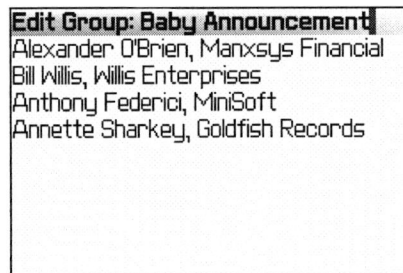

```
Edit Group: Baby Announcement
Alexander O'Brien, Manxsys Financial
Bill Willis, Willis Enterprises
Anthony Federici, MiniSoft
Annette Sharkey, Goldfish Records
```

Sending the Baby Announcement From Your BlackBerry!

After you have created at new group on your BlackBerry, you want to send everyone a welcome email. You'll notice that "Baby Announcement" group looks and acts like any other address in your Address Book.

1. Look up the group name in your Address book by typing "Baby" – it will filter your address book to show only the "Baby Announcement"

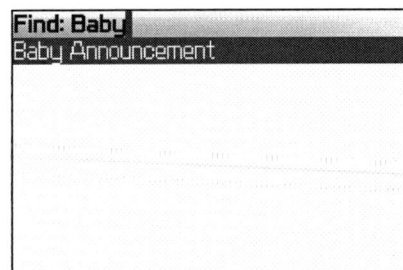

```
Find: Baby
Baby Announcement
```

2. Select "Email Baby Announcement":

```
Find: Bat  Filter
Baby Ann  View All
          New Address
          New Group
          View Group
          Edit Group
          Delete Group
          Email Baby Announcement
          Options
```

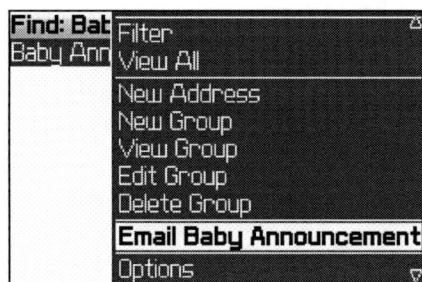

3. Compose your Baby Announcement Email and SEND it as you would normally do.

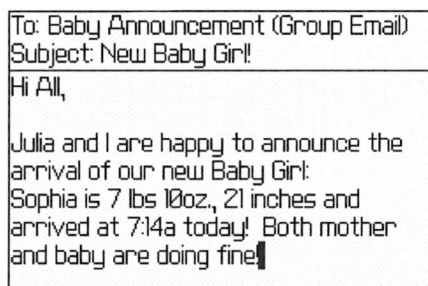

```
To: Baby Announcement (Group Email)
Subject: New Baby Girl!
Hi All,

Julia and I are happy to announce the
arrival of our new Baby Girl:
Sophia is 7 lbs 10oz., 21 inches and
arrived at 7:14a today!  Both mother
and baby are doing fine!
```

4. If you want to verify who is receiving your email, then you could open the email being sent, you will notice that there is a separate "To:" for each member of the group:

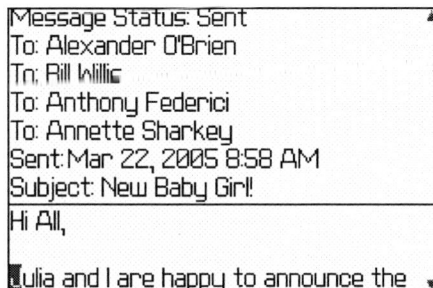

```
Message Status: Sent
To: Alexander O'Brien
To: Bill Willis
To: Anthony Federici
To: Annette Sharkey
Sent: Mar 22, 2005 8:58 AM
Subject: New Baby Girl!
Hi All,

Julia and I are happy to announce the
```

CALENDAR TIPS

TIP: Add a phone number to a scheduled CALL on your BlackBerry so you can dial from the calendar!

Dialing from the BlackBerry Calendar

When adding a Call to your calendar, add the contact's phone number to the scheduled appointment. Then you can instantly call them on your BlackBerry when the alarm rings.

Follow these steps to instantly call a contact from the BlackBerry calendar:

1. Schedule the call and include the contact's phone number and be sure to set an alarm on the activity.

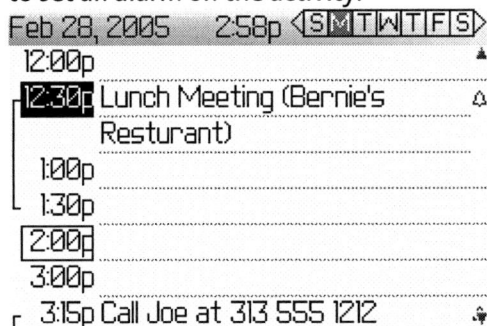

2. When the alarm rings (or your BlackBerry vibrates) then you'll see a screen like this:

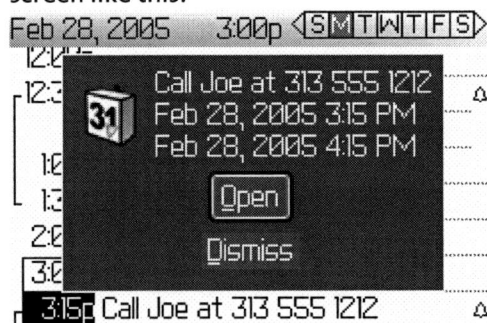

Tip!

Dialing your phone from your calendar is a fantastic way to save time when you have a scheduled call – just point and click on the phone number in the calendar event after the alarm rings!

3. Now Select "Open" to see the appointment like this:

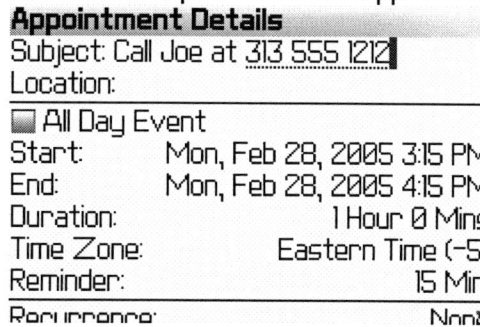

Appointment Details
Subject: Call Joe at <u>313 555 1212</u>
Location:
☐ All Day Event
Start: Mon, Feb 28, 2005 3:15 PM
End: Mon, Feb 28, 2005 4:15 PM
Duration: 1 Hour 0 Mins
Time Zone: Eastern Time (-5)
Reminder: 15 Min.
Recurrence: None

4. Highlight the phone number, by rolling up the trackwheel

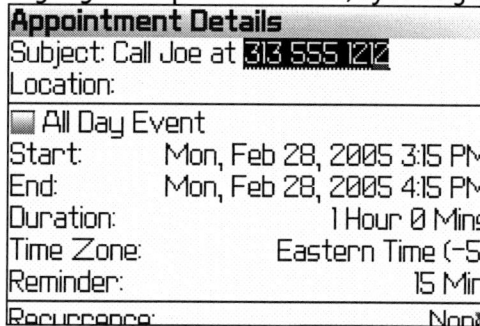

Appointment Details
Subject: Call Joe at **313 555 1212**
Location:
☐ All Day Event
Start: Mon, Feb 28, 2005 3:15 PM
End: Mon, Feb 28, 2005 4:15 PM
Duration: 1 Hour 0 Mins
Time Zone: Eastern Time (-5)
Reminder: 15 Min.
Recurrence: None

5. Click the trackwheel and select → Call:

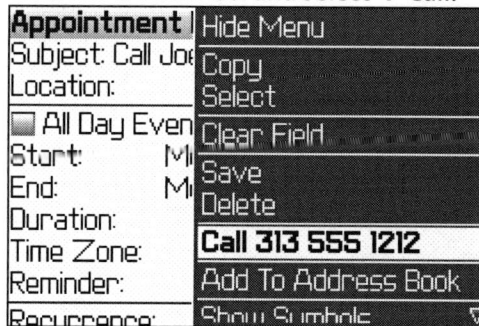

Appointment | Hide Menu
Subject: Call Joe | Copy
Location: | Select
☐ All Day Even | Clear Field
Start: M| | Save
End: M| | Delete
Duration: | **Call 313 555 1212**
Time Zone: | Add To Address Book
Reminder: | Show Symbols ▽
Recurrence:

Now you're talking in just 3 clicks from when you had the alarm ringing. What could be more simple or efficient!

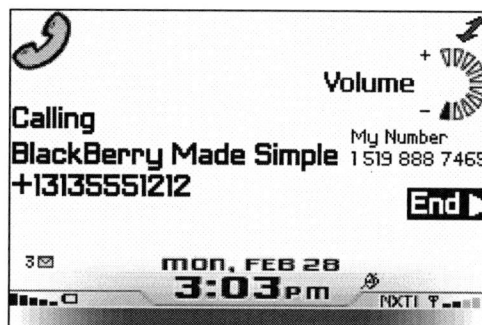

Calling
BlackBerry Made Simple   Volume
+13135551212
My Number
1 519 888 7465
End ▶

3 ✉   mon, FEB 28
                      3:03pm   NXT1

Write that Grocery List While on a Call

You get a call while you're in the Grocery Store – "Could you pick up a few extra things for me?"   The best way to handle this situation is to add to your Grocery List memo item while you're on the call!
To do this, follow these steps:

1.   You're on the phone call...

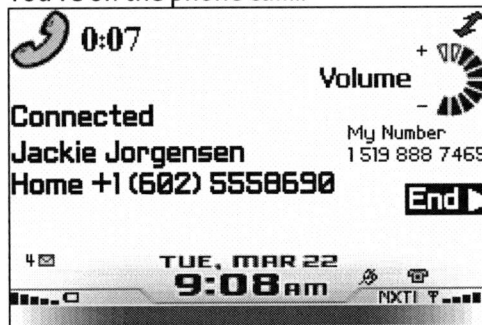

Tip!

Take notes in memo pad when on a call to make sure you don't forget anything important from the call.

2.   Use the ALT+ESC trick to switch over to the home screen

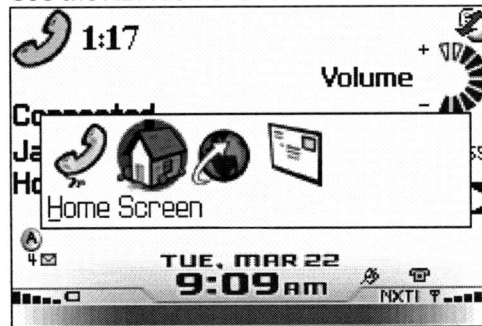

Then, find the memo icon (under the Applications icon on the 8700c)

Finding the Memo Pad Icon

8700 Series

Applications (sub-menu)

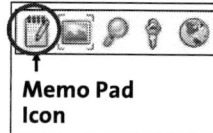

Use the Memo Pad Icon to take notes, write lists, store important information. They are fully searchable and can be organized with "Categories"

Memo Pad Icon

All Other Full Keyboard BlackBerries

Memo Pad Icon

8. Find your Grocery List and click "Edit" or create a new one on the spot.

```
Find:
Grocery     Hold
            Volume
            Mute
            Notes
            Filter
            New
            View
            Edit
            Delete
```

9. Open the Grocery List

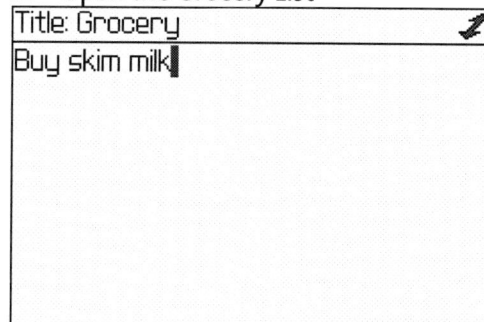

```
Title: Grocery
Buy skim milk
```

10. Now add the new items to your Grocery list from the call, check with the caller you've got everything and click SAVE:

Title: Groceri	Hide Menu
Buy skim milk	End Call
Half N Half	Hold
Bananas	Volume
Garlic	Mute
	Notes
	Select
	Clear Field
	Save

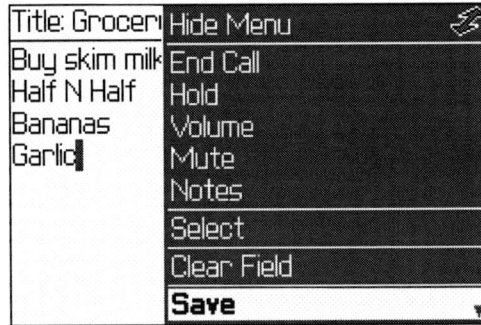

Now you can rest assured you will remember everything that was asked for during the call! Every time you return from the store you'll have everything that was requested!

ORGANIZING: Organizing Contacts with Categories

A great new feature has been added in v4.0 BlackBerry System Software is called "Categories". Categories are very useful if you have you have groups of information, such as: My Yoga Group, Children's Play Group, Tennis Group, Yoga Group, family, friends, etc. You can assign both Addresses & Tasks to Categories

To demonstrate how categories can help you better interact with groups of people we will use a hypothetical project called "Yoga Group". The Yoga Group includes:

Albert Barry
Allison Mikola
Cecil Carter

Assign Contacts to Categories

These contacts are already synced to the BlackBerry, so we need to assign them to the "Project Alpha" category.

To assign contacts to categories, follow these steps:

1. Enter the Address book and find Albert Barry, then click Edit.

```
Find: █            Hide Menu
Albert Barry, Mei  Filter
Alexander O'Brien
Allison Mikola, CH ( New Address
Annette Sharkey,  New Group
Anthony Federici,  View
Ariel Lorch, Mocki Edit
Benny Lender, Bes  Delete
Bill Craig, KKQS Ra Email Albert Barry
Bill Willis, Willis Ente Call Albert Barry
```

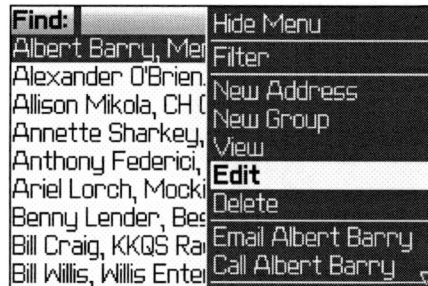

2.   Click the trackwheel again and select "Categories"

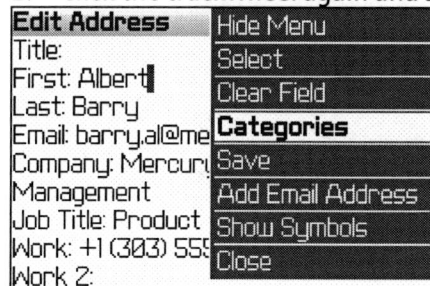

```
Edit Address      Hide Menu
Title:
First: Albert█     Select
Last: Barry        Clear Field
Email: barry.al@me Categories
Company: Mercur Save
Management        Add Email Address
Job Title: Product Show Symbols
Work: +1 (303) 55  Close
Work 2:
```

3.   Since the "Yoga Group" Category is not yet created, you need to create
      "New" to add it:

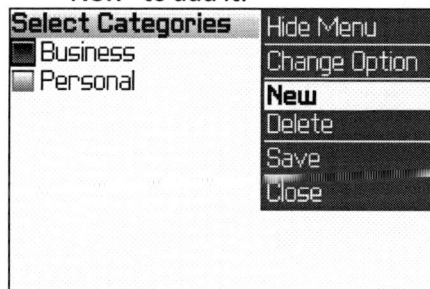

```
Select Categories   Hide Menu
█ Business
█ Personal          Change Option
                    New
                    Delete
                    Save
                    Close
```

4.   Type the name.

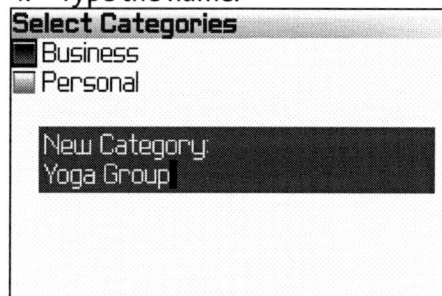

```
Select Categories
█ Business
█ Personal

     New Category:
     Yoga Group█
```

5.   Click the trackwheel to save the name, then use the SPACE bar to check
      the new category:

Select Categories
- ☐ Business
- ☐ Personal
- ■ Yoga Group

Select Categories | Hide Menu
- ☐ Business | Change Option
- ☐ Personal | New
- ■ Yoga Group | Delete
 | **Save**
 | Close

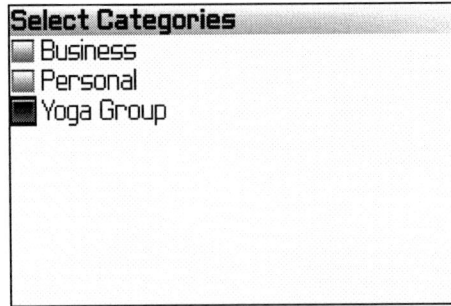

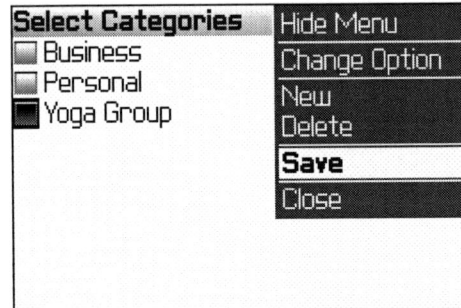

6. Click Save for the Category, and then Save for the Contact.

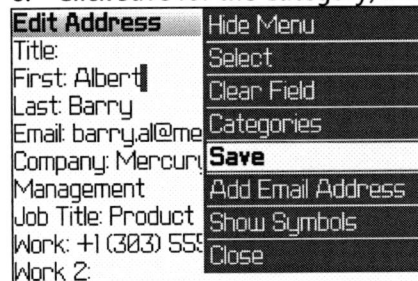

Edit Address | Hide Menu
Title: | Select
First: Albert | Clear Field
Last: Barry | Categories
Email: barry.al@me | **Save**
Company: Mercury | Add Email Address
Management | Show Symbols
Job Title: Product | Close
Work: +1 (303) 555
Work 2:

7. Now you've assigned Albert Barry to the new "Project Alpha" category. Add the rest of the team the same way. It's even easier to add new members, since the Category has already been created.

TIP: You can organize Contacts, MemoPad entries, and Tasks with Categories!

Filter by Categories

To view only contacts within a specific category, follow these steps:

1. In the address book contact list view, click in the trackwheel and select →FILTER

Tip!

Filtering by Categories is a great way to stay organized on your BlackBerry – and it uses the same Categories from your MS Outlook!

```
Find:
Cecil Carter, CH Go    Hide Menu
Chris Fierros, Inter   Filter
Chris Huffman, CH      New Address
Colleen McCarthy,      New Group
Danielle Middlebury    View
David Davis, R Com     Edit
Deiter Brock, CPQT     Delete
Dylan Nguyen, Bech     Email Cecil Carter
Edward Moets, MF       Call Cecil Carter
```

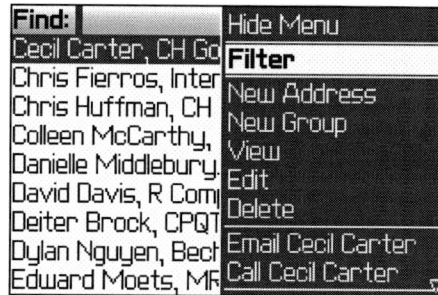

2. Find and check (using spacebar) "Yoga Group"

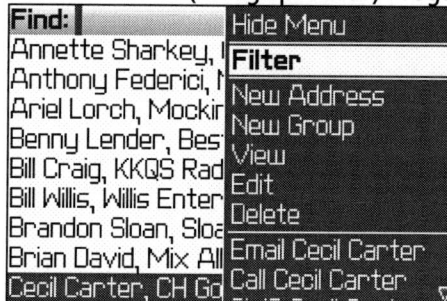

```
Find:
Annette Sharkey,       Hide Menu
Anthony Federici,      Filter
Ariel Lorch, Mockir    New Address
Benny Lender, Bes      New Group
Bill Craig, KKQS Rad   View
Bill Willis, Willis Enter  Edit
Brandon Sloan, Sloa    Delete
Brian David, Mix All   Email Cecil Carter
Cecil Carter, CH Go    Call Cecil Carter
```

3.   Check the "Yoga Group" Box by hitting the space bar when highlighted

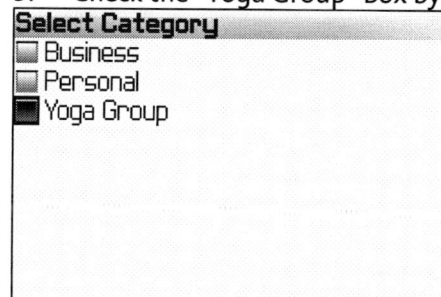

```
Select Category
□ Business
□ Personal
■ Yoga Group
```

4. The Address Book will now only show those people assigned to the
    category Yoga Group

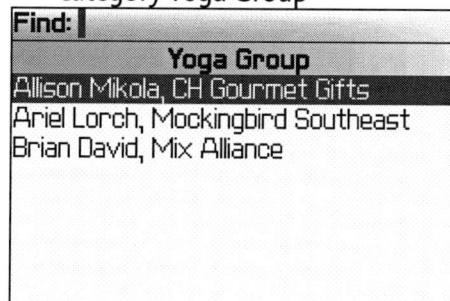

```
Find:
             Yoga Group
Allison Mikola, CH Gourmet Gifts
Ariel Lorch, Mockingbird Southeast
Brian David, Mix Alliance
```

Now you can instantly find all your Yoga Group members with a few clicks
and get in touch with them via phone or email!

TIME MANAGEMENT: Scheduling the Big Rocks First!

You can use your BlackBerry Week View to schedule your "Big Rocks" first.

You may have seen this example from Time Management trainers before:

You need these materials:

1 Large Bucket
=> Represents all your work hours the Week

6-8 Big Rocks (fills up the Bucket with space around them)
=> Represent those key tasks that you MUST get done this week!

1 Pile of Sand (fills up ½ of the Bucket)
=> Represent all those little "interruptions" calls, emails, conversations that are not related to helping you complete your "Big Rocks" tasks

The "Interrupted Joe" DOESN'T his key activities or ("Big Rocks"), but "try to fit them in" around everything else. Since you're not scheduling them, you pour all the "interruptions" first into the bucket; they take priority for the "Interrupted Joe". Then try to fit the Big Rocks into the bucket – THEY DON'T FIT! – In other words, all the interruptions have taken your precious time and now the "Interrupted Joe" <u>is not getting done all the important things he needs to get done!</u>

The "Scheduled Susan" plans out her week by scheduling time for each of her key activities "Big Rocks". In Susan's case, she "Schedules" or pours all the Big Rocks into the bucket first – they all fit! Then, Susan allows the sand (or "interruptions") to take second priority to all her "Big Rocks" in the week, so she so she pours the sand in on top of the Rocks and it fills in the empty spaces, but does not overflow the bucket – EVERYTHING GETS DONE!

You can "Schedule your Big Rocks" by using the Week View on your BlackBerry:

> ## Tip!
>
> In order to get your priority tasks or projects accomplished you need to block out meaningful "chunks" of time so you can focus uninterrupted on these items!

```
Mar 14, 2005    Week 11        3:03p
Mar   S   M   T   W   T   F   S
2005  13  14  15  16  17  18  19
9:00a
10:00a
11:00a
12:00p
1:00p
2:00p
3:00p
4:00p
```

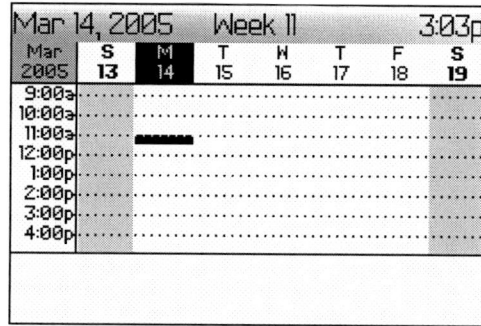

In the Case of Susan, she's an author an finds that she is a much more productive writer in the morning – so she plans blocks of 2 hours every morning to "Write Book" from 9a – 11a as shown:

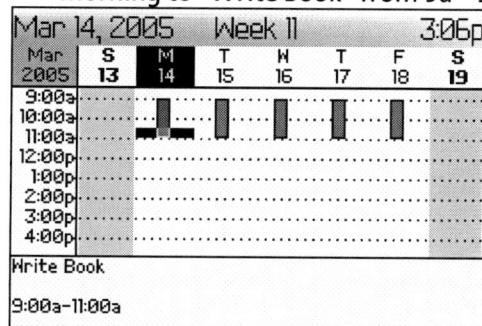

```
Mar 14, 2005    Week 11        3:06p
Mar   S   M   T   W   T   F   S
2005  13  14  15  16  17  18  19
9:00a
10:00a
11:00a
12:00p
1:00p
2:00p
3:00p
4:00p
Write Book
9:00a-11:00a
```

You have two options for scheduling this – you could create 5 separate appointments, or use the recurring feature to schedule the 1st one on Monday and have it repeat once a day for 5 days as shown here:

```
Appointment Details
End:       Mon, Mar 14, 2005 11:00 AM
Duration:              2 Hours 0 Mins
Time Zone:           Eastern Time (-5)
Reminder:                      15 Min.
Recurrence:                     Daily
Every:                              1
End:                            Date
                 Fri, Mar 18, 2005
Occurs every day until Mar 18, 2005.
```

Then in the afternoon she plans her other key activities – Promoting Her Book, Responding to Reader Email, Working on New Book Topics

Notice that she still leaves several hours every day for the "SAND" or interruptions that will come in fill up her day and decides to leave Friday afternoons empty.

TIP: Don't plan out every minute of each day – leave some "free" time for the "interruptions" that life throws at you so you can still get your "Big Rocks" done!

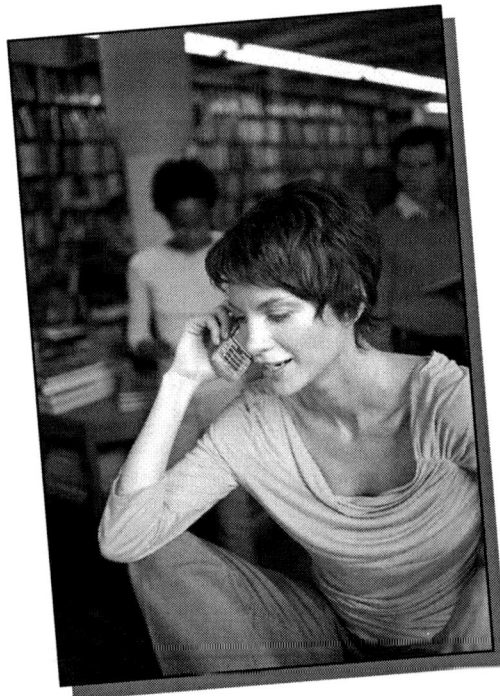

Using Memo pad for All Sorts of Lists

A great use for the memo pad is to manage and save lists with it. For example, just create a separate list for each store you regularly visit and add items to the list whenever they pop into your mind or someone asks for a specific item from a store. "Hey could you pick up some more Cinnamon Oatmeal, Milk and Eggs at the store".

Here's how to add a memo list:

1. Open the MemoPad

Finding the Memo Pad Icon

8700 Series

Applications (sub-menu)

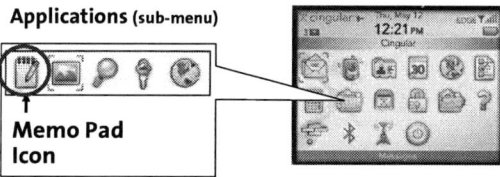

Use the Memo Pad Icon to take notes, write lists, store important information. They are fully searchable and can be organized with "Categories"

Memo Pad Icon

All Other Full Keyboard BlackBerries

Memo Pad Icon

2. Click "New"
3. Type the Title as "Grocery" and your items

```
Title: Grocery
Cinn Oatmeal
Milk
Eggs
```

4. Save it and now you have your instant grocery list.

5. Now you're working on a home improvement project and realize you don't have the correct screws, just open up a New memo item called "Hardware" and add the screws to it as shown.

Title: Hardware

1-1/2" drywall screws

Now you have a list for each store you regularly visit .

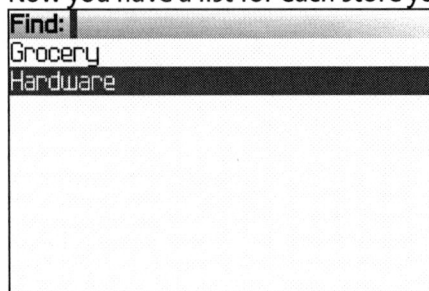

Find:
Grocery
Hardware

BlackBerry Wow! Stories

We are looking for great, fun or unusual ways in which you have used or benefited from your BlackBerry. It can be anything from work or play!

Below are a few of the Stories we've collected so far. Please visit our web site www.blackberrymadesimple.com and click on the "BlackBerry Wow!" link at the top of the page to read the latest or submit your own story!

Submit your own "BlackBerry Wow!" Story on our web site, if we include your story in a new book, we'll send you a free copy of the e-book (electronic PDF) version!

BlackBerry for Free Drinks!?
From Donna, a BlackBerry Enthusiast.
"I went out with some friends to the neighborhood pub for a bite to eat and it happened to be "Trivia Night". The DJ would ask a question, then play a few songs before requesting the answer. Plenty of time to send the question off to "Askmenow.com" and have them e-mail back the answer. I did not use the answers for personal gain, rather I fed the answers to a cute guy at the bar who ended up picking up our drinks tab at the end of the night. What fun!" Donna uses a BlackBerry 7520 from Nextel. Submitted: 21-Oct-2005

Traveler's Aid
From V.L., a BlackBerry Made Simple customer:
"I just came back from a trip to New York City. I needed bus and subway directions to get around town. I was able to use a FREE email service at NYC@hopstop.com. After you registering with them at www.hopstop.com, I simply emailed the following: "130 West 46th Street TO 102 Fifth Avenue." to NYC@hopstop.com. In less than 5 minutes, NYC Hopstop sent me an email reply with subway and bus directions! I saved a lot of time trying to find and figure out a subway and bus map! I use a Blackberry 7290 from Cingular" Submitted: 20-Sep-2005

70 MPH Homework Helper
From Martin Trautschold, author, BlackBerry Made Simple:
"I was driving home on the highway after picking up my daughter from school. She wanted to get a head start on her definitions homework on the drive. The only dictionary was at home. Instead of waiting, she used a "Google" search on my BlackBerry web browser to find the definition of each term by typing "(word) definition" into the Google Search field. It worked like a champ! I use a BlackBerry 7230 from T-Mobile."Submitted: 22-Sep-2005

<u>NOTES</u>

213710

Made in the USA